SOUTHERN ILLINOIS SALUKIS FOOTBALL

SOUTHERN ILLINOIS SALUKIS FOOTBALL

DAN VERDUN

FOREWORD by Jerry Kill

Southern Illinois University Press / Carbondale

Southern Illinois University Press
www.siupress.com

20 19 18 17   4 3 2 1

Funding for publication of this book was provided
by SIU Athletics.

Jacket illustrations: (*front, clockwise from top
left*) U.S. flag at homecoming (Steve Buhman,
SIU Communications); Grey Dawg, Saluki
mascot (SIU Athletics); Yonel Jourdain (39) in
the 1990s (SIU Athletics); Coach Jerry Kill (SIU
Athletics); SIU football helmet (Buhman, SIU
Communications); (*front flap*) 1896 Carbondale-
SINU football team (Huff, *Saluki Sports
History*); (*back flap*) 1983 national championship
plaque (SIU Athletics); (*top, back cover*)
players patting Tut's Tomb for good luck (SIU
Athletics); (*bottom right, back cover*) Houston
Antwine with Dick Towers (SIU Athletics).

Library of Congress
Cataloging-in-Publication Data
Names: Verdun, Dan, author.
Title: Southern Illinois Salukis football /
    Dan Verdun ; foreword by Jerry Kill.
Description: Carbondale : Southern Illinois
    University Press, [2017] | Includes
    bibliographical references.
Identifiers: LCCN 2017001150 |
    ISBN 9780809336197 (cloth : alk. paper) |
    ISBN 9780809336203 (e-book)
Subjects: LCSH: Southern Illinois University at
    Carbondale—Football—History. | Southern
    Illinois Salukis (Football team)
Classification: LCC GV958.S688 V47 2017 |
    DDC 796.332/6309773994—dc23
    LC record available at https://lccn.loc
    .gov/2017001150

To all who have worn the maroon and white over the years

CONTENTS

FOREWORD

JERRY KILL
SIU HEAD COACH, 2001–7

Southern Illinois University (SIU), the Carbondale community and the region as a whole will always be special to us. When I say *us*, I mean my wife, Rebecca. I mean our two children, Krystal and Tasha. Southern Illinois is the place we call home because that's where we raised our kids and where we lived longer than anywhere else we've been. Because the region was the perfect fit for us, we became part of it. I was diagnosed with my cancer there. We started the Coach Kill Cancer Fund there, and we're proud to say that it's still going. We get back whenever we can. We were there when Joel Sambursky, a terrific quarterback and a terrific kid, was inducted into the SIU Department of Athletics' Saluki Hall of Fame on the first ballot. Joel was very deserving of that honor. I spoke at the funeral of Dan Callahan, who was more than just a baseball coach; he was as wonderful a human being as you will find. My family and I still have a cabin on Lake of Egypt, where we like to relax and do a bit of fishing.

When I say *us*, I also mean my coaching staff. We were together as a core for a long time. As a staff, we went to Southern Illinois with a dream. SIU had struggled for over 20 years. There were even rumors about dropping the program. We had the dream of a revival.

That dream came true, thanks to great people and great support. We had a tremendous seven-year run. Look at the people who were at SIU in those days: Bruce Weber, Matt Painter, Chris Lowery, Rodney Watson, and Kerri Blaylock. During a five-to-seven-year period, we were all winning. There were Sweet Sixteen appearances, playoff runs, conference championships. I promise you that that degree of winning all at the same time will never happen again. It was something to behold.

On the football side, perhaps athletic director Paul Kowalczyk summed it up best when he said SIU had the biggest turnaround in NCAA history except for maybe Kansas State's revival under Bill Snyder. During Paul's tenure at SIU, the Salukis emerged as a nationally renowned athletics program with 15 conference championships in seven sports programs. We built the nicest NCAA Division I-AA stadium in the country. The people responsible for that stadium are all the players who sweated and worked hard in that old, crusty building known as McAndrew Stadium. Others got the ball rolling, but those players and their winning ways got that stadium built.

Turning around a program is never easy, but then nothing that's really worth doing is easy. I learned that lesson long ago from my parents, the two people who taught me more about life and what makes it worth living than anyone else.

Making our dream a reality at SIU proved to us that it can be done. That's what got us to the University of Minnesota, and beyond.

No matter where our careers and lives may take us, SIU, Carbondale and the southern Illinois region will always be a huge part of who we are.

ACKNOWLEDGMENTS

As with any project of this magnitude, there are so many people to thank. First and foremost are my wife, Nancy, and children, Tommy and Lauren. They have been understanding and supportive all the way through the late-night phone calls and early-morning writing sessions.

This book would not have been possible without the unfailing support and love of my parents, the late Paul and Marion Verdun. Like most of us, I never realized just how much parents do for their children until I began raising my own kids. Thanks also to my brothers, Jeff, Don and Ron. When I look back on my days growing up in our dwelling in Odell, I am reminded that it really was a home rather than just a house. I will always remember those formative years with fondness.

Meanwhile, a huge thank you goes out to my close friend Barry Bottino for all his advice, guidance and support along the way. Barry and I write a Chicago Now blog together (*Prairie State Pigskin*), which covers Illinois FCS football. Thanks for listening to me ramble on time after time about this book, Mister B.

Other friends have contributed in more ways than they will ever know. So thanks to Tom and Peg Doran, John and Karen Eisenhour, Mike Fitzgerald, Al Lagattolla, Tim and Dawn Lee, Jeff Long, John Ralph, John Ryan, Jeff Strohm and Dino Tiberi.

I also thank Southern Illinois University Press for all the hard work and dedication to making this book possible. Special thanks goes to Dr. Karl Kageff and his staff, highlighted by kudos to Wayne Larsen and Linda Buhman.

Huge thanks go out to each former coach, athlete, administrator, band director and dance team or cheer team sponsor who took time out of their lives to open their memory banks and share them with a complete stranger. This book is about you. Hopefully you will enjoy reading it as much as I did writing it.

Much of the information in this book comes from each of the universities involved. Behind all the media reports that hit newspapers, magazines, and radio and TV shows along with Internet sites are the people of the sports information offices and media relations departments. Thus I thank

Tom Weber, Jason Clay and John Lock of the SIU Sports Information Office. Much thanks go out to Sharon and Roger Lipe. This book would not be as good without them. Kathy Jones is another Saluki I wish to thank. A key resource for my book was Fred Huff's comprehensive *Saluki Sports History: 100 Years of Facts and Highlights*, published in 2005. I've been told by numerous people that Mr. Huff knows more about SIU athletics than anyone.

Additional thanks go to Mike Williams of Illinois State, Mike Korcek of Northern, Dave Kidwell and Rich Moser from Eastern, and Patrick Osterman of Western for all their incredible help.

From the NFL ranks, Jack Brennan and Danny Katz of the Bengals; Craig Kelley, Vernon Cheek and Pam Humphrey of the Colts; Rich Dalrymple and Jancy Briles of the Cowboys; Vince Freitas, Bill Johnston and Morad Shah of the Chargers; Reggie Roberts of the Falcons; Rob Crane of the Packers; Greg Bensel, Justin Marione, Michael C. Herbert and Sondra Egan of the Saints; and Robbie Bohren of the Titans deserve my gratitude.

From the Canadian Football League came the help of Jamie Cartmell (B.C. Lions), Kelly Forsberg (Saskatchewan Rough Riders), and Mitch Bayless and Melenee Mehler (Calgary Stampeders).

Invaluable assistance came from members of the media. Thus I recognize and thank the following for their help: Rick Armstrong of the *Aurora Beacon-News*; Bob Asmussen of the *Champaign News-Gazette*; Taylor Bell, formerly of the *Chicago Sun-Times*; Todd Hefferman and Les Winkeler of the *Southern Illinoisan*; Michael MacCambridge, author of so many landmark sports histories; Murray McCormick of the *Regina Leader-Post*; Bob McGinn of the *Milwaukee Journal Sentinental*; Brian Nielsen of the *Journal Gazette and Times-Courier*; Randy Reinhardt of the *Bloomington Pantagraph*; Mike Reis, Voice of the Salukis; Carl Walworth of the *Journal Gazette and Times-Courier*; and Len Ziehm, formerly of the *Sun-Times*.

Fellow sports historians and writers Bob Gill, John Maxymuk and Roger Snell offered not only support and information but also key pieces of advice and insight.

SIU SALUKIS FACT PAGE

Institution Founded—1869

Location—Carbondale

Football Established—1913

Colors—Maroon and white

Website—http://SIUSalukis.com/

Mascot—Grey Dawg and Brown Dawg

Home Stadium—Saluki Stadium

National Championship—1983

Highest NFL Draft Picks—Lionel Antoine, Chicago Bears, 1st round (3rd overall choice); Terry Taylor, Seattle Seahawks, 1st round (22nd overall choice)

Famous Alumni in Other Sports—Chris Carr (basketball); Mike Glenn (basketball); Steve Finley (baseball); Walt Frazier (basketball); Connie-Price Smith (four-time track and field Olympian); Dave Stieb (baseball)

Famous Nonsport Alumni—Jim Belushi (actor, comedian); John Belushi (actor, comedian); Roland Burris (politician); Shawn Colvin (musician); Don S. Davis (actor); Dennis Franz (actor); Dick Gregory (civil rights activist, comedian); Joan Higginbotham (astronaut); Curt Jones (founder of Dippin' Dots); Rodney P. Kelly (retired major general, U.S. Air Force); Donald McHenry (ambassador); Melissa McCarthy (actress, comedian); Bob Odenkirk (actor, comedian, writer, director, producer); Sir Curtis Price (musician); Richard Roundtree (actor); Jackie Spinner (journalist); Robert K. Weiss (movie producer)

SOUTHERN ILLINOIS SALUKIS FOOTBALL

The 1896 Carbondale-SINU football team featured students and nonstudents and played without faculty approval.

EARLY DAYS

In 1898 America was at war with Spain. Meanwhile, several years of dispute at Southern Illinois Normal University (SINU) finally came to an end.

According to Fred Huff's book *Saluki Sports History: 100 Years of Facts and Highlights*, SINU's faculty gave its approval on November 15, 1898, for students to participate in football.

There were, however, several stipulations for potential players, according to Huff's book. Among them were guidelines for eligibility.

"Reportedly, these rules did not sponsor or in any way encourage the organization of a football team. They were simply formulated for the purpose of regulating any team organized by students," Huff wrote.

A common practice of the time had the competing teams providing game officials. Generally one referee worked the first half of a game and the other team's official took over for the second half. Disagreements were commonplace.

Those early SINU teams went by the moniker "Maroons," after the school colors.

Though many on the SINU roster were students, nonstudents frequently filled in when they were needed. Scores from the early 1900s are difficult to confirm. According to Huff's book, one report claimed SINU played a game against Du Quoin High School on January 26, 1912. The report also stated SINU's record was 26-13-1 during the previous six years.

William McAndrew became the first SINU athletic director in 1913. McAndrew began the first "organized" Maroon football team. He would serve the university until his death in 1943 (with the exception of two years when he served the country during World War I). McAndrew coached football for 20 years, basketball for 25 years, baseball for four years and track for two years. His 1930–31 football teams did not lose a game for a season and a half. McAndrew was friends with College Football Hall of Fame members Amos Alonzo Stagg and Knute Rockne.

In 1916 SINU dedicated its new football facility—Bayliss Field—east of the railroad tracks and the building that later became known as Lincoln School, and northeast of campus.

With McAndrew away serving in the military, Sam Patterson took over the coaching

The opening game of the 1916 season coincided with the dedication of Bayliss Field, east of what later became known as Lincoln School.

reins in mid-fall 1917. Often regarded as SINU's first four-sport athlete, Patterson played tennis, baseball and basketball, and quarterbacked the football team from 1908 to 1912.

With World War I continuing to rage in Europe, organized athletics at SINU were shut down for the 1918–19 school year.

McAndrew—a brigadier general with a law degree—returned to SINU during the 1920–21 academic year.

The Maroons registered their first six-win season in 1924 and, under McAndrew, continued to post winning records even as SINU improved its schedules. McAndrew's 1928 team went 7-1-2; his 1929 team was 5-3-1. Those teams were led by Carbondale's Harry "Dutch" Lutz as quarterback and captain, while Glenn "Abe" Martin transferred in from McKendree College.

Perhaps McAndrew's finest hour came in 1930 when his Southern Illinois Teachers College (SITC, as the school was called during the Great Depression) went untied

and undefeated and captured the school's first conference championship. The Maroons recorded their first unbeaten season with a 9-0-0 mark, outscoring opponents 224-24 and registering six consecutive shutouts.

The Little 19 Conference champions featured nine returning lettermen. Clarence "Fuzz" Harriss and Abe Martin were the team captains. That pair combined with Frank Eovaldi in the dynamic Maroon backfield. Martin scored 64 points to lead the team.

SITC extended its winning streak to 15 games until losing at Illinois State on Halloween of the 1931 season. Amazingly, the Maroons began the 1931 season with five consecutive shutouts before falling 14-0 to Illinois State Normal University. The Maroons finished the season with a 7-2 record.

A narrow 6-2 loss to Illinois Wesleyan cost SITC its second conference title in the final game of the 1934 season. As was common at the time, both teams frequently punted on third downs (and occasionally on second downs) in an effort to avoid offensive mistakes. William Morawski accounted for the Maroons' score when he blocked a Wesleyan punt that resulted in a safety. However, the Titans scored on a long pass to open the fourth quarter.

Former SITC standout Abe Martin took over head coaching duties from McAndrew for the 1939 season. Martin's 1941 team broke a spell of six straight losing seasons with a 5-3-1 mark. Martin stepped in as basketball coach when McAndrew died suddenly on February 11, 1943. Roscoe Pulliam, SITC's president, announced his intention to name the football stadium after McAndrew.

The stadium "would stand as a monument to a great man's vision, planning and perseverance," states Pulliam in Huff's book.

The university's official name, Southern Illinois Normal University, returned in 1943. However, SINU canceled its football schedule that year due to the shortage of male athletes caused by World War II.

The 1930 SITC team was undefeated. *Front row, left to right*, Richard Watson, Robert Fox, Albert Patton, Paul Gene Brown, Ellsworth Robertson, Robert Doty, Harry Canada, Cannon Storment, and Lindell Rockwell. *Middle row, left to right*, Taylor, Dryden, Wiggins, Paul McKinnis, Glenn "Abe" Martin, Frank Eovaldi, Dan Foley, and James Lauder. *Top row, left to right*, Bannister, George Sauerwein, Clarence Stephens, Eugene Bricker, captain Clarence Harriss, and Clarence Hodge. Paul Swafford also lettered but was not present for the photo.

Members of the Salukis' 1947 Corn Bowl team line up in formation. The linemen (*left to right*) are Bob Colborn, John Corn, Bob Etheridge, Bill Cosgrove, Jim Lovin, Charlie Lathieu, and Joe Hughes. The quarterback is Bill Malinsky, with George Sawyer (65), John Riggs (behind Malinksy), and Dick Seelman (59) completing the backfield.

THE IIAC

It's been nearly 50 years since the Illinois Intercollegiate Athletic Conference (IIAC) last crowned a championship football team. Yet, for those who competed, the memories are as fresh as the smell of cut grass on the first day of fall practice.

"It was great," said Bob Heimerdinger, the 1951 conference most valuable player from Northern Illinois University. The conference "was made up of the people you knew from high school, and you saw them every year."

Heimerdinger, the father of the late NFL offensive coordinator Mike Heimerdinger, added that the IIAC's strength was the men who ran it.

"They were the whole ball of wax," he said. "In those days those men were everything. They coached the sports, and they ran the PE departments."

Those men included Heimerdinger's coach, George "Chick" Evans. Others were Charles Lantz and Maynard "Pat" O'Brien of Eastern, Vince DiFrancesca of Western and Ed Struck of ISU. Southern was coached by the likes of Glenn "Abe" Martin (1939–49), Bill Waller (1950–51) and William O'Brien (1952–54).

"It was just those five state schools when I played," said 1947 conference MVP Red Miller of Western, who later coached the Denver Broncos in the Super Bowl.

"Northern and Southern were the biggest schools, ISU was in the middle, and Western and Eastern stayed about the same size," said Lou Stivers, captain of Eastern's 1948 conference champions.

"(The IIAC) was every bit as tough as the Mid-American Conference," said Jack Pheanis, who played with Heimerdinger and later coached under both Evans and Howard Fletcher at NIU. "The Mid-American was better at publicizing themselves. They also had a number of people on all the (NCAA) committees."

One of the attractions of the IIAC was its wide-open play.

"The Big 10 was known for its running game," said Pheanis, who began his playing career at the University of Illinois. "We (the IIAC) were a passing league."

Tom Beck, named all-conference on both offense and defense in 1961, enjoyed playing in the IIAC.

"It was a great time," Beck said. "I loved going on the trips and being with the guys. We traveled by bus to the games. We did take the train down to Carbondale to play

Southern. We took a bus to Kankakee and then boarded the train."

Jack Dean played halfback for NIU's 1963 national championship team and later served as the head coach at Eastern.

"(The IIAC) was special because people don't realize how many great players came out of that league," Dean said. "You look at Western. They had guys like (future AFL star) Booker Edgerson and (first-round NFL draft pick) Leroy Jackson. You went down to Southern, and they were always loaded."

> *(The IIAC) was special because people don't realize how many great players came out of that league.*

"Eastern Michigan had Hayes Jones, who was an Olympic hurdler (who won gold in the 110-meter hurdles in the 1964 Games). Central Michigan was just so tough in football."

When asked just how strong the IIAC was, Dean used an analogy.

"I consider it very close to what the Mid-American Conference is today," he replied.

According to a 1970 article in the *NCAA News*, the league claimed most of the Illinois institutions of higher education. It was nicknamed the "Little Nineteen," though in 1928 it had a membership of 23 schools.

Former Illinois State track coach Joe Cogdal noted that the IIAC had roots in the 1870s, when a number of schools banded together for oratorical contests. Cogdal was associated with the conference for 43 of its 62 years of existence.

The first intercollegiate football game in the conference region was played in 1881 between Illinois State Normal University and Knox College. By 1894 a football association had been established.

The conference was officially formed in April 1908 with eight charter members—Illinois State, Illinois Wesleyan, Bradley, Millikin, Monmouth, Knox, Lombard College and Illinois College.

The first track meet was held on May 22, 1908. The league expanded rapidly, With Eastern and Western joining the league in 1912 and 1915, respectively.

The newly appointed director of athletics William McAndrew developed the Southern Illinois Normal University program, and SINU gained acceptance into the conference in the spring of 1914.

In 1920 the name "Illinois Intercollegiate Athletic Conference" was adopted. Conference membership reached a peak of 23 schools in 1928, when virtually all of the small colleges of Illinois were included.

An interesting footnote is that Eastern's 1928 conference championship roster included future actor, writer and folk singer Burl Ives as a lineman.

Private schools withdrew during the 1930s, until in 1942 only Eastern, Northern, Southern, Western and Illinois State remained.

In 1947 "Southern Illinois University" (SIU) was officially adopted as the school's name. SIU posted a 7-2-1 record under head coach Abe Martin. The Maroons won the IIAC title and earned a berth in the inaugural Corn Bowl, an annual event held in Bloomington from 1947 to 1955. SIU shut out North Central College of Naperville 21-0 to win the November 27 bowl.

Five SIU players—Bob Colburn, John Corn, Jim Lovin, Bill Malinsky and Don Riggs—earned All-IIAC First Team honors. Joe Hughes and Bill Cosgrove were named to the second team. Galen Davis, Bob Etheridge, Bob Johnson, Howard Jones, Charles Mathieu and George Sawyer received honorable mention awards.

Lovin earned All-IIAC First Team accolades each of his four seasons at Southern, an unprecedented honor. Lovin, who played both offense and defense, was the first Saluki to have his jersey (78) retired by SIU. A 1978 SIU Athletics Hall of Fame inductee, he enjoyed a distinguished career as a prep football coach.

In 1950 the league became the Interstate Intercollegiate Athletic Conference when Central Michigan and Eastern Michigan joined, upping membership to seven schools.

That same academic year SIU officially selected "Salukis" as its mascot name. According to Fred Huff's *Saluki Sports History: 100 Years of Facts and Highlights*, the nickname was reported in the March 6, 1951, edition of the *Southern Illinoisan*. "Salukis" was chosen after several SIU coaches, lettermen and faculty representatives suggested the name. The newspaper stated that the students "had recently voted on names such as 'Knights,' 'Egyptians,' 'Marauders' and 'Rebels,' and the like without reaching a decision."

"For the record, 526 voted for 'Salukis' as compared to 144 for 'Rebels' and even fewer for the other suggested names," stated Huff's book.

Meanwhile, Carver Shannon, an African American from Mississippi, came north to star in the Southern Illinois backfield during the 1950s.

"It was exciting to play (at Southern)," said Shannon, who later played for the Los Angeles Rams. "We had many talented performers in many sports all across campus.

"Things really took off," Shannon, now living in California, said. "Sometimes they would have to put seats in the end zone to get everybody in."

Shannon was one of the main reasons. As a sophomore in 1956, he ran the ball for seven yards per carry en route to the IIAC MVP award. By 1958, Shannon's senior season, the Salukis had revitalized football in Carbondale. SIU posted its best record in more than a decade with a 7-2 mark. Teammate Cecil Hart took home conference MVP honors.

The 1958 IIAC season could have gone down as one of the all-time greatest in SIU history had the Salukis not stumbled twice, losing to a pair of tail-end conference foes. As the record books show, SIU finished at 7-2 overall, with the losses to Illinois State (21-8 at home) and Northern Illinois (17-7 on the road) preventing an undefeated season.

Nevertheless, the Salukis pulled off an exhilarating 32-31 home victory over rival Western Illinois. Decades later, athletic director Donald Boydston would call it "the most exciting football game I ever saw."

Played in just the third week of the season, SIU roared to an 18-0 halftime lead. WIU rallied to take a 25-18 lead. The Leathernecks held a 31-24 lead with just 15 seconds remaining in the game. The Salukis faced a seemingly daunting task with the ball resting on their own 33-yard line.

Yet SIU pulled off a miraculous 67-yard touchdown play as quarterback Bill Norwood connected with Lane "Night Train" Jenkins. The score pulled SIU to within a point of Western. Having failed four times to kick an extra point in the game, head coach Al Kawal chose to go for a two-point conversion. According to Huff's book, "Jenkins ran wide, broke a tackle on the sidelines and scored" the game-winning conversion.

The loss was the lone defeat for the Leathernecks that season, yet Western Illinois won back-to-back conference championships in 1958 and 1959 under head coach Lou Saban. The '59 Leathernecks posted an undefeated season in which they outscored opponents by a 303-104 margin. WIU shut out its final two opponents.

"Lou Saban was all business," said WIU tackle Wayne Lunak. "He was more like the legendary Paul Brown. He was the hammer. I remember one of our running backs came out of his office and said Lou just kicked me out of school. I told him that the football coach can kick you off the team, but not out of school. It didn't matter; the running back left (school)."

Robert "Red" Miller, a Macomb native, returned to his alma mater and served as one of Saban's assistants along with Joe Collier, Art Duffelmeier and Guy Ricci.

"That was a special group of players through and through," said the 82-year-old Miller from his home in suburban Denver.

When Saban left WIU for the Boston Patriots of the newly founded American Football League, the Leathernecks took a hit.

"Lou needed coaches he could trust so he took Joe Collier and Red Miller with him," Leatherneck star Booker Edgerson said. "Of course, that hurt us."

In 1960 SIU captured the IIAC crown by posting a 6-0 conference record. Head coach Carmen Piccone's Salukis were 8-2 overall (losing at Bowling Green and Ohio). Saluki football set the stage for one of the most successful sports years in the school's history, as eight other SIU teams also won conference championships.

Amos Bullocks rushed for 996 yards, breaking Carver Shannon's mark set four years earlier.

"Being a part of SIU's first Intercollegiate Athletic Association championship (was a highlight of my career). We played for the championship in 1959, and it was a rough one against Eastern Michigan. It was most enjoyable because we wrecked their homecoming," said Bullocks.

Houston Antwine was chosen MVP in addition to earning All-American honors from the National Association of Intercollegiate Athletics. Antwine was also named to the Associated Press Little All-America team. Gene Williams was a second-team choice. Antwine, Bullocks, Ron Winter, Tom Bruna, Paul Brostrom, Greg Secker and Dennis Harmon each received all-conference recognition.

SIU repeated as IIAC champion in 1961. Bullocks, a three-year starter, returned to star in the Saluki backfield. Bullocks would leave SIU with 2,441 rushing yards. Meanwhile, Winter, the SIU quarterback, earned team MVP honors. Ends Jim Battle and

Charles O'Neil caught 25 and 23 passes, respectively, for the Salukis.

"We were as tough as anyone in those years," said tackle Sam Silas, who would later play professional football.

The IIAC began to change following SIU's back-to-back championships. The Salukis and Eastern Michigan withdrew from the league. Northern Illinois followed suit in 1966.

SIU's first season as an independent team (1962) proved to be difficult: the Salukis faced five new opponents and lost to three of them—Texas A&I, Northern Michigan and North Texas State. In fact, SIU would experience losing seasons until Coach Dick Towers's Salukis posted a 5-5 record in 1969.

Northern Illinois won three straight IIAC championships from 1963 to 1965. In fact, the Huskies captured the '63 NCAA College Division national championship under head coach Howard Fletcher. NIU featured a shotgun-spread passing attack that took college football by storm.

Sports Illustrated featured quarterback George Bork in a three-page article titled "A Big Man in Any League." Bork and his Northern teammates found their way into *Time* magazine. CBS aired game highlights nationally. Bork was interviewed on NBC radio. Pro scouts from the likes of the Green Bay Packers, Dallas Cowboys and San Francisco 49ers came to see him play.

"That 1963 season is my greatest memory (of my career)," said Bork, a College Football Hall of Fame member. He and his wife still return to DeKalb on a regular basis.

The conference officially disbanded at the end of the 1969–70 academic year. Thus Western Illinois was the last IIAC champion, winning the conference title in the fall of 1969 under College Football Hall of Fame coach Darrell Mudra.

"We kicked people all over the field pretty good when I was at Western," Mudra said from his retirement home in Florida.

We were as tough as anyone in those years.

Mike Wagner, who later won four Super Bowls with the Pittsburgh Steelers, earned NAIA All-American honors that championship season for the Leathernecks.

"It was a big thing for a small program at the time," Wagner said from his home in Pennsylvania.

"Mike Wagner was the all-American boy," said former WIU assistant coach Pete Rodriguez. "He was blonde-haired and blue-eyed. He had all the attributes to be a fine player. You don't find someone like him at Western Illinois usually. He got overlooked by a lot of people and bigger schools. He really blossomed at Western."

While Northern became a Division-I football program in 1969, the rest of the Illinois schools played at the NCAA College Division and then Division-II levels through the 1970s.

Eastern, under Mudra, won the 1978 Division-II national championship. Mudra's coaching staff included Mike Shanahan as offensive coordinator and John Teerlinck as defensive coordinator.

Shanahan later won consecutive Super Bowls as the Denver Broncos head coach. Teerlinck, recently retired defensive line coach for the Indianapolis Colts, has been part of four Super Bowl coaching staffs. Pro Football Hall of Fame member John Randle chose Teerlinck to give his introduction speech in Canton.

With NIU continuing to play at the Division I-A level, the four remaining schools all transitioned from Division-II into I-AA (now called the Football Championship Subdivision) football in the early 1980s. Interestingly, Illinois State played at the I-A level from 1978 to 1981 before moving to I-AA status.

When the Gateway Conference was formed in 1985, Eastern, Southern, Western and ISU became charter members. Eastern left the league in 1996 to join the Ohio Valley Conference in all sports.

"You wonder where is the rivalry?" said Eastern quarterback Roger Haberer who played in the 1960s. "Today when Eastern plays Eastern Kentucky, it just isn't the same. Maybe it will be someday, but there was more rivalry in those days (of the IIAC)."

Southern, Western and ISU remain together in the Missouri Valley Conference (the Gateway officially changed its named in 2009).

"When you look back now it would be nice from the traveling and financial aspect (to still be together)," said Lou Stivers.

IIAC STATISTICS

ILLINOIS INTERCOLLEGIATE ATHLETIC CONFERENCE FOOTBALL CHAMPIONS

1914	Eastern Illinois, Millikin
1915	Illinois College
1916	Millikin
1917	Lombard
1918	No champion
1919	Unknown
1920	Unknown
1921	Unknown
1922	Unknown
1923	Unknown
1924	Bradley
1925	Bradley, Monmouth
1926	Bradley, Monmouth
1927	Bradley
1928	Eastern Illinois, Millikin
1929	Knox, Lombard
1930	Millikin
1931	Monmouth
1932	Illinois Wesleyan, McKendree
1933	Illinois Wesleyan
1934	Augustana, Millikin
1935	Millikin, Monmouth
1936	Illinois Wesleyan, St. Viator
1937	Bradley, Illinois College, Illinois State
1938	Northern Illinois
1939	Illinois State, Western Illinois
1940	Carthage (Wisc.), Illinois State
1941	Illinois State, Northern Illinois

1942	Western Illinois
1943	No champion
1944	Northern Illinois
1945	Illinois State
1946	Northern Illinois
1947	Southern Illinois
1948	Eastern Illinois
1949	Western Illinois

INTERSTATE INTERCOLLEGIATE ATHLETIC CONFERENCE FOOTBALL CHAMPIONS

1950	Illinois State
1951	Northern Illinois
1952	Central Michigan
1953	Central Michigan
1954	Central Michigan, Eastern Michigan
1955	Central Michigan, Eastern Michigan
1956	Central Michigan
1957	Eastern Michigan
1958	Western Illinois
1959	Western Illinois
1960	Southern Illinois
1961	Southern Illinois
1962	Central Michigan
1963	Northern Illinois
1964	Northern Illinois, Western Illinois
1965	Northern Illinois
1966	Central Michigan
1967	Central Michigan, Illinois State
1968	Central Michigan, Illinois State
1969	Western Illinois

INTERSTATE INTERCOLLEGIATE ATHLETIC CONFERENCE FOOTBALL MVPS

1950	Dean Burridge, Illinois State
1951	Bob Heimerdinger, Northern Illinois
1952	Wes Bair, Illinois State
1953	Charles Miller, Central Michigan
1954	Bob Middlekauff, Eastern Michigan
1955	Bernie Raternik, Central Michigan
1956	Jim Podoley, Central Michigan, and Carver Shannon, Southern Illinois
1957	Kerry Keating, Eastern Michigan
1958	Walter Beach, Central Michigan, and Cecil Hart, Southern Illinois
1959	Lew Finn, Northern Illinois, and Willie Brown, Southern Illinois
1960	Leroy Jackson, Western Illinois
1961	Leroy Jackson, Western Illinois
1962	George Bork, Northern Illinois
1963	George Bork, Northern Illinois
1964	Jack Dean, Northern Illinois
1965	Ron Christian, Northern Illinois
1966	Bill Brockhouse, Western Illinois
1967	Steve Bjornstad, Illinois State
1968	Craig Tefft, Central Michigan
1969	Ron Wilson, Western Illinois

Glenn "Abe" Martin (*left*) and Bill O'Brien oversee a Saluki practice in the post–World War II era.

1950s

MARION RUSHING

Marion Rushing not only starred on the football field at Southern Illinois but also earned more varsity letters than any athlete in school history.

Rushing, a native of Pinckneyville, earned 13 varsity letters while participating in four sports: football, basketball, wrestling and track. According to Fred Huff's *Saluki Sports History: 100 Years of Facts and Highlights,* "unquestionably his finest contributions were in football as he later enjoyed a multi-year career in the NFL, playing with the St. Louis Cardinals."

Rushing competed at Southern from 1954 through 1957. He played in the defensive line and earned All–Interstate Intercollegiate Athletic Conference (IIAC) honors in 1956 and 1957. Rushing set school records in the javelin in 1958 and was a two-time winner of the Henry Hinkley Award, which is annually given to SIU's top athlete. Rushing was inducted into the inaugural Saluki Hall of Fame class in 1978. In 2010, SIU renamed Tennis Drive in his honor.

"Marion was so tough," said former Saluki running back Carver Shannon. "He never

Marion Rushing earned more varsity letters than any other athlete in SIU history.

said a word, but his play spoke for him. What an athlete he was."

After his illustrious SIU career, Rushing played 10 seasons of professional football in both the NFL and the AFL. A pro linebacker, Rushing played for the Chicago Bears, the St. Louis Cardinals and the Houston Oilers. He played in 105 games, finishing his career in 1968.

Rushing was diagnosed with Parkinson's disease at age 46.

"Marion's roots go very deep in Pinckneyville," Bonnie Rushing, Marion's wife, said at the ceremony naming the street after him. "There is no question of where his permanent residence would be."

Rushing passed away on April 26, 2013, at the age of 76.

CARVER SHANNON

The unwritten rules of his era didn't allow Carver Shannon to play for his home-state Ole Miss Rebels. That prejudice proved to be a bonanza for Southern Illinois University.

"(Going to Ole Miss) never even crossed my mind," said Shannon from his home in Los Angeles. "Maybe I was too young to see (racism). Of course, I went to separate schools from my (white) friends. Friday nights we'd play our (separate) games, but Sunday we would all meet down at the stadium to play for fun. I had white friends on the same street (that I lived on). (Racism) was there, but it didn't register with me."

Though Shannon couldn't play for Ole Miss in the 1950s, he still had plenty of offers. Historically black universities such as

Tennessee State and Jackson State wanted him. Somehow Utah State was in the mix. Yet Shannon appeared set to enroll in Big 10 country.

"I was training to go to Indiana," Shannon said. "That's where my mother worked on her doctorate."

That's when fate intervened in the form of legendary Donald "Doc" Boydston.

"(SIU head coach) Al Kawal sent Doc out looking for players," Shannon said. "He told him, 'Why don't you bring me one of those black running backs from down there (in Mississippi)?'"

Boydston had somehow stumbled across Shannon, the multisport star of Mississippi's Corinth High School.

The persistence of Boydston and a promise paid dividends for SIU.

"I finally told Doc that I'd go to Southern," Shannon said. "But I told him that just to get rid of him."

Shannon's plan didn't work. Boydston showed up at his door with the engine running.

"Mom, look, that man's back again," Shannon recalled a conversation from more than 50 years earlier. "She told me, 'You told him you'd go, so you'd better get ready to leave.'"

Thus Carver Shannon made the trek to Carbondale.

"When I got there, I was early," Shannon said. "I was the only somebody in Anthony Hall. No one else had moved in yet."

Shannon spent three days in the otherwise empty residence hall.

"I was lonely," he said. "But in those days I played the saxophone. So I played in the

Carver Shannon (*center*) holds the SIU single-season record for yards per carry (8.22 in 1957).

bathroom. I played in the stairwell. I played all over that hall. It was just me and my saxophone to keep me going."

When his fellow students arrived, it was time for football.

"I remember going in and getting this old, beat-up equipment," Shannon said. "I was something like the 14th-string running back to start."

Yet, there were people who believed in him.

"(Equipment manager) Mr. Grimes gave me something better to wear at practice," Shannon said. "I found out years later that he and (varsity player) Hank Warfield always bet on which new guys would make it. Mr. Grimes said he saw something in me."

Soon the entire SIU football team saw it too.

"I did whatever it took," Shannon said. "I'd bust a gut to be first in the sprints. I'd try to kill the tackling dummy. One day the coaches said they needed someone to kick off. I told them I could do it. I put seven out of 10 balls out of the end zone."

I did whatever it took. I'd bust a gut to be first in the sprints. I'd try to kill the tackling dummy.

Shannon also remembers going head-to-head with the veteran Warfield in practice.

"That was the day that it all changed for me," he said.

Soon Kawal was telling assistant coach Carmen Piccone to insert Shannon into the offensive backfield.

"I played the second half and scored two or three touchdowns," Shannon said. "The next week was Homecoming, and I was starting."

Shannon said that he was spurred on by dreams—both figuratively and literally.

"I used to have these dreams that I'd be running the ball through and around everybody," he said. "I'd wake up and those dreams were pretty much coming true in the real games."

Shannon also realized that any running back's success is dependent on his line.

"So I started recruiting for us," he said. "I went to places like Memphis and got players like Houston Antwine and Willie Brown."

Antwine became an NAIA wrestling champion at SIU and later earned All-Pro honors six straight seasons in the American Football League. Brown, a guard, managed to be selected as the IIAC most valuable player in 1959.

As a sophomore in 1956, Shannon ran the ball for seven yards per carry en route to the IIAC MVP award. He set an SIU scoring record by amassing 90 points (13 touchdowns and 12 points after touchdowns).

"I got letters from the Bears, Rams and Colts that year," he noted.

A season later, he was even better, carrying the ball for an astounding 8.22 yards per rush. This mark still stands as a single-season Saluki record.

Carver Shannon "was the money ballplayer on that team," said former Western Illinois lineman Jerry Auchstetter.

By 1958, Shannon's senior season, the Salukis had hit full stride. SIU posted its best record in more than a decade with a

7-2 mark. Teammate Cecil Hart took home conference MVP honors. Shannon, however, was slowed by injuries. Though he rushed for only 388 yards, he scored seven touchdowns.

Shannon ranks 13th in school history for his 1,805 career rushing yards. In addition, he averaged 6.6 yards per carry, second only to Brandon Jacobs (6.61). Jacobs, however, played just one season at SIU.

Shannon had many skills as a runner.

"I could adjust to what was needed," he said. "I could be a power runner if I had to, or I could use my speed. Actually, it's better to be quick than fast. Being quick means you avoid the defense more effectively."

Vision was one of Shannon's greatest strengths.

"As a runner you have to see the field, you have to anticipate what's going on around you," he said. "You've got to see. That's a major part of any back's success. If you cut against the grain, you've got to see green."

Shannon also cited his desire to compete.

"Every time we stepped on the grass I felt like we would win," he said.

During his time at SIU, Shannon also tried out for the basketball team and ran track. He roomed with Charles "Chico" Vaughn, the high-scoring guard from Tamms High School who later played in both the NBA and the ABA.

On the track, Shannon broke the SIU 100-yard dash record with a 9.8 clocking at the 1958 state meet.

Asked if he experienced any racism while at SIU, Shannon mentioned two events. He was once given a "to-go" cup at a Carbondale malt shop while his two white friends were served. The other occurred in a local barber shop.

"They offered free haircuts for touchdowns scored," Shannon said. "I waited for over two hours and kept getting passed over."

Shannon took his concerns to the university president.

"That got them started looking into things," he said. "They sent out blacks and whites to restaurants and to rent housing, things like that. What they found was there was more (racism) there than we realized."

Yet Shannon said he still looks favorably on his time in Carbondale.

"I considered (the acts of racism) to be individuals, not the Carbondale community," he said. "I dated white girls, I dated black girls. I had fun."

When his time at SIU ended, pro football beckoned. The Los Angeles Rams picked Shannon in the 19th round of the 1959 NFL draft. However, the 6-foot-1, 198-pounder instead chose the Canadian Football League.

"The Winnipeg Blue Bombers offered me more money than the Rams; it's as simple as that," Shannon said.

Shannon played three years in the CFL, mostly with Winnipeg. The Blue Bombers won the 1959 Grey Cup under head coach Bud Grant.

"Bud was a lot like the Lakers' coach (Phil Jackson)," Shannon said. "He was quiet, but when he says something, believe it. He means it."

In his final CFL season, Winnipeg wanted Shannon to sign a contract extension. Shannon refused because he wanted to return to the United States and play for the NFL.

"They let me go, but I got signed by the Hamilton Tiger-Cats," Shannon said.

Ironically, the Grey Cup was a rematch of the same two teams. Again, as in '59, Winnipeg defeated Hamilton for the CFL championship.

"After the game I went over and celebrated with Winnipeg," Shannon said. "They were the ones with the champagne."

Shannon returned to the States and joined the Los Angeles Rams for the 1962 season. He spent the next three seasons playing defensive back and halfback for that team. Shannon, however, excelled as a return man on special teams.

"I always felt like I could break a long one," he said. "I still had my dreams like in college, but in the pros something would usually trip me up."

That didn't happen in a 1963 game against Minnesota. Shannon returned a kickoff 99 yards for a touchdown.

"Sure, I remember it," Shannon said. "At the 40-yard line I was clear."

When football ended, Shannon took a position with Hughes Aviation in Los Angeles.

"No, I never met the man (Howard Hughes)," he said.

But Shannon did find success. While working for the corporation, he earned a master's in business from UCLA. Shannon retired in 2003 after a 34-year career with Hughes.

In addition, Shannon also worked as a line judge on officiating crews in both the Pac 10 Conference and the NFL for over a decade.

"I had to give it up," he said. "My wife had postpartum depression. Back then, people didn't understand it like today. I had to keep my babies safe. The NFL wouldn't grant me a leave."

Early on, Shannon developed a love for community service. He became involved with the Big Brothers program. He also worked with the Special Olympics.

Today he belongs to a group called Goals for Life. In fact, he serves on its board of directors.

"We go out to schools and teach kids how to accomplish things in life," he said. "Being a football player, (I) can get their attention."

Shannon also belongs to the National Football Foundation. In fact, he has a vote to determine the initial candidacy of potential College Football Hall of Fame inductees.

"We vote our recommendations and then it goes to a committee," he said.

Asked if perhaps his name might someday join those enshrined among the all-time greats, Shannon said, "Somebody from SIU should be there; if not me, then someone else."

For now, Shannon is a member of the SIU Hall of Fame.

"It was an honor," he said. "It showed appreciation for what I did."

Shannon also works as an independent contractor for football broadcasts. He's the guy you'll see wearing the bright orange sleeve keeping the game officials alert to TV timeouts.

"Every weekend UCLA or USC is home, so I don't have to travel," he said.

Shannon also spent time visiting his former Rams teammate Ollie Matson, the man the Rams traded nine players to get from the Chicago Cardinals.

"Ollie has Alzheimer's," Shannon said shortly before Matson's death in 2011. "He doesn't know me, but I keep going (to see him). I do it for me, and I do it because he's still my friend and it's the right thing to do."

When asked how football has changed since his playing days, Shannon didn't pull any punches.

"I tell you what, the game is more selfish," he said. "If you run for a touchdown, we all saw it. You don't have to do flips. If I were still playing defensive back you may as well give me the 15 yards (for a personal foul penalty) because I'm going to knock the shit out of him. You already know you messed up by letting him score so why does he have to rub it in?

"These receivers are all yelling, 'Throw me the damn ball!' What about winning the damn game? Shouldn't that be your goal?"

Shannon didn't just pick on the offensive players.

"There are too many defensive backs playing for the interception. They're not putting the team first. That's not how it should be."

Carver Shannon would know about how things should be. With football at Ole Miss in the mid-1950s being unattainable, the Salukis beckoned and won his attention.

"It was one of the best decisions I ever made," said Shannon. "The timing of it all was just right."

FOUR DOWN TERRITORY

Favorite Football Movie—*Jim Thorpe, All-American.*
First Car—It was an old Cadillac I had in college.
Worst Summer Job—In Chicago I worked for a painter. You'd be up on a ladder trimming under the brick on these tall buildings. Inside these buildings were these really tall

Massive Houston Antwine, shown here with SIU head coach Dick Towers, is a member of both the SIU and Patriots halls of fame. In addition, Antwine was an NAIA wrestling champion.

closets. The contractor worked you hard because the sooner we got done, the sooner he got paid.
Favorite Subject in School—Growing up it was history. In college, believe it or not, it was poetry. I had this teacher who made me fall in love with it.

HOUSTON ANTWINE

On the surface Houston Antwine appeared bigger than life. At the core, the 6-foot-tall, 270-pound native of Louise, Mississippi, was simply the greatest two-way lineman in Saluki history.

"In my honest opinion, using every piece of information that I have and trying to be objective and respectful of those who played before and after us, Houston Antwine was the best lineman ever to play football at Southern Illinois University," said former teammate Sam Silas. "It's hard to believe that anyone was better."

Antwine, or "Twine" as he was nicknamed, was virtually impossible to move out of the middle of the line from his defensive tackle position. That quality, coupled with his presence in the offensive line, made Antwine double trouble for SIU opponents.

"He had a terrific offensive game and a terrific defensive game," Silas said. "He was the best I ever saw."

SIU running back Carver Shannon was instrumental in getting Antwine to Carbondale.

"My first years at Southern Illinois, most of the linemen were my size," said the 6-foot-1, 198-pound Shannon. "I told (SIU athletic director Donald) Doc (Boydston) we needed to recruit some big linemen."

Shannon suggested recruiting in the Memphis, Tennessee, area.

"I was from Mississippi," he said, "I didn't know Willie Brown or Houston Antwine personally, but I knew that there was good competition among those Memphis high schools."

Both Brown and Antwine soon found their way to the Salukis.

"Twine had quickness for his size," Shannon said. "He really blossomed."

Of course, Shannon also benefited from Antwine's presence in the line.

"Twine and I worked out a little system," Shannon said. "He would swipe his hand on his butt for which direction I should go. If he swiped left, I went left. If he swiped right, I went right. That worked out pretty well for us. We had great success."

During his time in Carbondale, Antwine became the most celebrated lineman ever to don a Saluki jersey. He was the dominating defensive force who led SIU to a pair of second-place conference finishes as a sophomore and a junior. As a senior, Antwine anchored the Salukis' run to the 1960 IIAC title.

On October 22, playing in front of a record Homecoming crowd of 12,000, Antwine blocked an Illinois State punt that Silas returned to the Redbirds' 10-yard line. Moments later, SIU scored to take a 14-0 lead en route to a 30-6 triumph.

A week later, the Salukis routed Eastern Michigan 66-8 at McAndrew Stadium. The victory allowed SIU to clinch a tie for the conference title for the first time in 30 years. The Salukis jumped out to a quick 14-0 lead and never looked back. Jim Thompson returned the opening kickoff 75 yards for a touchdown. Running back Amos Bullocks, who set an SIU record with 996 yards in a single season, scored twice in the game. His first touchdown came on a 21-yard run, keyed by an Antwine block.

Jack Dean played in the backfield for Northern Illinois University during the early '60s. Dean, who later coached at Eastern Illinois University, remembered playing against SIU and Antwine.

"We took the Illinois Central Railroad from Geneva to Carbondale on Friday. We played the Salukis the next night. I was a freshman and this was my first road trip," Dean said. "They had a large crowd that night, and we won the toss to receive. I lined up on about the goal line to receive the kick-off. I was a 17-year-old frosh at about 145 pounds. The SIU cheerleaders were all in the end zone behind me; each one had a big barking dog. Salukis. I had these dogs barking at my heels and looked down the field and bench and (saw) the likes of Houston and that big Maroon mob.

"I think we played Wheaton College the week prior for our home opener, and this was a different breed of cat. I think I had a pretty good return, running from the dogs, but was welcomed to Carbondale by a smashing tackle of several of them, who drove me out of bounds and into the cinder track that circled the field. I made it through the game, which I am sure Southern won, with just cinder burns from the first play."

Antwine lettered four times in his collegiate career. Moreover, SIU won 25 of 35 games during his tenure. Antwine earned IIAC First Team honors in 1957, 1958 and 1960. He was an Associated Press Second Team All-American in 1960 and was named MVP after the Salukis' championship run.

As a college wrestler, Antwine captured the 1960 NAIA heavyweight national title after finishing as the runner-up a year earlier.

Prior to leaving college, Antwine played in the 1961 College All-Star Game against the NFL champion Philadelphia Eagles. Though he suffered an injury during the game, Antwine's pro prospects were hardly damaged.

With the National Football League and the American Football League in full operation, Antwine was a hot commodity. The Detroit Lions selected him in the NFL draft's third round as the 38th overall pick.

Meanwhile, the Houston Oilers of the AFL chose Antwine in the eighth round as the 64th overall selection.

Antwine opted to sign with the AFL. He was traded, however, to the Boston Patriots, then coached by former Western Illinois head coach Lou Saban.

Antwine excelled in the AFL, earning All-Star status six straight seasons (1963–68). Moreover, he was named to the All-Time All-AFL Team and to the Patriots All-1960s Team.

He *was the best all-around. Twine was a total player.*

Antwine was recognized as one of the premier AFL pass rushers. He generally drew double-team blocking. In 142 games with the Patriots, Antwine registered 39 sacks, recovered four fumbles and intercepted a pass. He led the team in sacks three consecutive years (1967–69).

"In my era, I did not run across any professional who played defensive tackle who was any better than he was," said Sam Silas, who played 1963–70 in the NFL. "Some rushed the passer better but were not as strong against the run as Twine was. He was the best all-around. Twine was a total player."

Silas, a Pro Bowler at defensive tackle in 1965, elaborated.

"The Patriots, in a crunch, could have taken him off the offensive line and put him on defense. And you would not find five linemen in our era who could have done that," Silas said.

Silas also credited Antwine with his own success in pro ball.

"He came back to campus after his first year with the Patriots," Silas said. "None of the (SIU) coaches knew enough about pro football, or even seemed interested in helping me with my aspirations. I went to Twine and asked him what I needed to know and how to make it. He was willing to show me and was patient enough to do so."

According to Jeff Miller in his book *Going Long: The Wild 10-Year Saga of the Renegade American Football League in the Words of Those Who Lived It*, Antwine was a key player in a time of segregation and civil rights discrimination.

When I first came to Houston in 1961, we didn't stay in different accommodations, but we stayed at some motel outside of town . . .

"When I first came to Houston in 1961, we didn't stay in different accommodations, but we stayed at some motel outside of town because they couldn't find anywhere where we all could stay together," Antwine told Miller. "I was impressed with the fact that they didn't want to split the team up. The years after that when we went in to play, it seemed as though they had corrected that situation.

"We were going to New Orleans in 1962 to spend a week there and play an exhibition game. The team didn't let the ballplayers know what the situation was in New Orleans

until we left Buffalo: 'Look, we can't stay as one team in the hotel.' They put the black ballplayers in some hotel way across town."

Antwine was front and center in a controversy over the AFL All-Star Game in New Orleans.

"I was staying at the Fontainebleau Hotel with the Eastern squad," Antwine told Miller. "Cookie Gilchrist and some of the other guys came in and wanted to go over and visit with the guys on the Western team. We couldn't get cabs to go over to the Roosevelt. The cabdrivers said, 'We can't haul you guys. We're going to call you some colored cabs.' And Cookie raised a whole bunch of noise. We eventually got over to the Roosevelt, and it seemed like the black ballplayers there were having the same problems. During the course of the evening, the problem persisted. Late in the evening, everybody was comparing notes: 'You couldn't do this, and you couldn't do that, and you were insulted here.'"

League officials and New Orleans businessmen quickly scrambled to head off the player boycott. However, Antwine and his fellow African American All-Stars didn't budge.

"They were promising us cars. They were promising us everything, if we just stayed there and played. But if we did that, we would be accepting the conditions. Everybody made plans to leave," Antwine told Miller.

And leave they did. Meanwhile, the AFL hastily threw together an alternative. The "new" All-Star Game, which took place at Jeppesen Stadium in Houston, was won by the West, 38-14.

In his book Miller noted, "There are no plaques, no citations that note the action taken in Room 990 of the Roosevelt Hotel that led to the All-Star Game leaving New Orleans. So the following notation will have to do. Twenty-two black players made the collective decision; some have said since that the decision was unanimous while others have indicated there was at least some dissent and disagreement."

"It didn't get the publicity that I think it should have," Antwine told Miller. "We didn't feel it was properly addressed. Back in Boston, there was one little blip in the paper showing me with my bag leaving the hotel. That was basically it. The hostility and the treatment that we received in New Orleans was never, never really publicized. I've talked to Cookie, and he was really ticked off about it. Right now, if you ask somebody, 'Do you remember the AFL All-Star Game that was supposed to be played in New Orleans?' nobody remembers what happened."

When the AFL and the NFL merged for the 1970 season, Antwine remained with the Patriots through the 1971 season.

In the New England media guide Antwine was noted for "a habit of destroying training camp tackling dummies."

He finished his pro career with the Philadelphia Eagles in 1972.

"Twine had back trouble from his playing days," Silas said. "He had pain that ran down the back of his legs."

According to Silas, Antwine returned to Boston and became a successful insurance agent.

"At some point he moved to Davis, California," Silas said.

"That's true," Shannon said. "Twine lived in the (San Francisco) Bay area. He was retired. Since I lived in Los Angeles, we reconnected. Then he and his wife moved back to Memphis."

Antwine died on December 26, 2011, of heart failure. His death was followed by that of his wife, Evelyn, who passed away from lung cancer less than a day later.

"For those of us who grew up watching the Boston Patriots, this is a really sad day," Patriots owner Robert Kraft said afterward. "In the 1960s, the defensive tackle tandem of 'Twine' and Jim Lee Hunt were as good as any in the league and helped propel the Patriots to the franchise's first division championship in 1963.

"I loved hearing Houston's stories about those early days in Boston. It was such a thrill for me, personally, to spend time with the players from that era.

"I am saddened to learn of the deaths of both Houston and Evelyn and want to express my deepest sympathies to the Antwines' daughter, Regina, and all who mourn her losses. Let us all cherish life and remind loved ones how we feel about them daily."

For Silas and Shannon, the news of Antwine's death came as a surprise.

"I think of him so fondly," Silas said. "First of all, he was very helpful to me. He had such a fantastic personality. Houston was a better football player than me. I recognize that. But he was also my friend and such a wonderful human being."

Shannon said, "Everybody was shocked. I read it in the newspaper. I talked to seven or eight former teammates. None of us got word about it. I imagine that Twine's family had their hands full with two deaths so close together.

"Twine had a great personality. He had a very soft side, which people didn't expect. He loved to laugh. Believe me, Twine will be missed by those who knew him best."

SAM SILAS

At a time when most Americans were mourning, Sam Silas had reason to celebrate.

"President Kennedy had been shot and killed," recalled the SIU defensive star of the early 1960s.

Silas, a member of the St. Louis Cardinals, was in New York to play the Giants at Yankee Stadium. NFL commissioner Pete Rozelle had made the decision—one he later called his greatest mistake—not to cancel the Sunday schedule of NFL games.

"Many of the players did not want to play," Silas said. "There was ice on the field in New York. Our starting left tackle got hurt, and I was sent in for him. I got two and a half sacks in three plays. I never did that again in my career."

Thus, while the country was dealing with a tragedy, Silas had reached a turning point in his pro football career.

Silas said, "People were asking, 'Who is this guy?'"

The answer to that question starts in Homeland, Florida, where he lived until he was two years old.

Silas attended high school at Union Academy in Bartow, Florida. It was there that Silas honed his craft as a student and as an athlete.

"I wanted to be a doctor," he said. "I played football, basketball (and) track, and in the summer I was on a swim team."

Though he stood 6-foot-4 and weighed 230 pounds by his sophomore year, Silas struggled on the basketball court.

"My coach, my classmates and me included, all agree that I was the world's worst basketball player," he said. "My coach kept me on the team as a means of keeping me in shape around the clock."

According to Silas, many northern college coaches flocked to Florida in search of speedy athletes such as Bob Hayes, the Jacksonville sprinter who won Olympic gold and later starred for the Dallas Cowboys.

Famed Florida A&M head football coach Alonzo "Jake" Gaither drew national attention for his comments that the Sunshine State's athletes were "mobile, hostile and agile."

Silas said, "That brought national attention to Florida. Coaches came down from everywhere."

Among those traveling to Florida were SIU athletic director Doc Boydston, the man who had helped deliver Carver Shannon to the Salukis.

"He and the assistant athletic director—his name was Bill O'Brien, if I recall correctly— had decided to vacation in Florida. You know, mix a little business with pleasure," Silas said.

Word got to the SIU duo about Silas. Working in the Salukis' favor was the fact that schools such as Florida, Florida State and Miami weren't actively recruiting African Americans at the time.

After starring at SIU, Sam Silas became an All-Pro player with the St. Louis Cardinals.

"They came to basketball practice and watched me," Silas recalled. "Fortunately that day we were doing training. I wasn't shooting or dribbling or anything like that. I was just running up and down the court."

Boydston and O'Brien liked what they saw. In fact, following practice, they went home with Silas and offered him a scholarship.

"They met my grandmother, who was two-in-one for me. She was my grandmother and my mother," he said.

Silas picked SIU over Florida A&M and a last-minute offer from Indiana University because "when a Southern country boy gets a chance to fly on a plane up north it was just majestic. I was won over."

Silas quickly worked his way into the starting lineup for the Salukis—though it wasn't quick enough for him.

"I was naïve," he said. "I lived in a synthetic world for quite a long time in my athletic career. I felt all along I would play. When I became a starter in my second year I wasn't even excited. Call it arrogance, perhaps, but from the day I first set foot on the field, I felt that only one person playing was better than me. That other person was Houston Antwine."

The Salukis of the early 1960s were a powerful lot. Featuring players such as Antwine, Silas and Willie Brown, SIU won consecutive Interstate Intercollegiate Athletic Conference championships under head coach Carmen Piccone.

"I don't remember any particular games per se," said Silas, "but I do remember a few things here and there."

One of the most memorable was when Silas split his football pants down the back seam during a game against rival Western Illinois.

"Like most players, I just wore my jockstrap under the pants with no shorts or anything over it. I was playing both offense and defense and the game was close so I couldn't go to the sidelines and change," he said.

Meanwhile a photographer took a photo from the end zone behind the Salukis.

"The photo appeared a couple of days later in the *Southern Illinoisan.* The way it was taken our linebacker Jim Minton's hand was positioned in such a way to block the revealing area. The caption said, 'Protection for Sam.' That photo was a real keepsake," Silas laughed.

Another time Silas played with a shoulder injury.

"I was married at the time," he said. "My wife had to dress me at home because I could only move my shoulder certain ways. When I got to the locker room, my teammates had to undress me and get me into my uniform. I remember having a good game and that we won."

Toward the end of one season, Silas broke his jaw in a collision with a teammate during practice.

"I had no idea of the nature of the injury," he said. "It wasn't until after the season when I was opening my mouth I heard a cracking sound. The doctor wired up my mouth for two or three weeks."

When his Saluki career ended, Silas got no guidance in regard to pro football.

"It seems as though once I was finished playing I didn't have as much contact with the coaching staff," he said. "I didn't lose sleep over it, but they didn't seem concerned with me. Maybe they felt I'd be okay. Maybe they felt, ever so quietly, that I wouldn't make it."

Whatever the case, the Boston Patriots of the American Football League chose Silas as their sixth round pick in the 1963 draft.

However, Boston's contract offer was for only $9,000 with a $1,000 bonus.

"I was elated to be drafted by the Patriots, but it seemed to be a very modest contract," he said.

In addition, Silas felt the National Football League was the stick by which he wanted to be measured. Therefore he signed as a free agent with the St. Louis Cardinals.

"They lured me into signing before I even knew it," Silas said. "Instinctively I wanted to play the better brand of football in the NFL. I wanted to compete against the best."

Silas signed for $10,000 with a $2,000 bonus.

"Sometimes, even today, I wonder how things would have turned out had I signed with the AFL, but I have no regrets," he said.

For Silas, making the Cardinals' roster proved to be a daunting task.

"The best player does not always make the grade," he said. "I learned that a set of circumstances all going in one direction determines what happens."

For Silas, those circumstances included overcoming players from larger schools who had signed more lucrative contracts and been given off-season jobs with Anheuser-Busch.

"If you had asked the coaches how to rate me on a scale of 1 to 10 with 1 being the best, they'd have ranked me a 20," Silas said. "I didn't have a snowball's chance in hell of making it."

Yet Silas didn't want to return to Florida without giving his all for his once-in-a-lifetime shot.

"I never quit. I sprinted everywhere," he said.

Silas also developed a friendship with Bill "Thunder" Thornton, a fifth-round St. Louis draft pick.

"Thunder told me, 'Make the job of those bastards very difficult. Don't let them break you,'" Silas said.

> **T**he best player does not always make the grade. I learned that a set of circumstances all going in one direction determines what happens.

Still, his roster spot wasn't guaranteed until the final game of the exhibition season.

"We played the Minnesota Vikings in St. Louis," he said. "They beat the hell out of us, but I have the Minnesota Vikings to thank. They made everyone on our team look bad except for a few of us. I was one of the few Cardinals who had a decent game. I played mostly special teams, but I was able to come through and make a few plays."

Silas made enough plays to make the final St. Louis roster. His spot was secured on those three plays against the New York Giants on that fateful November Sunday.

In all, Silas played eight years in the NFL. He played in the Pro Bowl in 1965. Silas spent five seasons with St. Louis before playing for the Giants in 1968. He finished his career with the San Francisco 49ers.

Silas used his status as a professional football player to continue his education. While still playing, Silas earned a master's degree from SIU while also providing some public relations for the university.

"It was a benefit for both sides," he said. "They got good PR from me, and I got a break on the cost of my schooling."

Silas worked for SIU briefly until budget cuts ended his job. However, he was hired to teach at William Paterson University in New Jersey shortly thereafter.

"I retired after 34 years there," he said.

Silas has spent his golden years "bouncing back and forth between New Jersey and Florida."

"I still have the house I grew up in. My grandmother willed it to me," he said.

In the summer of 2011 Silas attended a reunion of his high school class. It proved to be the perfect time for reflection.

"It was so wonderful to see so many faces that we haven't seen in so long. It was reenergizing," he said.

When asked to reflect on the 1963 game in New York that stands as a landmark in his pro football career, Silas smiled.

"That game put me on the map," he said.

A map that includes a road running through SIU in Carbondale.

FOUR DOWN TERRITORY

Favorite Football Movie—Actually, no, I don't have any, but I do have those two games (in 1963) that we filmed. Those recorded performances are what I'm happy about. Those two and a half sacks in three plays against the Giants and then the following week we played in Cleveland. We didn't play the Cleveland Browns; we played Jim Brown. Of course, they ran my way since I was the unproven player on the line. We held him to a net of six yards. Those films would be my choice.

First Car—My grandmother could not drive, so I drove her. She had a 1957 Ford, brand-new. When she was trying to teach me a lesson or keep me from getting into something I shouldn't, she'd take that car away. The first car I bought was a 1954 Plymouth. I bought it from a fella in Carbondale. I paid $85 for it. I drove it back and forth from Carbondale to Florida four times. Then I had to get rid of it because I couldn't afford new brakes. When I was playing with San Francisco I bought the same 1954 Plymouth model for $160. I drove it to Carbondale and put it in storage. I later drove it to New Jersey, and it's been in my garage ever since. Oh, I drive it now and again, but I keep it to remind me of those days long ago.

Worst Summer Job—There are two jobs. As a youngster—I was probably 10 or 12 years old—I worked on farms. I picked string beans. It was so hot. It took so much effort to pick the volume they wanted just to earn a small amount of money. After my senior year in high school I took one class at Florida A&M and worked construction. That was hot! That tar paper was something. I hated that.

Favorite Subject in School—I majored in zoology with hopes of becoming a doctor. I soon discovered it wasn't my forte. I realized that I could not make the right grades unless I quit football, and I loved it too much to do that. But as much as I enjoyed zoology, the class I loved the most was English, even though I'm not very good at it. But I loved it. There was a professor, Dr. Georgia Wynn, who really made it so enjoyable. Later, I really enjoyed exercise physiology, but if I had to pick, it's English.

Jim Hart (16) in action during the 1960s.

1960s

JIM HART

While noted novelist Pat Conroy penned the autobiographical *My Losing Season*, quarterback Jim Hart could have just as easily told his story.

Conroy's 2003 memoir told of his struggles as a basketball player at the Citadel during the 1960s. Hart has enough material to vividly describe his days as a football player at Southern Illinois University in those same terms during the same era.

"I probably remember more negative things than positive," said Hart from his home in southwestern Florida. "We were not very successful."

During Hart's playing days in Carbondale, the Salukis were bent on upgrading their schedule. Southern, however, didn't offer the full athletic scholarships that many of its opponents did.

"When we talk of a full NCAA scholarship, that's room, board, books, fees, tuition and $15 a month," Hart recalled. "It wasn't until (basketball star) Walt Frazier came along in 1964 that someone at SIU got one of those.

Jim Hart set numerous records at SIU and later starred in the National Football League. Hart also served as athletic director for his alma mater.

"Coach Carmen Piccone and his staff recruited me," he said. "When I first went there the offense was the traditional three yards and a cloud of dust (run-oriented) offense. But, after my freshman year, he changed to a pro-style offense. I owe that to Carmen."

Hart's junior and senior seasons were played under former St. Louis Cardinals assistant coach Don Shroyer.

"He was a hard-nosed guy," Hart recalled. "He kept us going even during the tough times."

Those teams we played were just so much bigger than us. I remember just getting hammered.

And the tough times were abundant. SIU posted just an 8-21 record during Hart's varsity days.

"We played schools like Tulsa with (Heisman runner-up) Jerry Rhome and (receiver) Howard Twilley," Hart said. "We played Bowling Green, Wichita State and Toledo."

Hart also recalls playing in Louisville, where SIU's African American players couldn't stay at the same hotel as the rest of the team.

"Being from (more liberal) Evanston, that just blew my mind," said Hart. "It's something that was going on during those times."

The Salukis were also struggling on the field during those years.

"Those teams we played were just so much bigger than us. I remember just getting hammered. I barely had time to throw the ball," he recalled.

Hart also remembers the final game of the 1964 season when the Salukis hosted Evansville.

"On Friday it was 50 degrees and raining like crazy," Hart recalled. "Coach Shroyer had us practice on the stadium field, because it was the last game of the season. Well, overnight the temperatures dropped into the teens and the field froze. There were shoe marks and holes everywhere. You could count the number of people in the stands. We lost 2-0 when our center snapped the ball over the punter's head."

Despite playing for often overmatched teams, Hart managed to set the SIU career passing record with 3,779 yards. That mark stood until 1983. Hart's 34 career touchdown passes are still sixth on the all-time Saluki charts.

So does Hart ever wish he'd have gone to a bigger school? After all, large universities like Northwestern, Illinois and Arizona made him offers following his prep career at Niles West High School in the Chicago suburbs.

"Shoot, no," Hart said emphatically. "I've had more fun at every level that I played at. Look at the pros today. Sure, they make big money, but they don't have fun. People I talk to tell me these guys go their separate ways after the games and practices. We did all kinds of things on and off the field back when I played.

"If I were making $15 million a year like some are now, I'd have lived at the stadium."

Hart saw other advantages to playing at a school like SIU.

"The pressures aren't as great as (those at) a place like U of I or the Big 10 or the Big 12 or wherever," Hart explained. "Those guys are on TV all the time. Everyone wants to be a pro. There's a lot of pressure on every play."

After his days ended at SIU, Hart wasn't taken by any NFL teams in the 1966 draft. He did receive some attention though. Hart recalls getting letters from Dallas, San Francisco and Los Angeles.

"The Cowboys sent letters to everyone in those days," Hart said.

It was at that same time that Shroyer returned to his job as a St. Louis Cardinals' assistant coach, a position he had held prior to coming to Carbondale.

"Don was disappointed like I was that I didn't get drafted," Hart said. "But he got the Cardinals to sign me (as a free agent). They sent their ticket manager to sign me. That shows you where I ranked."

In the days of Joe Namath's record $600,000 deal with the New York Jets of the AFL, Hart signed for $12,000 and a $1,000 bonus.

"I was hoping for something like $15,000 and a $5,000 bonus, but the guy who signed me kept saying he wasn't authorized for that," Hart said. "It was late at night, and he said there was no one to call from the Cardinals. I started to worry that if I didn't sign, they'd think I was trying to squeeze them for more money and then there would be no offer."

Once into the Cardinals' camp, where Hart found himself listed sixth on a six-man depth chart, he had to work his way up the ladder. When starter Charley Johnson had to leave the team to fulfill an ROTC commitment in 1967 and '68, Hart found himself in the starting lineup.

For the next few seasons, Hart fought for playing time with the likes of Pete Bethard and Gary Cuozzo. His play and playing time were sporadic.

Then came Hart's big break in 1973. The Cardinals hired Don Coryell as their new head coach. Coryell, known for his passing game, made Hart the starter. It was a position he would hold for the next decade in St. Louis.

"Coryell was innovative and fun to play for," Hart said. "You wanted to play for a guy like him."

Hart enjoyed his finest seasons under Coryell's leadership. Statistically, Hart's biggest seasons occurred from 1974 to 1976. He led the team to 10 or more victories and two division titles during those years.

Then things began to fall apart. First, St. Louis owner Bill Bidwill wouldn't sign star running back Terry Metcalf. Then Coryell left to become the head coach of the San Diego Chargers.

Hart remained in St. Louis through those turbulent years under head coaches the likes of Bud Wilkinson, Larry Wilson and Jim Hanifan. By the beginning of the 1984 season, Hart was pushed aside in favor of promising young quarterback Neil Lomax.

Hart spent one more season in the NFL with the Washington Redskins before retiring as a player.

In his 2008 research-based book *The Pro Football Historical Abstract*, sports historian Sean Lahman ranked Hart as the 53rd greatest quarterback.

In his book *Quarterback Abstract*, writer John Maxymuk rates Hart as a "good quarterback," awarding him a score of eight on a 10-point scale.

"Jim Hart was a baby-faced gunslinger at quarterback," Maxymuk wrote. "He wasn't brash like Bobby Layne or cocky like Dan Fouts or emotional like Brett Favre, but Hart lived and died by the long ball, flourished and perished by forcing the ball into tight coverage. While not as talented or successful as those three Hall of Famers, Hart was a very good quarterback over a long career and guided the woeful Cardinals to their only period of success in the past 60 years, three straight 10+ win seasons and consecutive division championships under Coach Don Coryell in the mid-1970s."

Hart followed his playing career by starting two new ones. He worked alongside NFL Hall-of-Famer Dick Butkus as an analyst on Chicago Bears' broadcasts. Then came an offer to return to SIU as its athletic director.

For two years, Hart did both jobs before giving up the broadcasting to devote more time to being SIU's A.D. following the 1989 NFL season.

We really liked it (at SIU). Some of our greatest friends are from those days.

"WGN asked me if I wanted to do something for them full-time," Hart explained. "I didn't want to leave SIU, because the SIU job seemed more long lasting."

Long lasting turned out to be 12 years.

"We really liked it (at SIU)," said Hart. "Some of our greatest friends are from those days."

Hart said the honeymoon as A.D. lasted about six years.

"When you start to win games, the pressures grow and become a reality," Hart said. "There begins to be a familiarity. More people want to be in on the decision-making process. I just wanted to do my job."

In addition, the fiscal picture began to deteriorate. The state of Illinois ruled that university funds could no longer be used for athletic scholarships.

"It didn't hurt a school like U of I," Hart said. "They had their own fund-raising foundation separate from that.

"But, for a school like SIU, you were talking about losing $1.5 million from a budget that was maybe $3.5 million total."

Fund-raising soon took its toll.

"For the Chicago alums contributing money back, they never got to see what was being done with that money. It wasn't long before some of them began to question why they were giving money," Hart said. "Even many of the guys I played with never went back to Southern because it's such a long distance from Chicago."

In 1999 Hart left SIU to return to St. Louis. He opened a restaurant with former Cardinal teammate Dan Dierdorf in the Gateway City.

Today Hart spends his retirement years with Mary, his wife of over 50 years. He spends time playing golf and entertaining friends. Still, Hart manages to follow Saluki football.

"I've got them on my computer (favorites)," Hart said. "I listen to the games on the Internet. SIU has had success. They've made the playoffs on a consistent basis."

So while Hart's story may not have the same best-selling power as the one written by Conroy, it's still a gripping tale.

Indeed, Jim Hart's Southern story is one that proves good things do sometimes come from adversity.

FOUR DOWN TERRITORY

Favorite Football Movie—*Paper Lion*; I had a part in that one.
First Car—1966 Pontiac Lemans after signing my rookie contract with the Cardinals.
Worst Summer Job—The toughest was as a "packer boy" with W. F. Hall Printing Company in Chicago.
Favorite Subject in School—Kinesiology.

CARL MAUCK

Carl Mauck remembers watching the landmark 1958 NFL championship game between the Baltimore Colts and the New York Giants that many sports historians say thrust pro football into national consciousness.

"I was 11 years old and watched it on a 12-inch black-and-white TV," said Mauck. "Ten years later I was snapping the ball to Johnny Unitas."

Much happened to Mauck between those two events. Perhaps even more happened to him afterward.

Born in 1947, Mauck grew up in McLeansboro.

"Home of the Foxes," noted Mauck. "There are three of us (that made it in professional sports). There was a guy named Ray Blades who played with the old Gas House Gang (the nickname given to the St. Louis Cardinals of the 1930s). Of course, there's (former Chicago Bull and ex–head coach of the Utah Jazz) Jerry Sloan, and there's me."

Before he was a pro football player, Mauck starred as a four-sport athlete for McLeansboro High School. He competed in football, basketball, baseball and track.

"There were 22 juniors and seniors on the football team," Mauck said. "All the other sports were no cut because we needed the participants."

Mauck's prowess in football and basketball caught the attention of more than a few colleges and universities. Among these were Dartmouth, Missouri and the military academies. Yet Mauck decided on Southern Illinois University.

"(SIU) was 60 miles from home," he said. "They wanted me the most. I never went on an official visit."

Mauck signed up not only for football but also for basketball.

"Don Shroyer was the football coach then, and Jack Hartman was the basketball coach," he said.

Mauck didn't really get to know either coach very well. Shroyer left after one season, and Mauck played just one year of basketball.

"Remember, those were the days when freshmen weren't eligible to compete at the varsity level," he noted. "When the decision came to play spring football, that was the end of my basketball."

Still, Mauck vividly remembers playing with future basketball Hall of Famer and SIU legend Clyde Frazier.

"All I can tell you is that he was a great athlete," Mauck said. "We played Louisville when they had (future Hall of Famer) Wes Unseld and (future NBA player) Butch Beard. Frazier outrebounded Unseld and outscored Beard."

McLeansboro native Carl Mauck (52) enjoyed lengthy careers as both player and coach after his time at SIU ended.

Furthermore, Mauck remembers Frazier on the spring football practice field.

"He had been a high school quarterback in Atlanta, Georgia," Mauck said. "He threw the ball 65 yards in the air right-handed. Then he turned around and threw the ball 65 yards in the air left-handed. He was ambidextrous.

"He could have played football easy, very easy."

While Frazier enjoyed his success on the hardwood, Mauck quickly gained fame on the football field. When Shroyer left to return to the St. Louis Cardinals in the NFL, Ellis Rainsberger took the SIU helm.

"We beat Wichita State at home; we hadn't done that before, as far as I know," Mauck said. "We finished one game under .500 (with a 4-5 record for the 1966 season)."

Rainsberger left Carbondale, however, to take an assistant's job at the University of Illinois.

"He had a lot of juice," Mauck said. "Everybody was disappointed when he left."

Former assistant Dick Towers was then promoted and took over as the SIU head coach.

"We were not very good my junior year (3-7 record)," Mauck said. "We went down to North Texas State in Denton. They had (future Pittsburgh Steeler Hall of Famer) Joe Greene. They just whipped us (37-0).

"The next week we played Tulsa. They had just beaten Arkansas and were ranked number 5 or 6 in the nation. They came in 6-0, and we were 1-5. They threw the ball about 40 times a game. It was Homecoming for us. Tulsa was something like a 40- or 45-point favorite."

After falling behind early, SIU whittled away at the Tulsa lead. Eventually, the Salukis forged ahead 16-13.

"Tulsa was driving on us," Mauck said. "It was fourth-and-five. They threw a little flare pass. We got the guy down half a yard short (of the first down). The fans stormed the field, tore the goal posts down and ran them down the street. It's still called one of the greatest games in SIU history."

The Salukis were 6-3 in Mauck's senior season.

"We beat some pretty good teams that season," he said of the SIU schedule that included Dayton, Drake and Tampa.

"Tampa was NAIA, which meant they could get anybody to play (regardless of academic requirements). They were stacked. They had a running back named Leon McQuay who later played in the Canadian Football League. They had Jim Del Gaizo, who was the Miami Dolphins' backup quarterback, and they had John Matuszak of the Oakland Raiders."

SIU prevailed 23-20 in the late-season game played in Tampa.

With his collegiate career over, Mauck was selected by the Baltimore Colts in the 13th round of the NFL draft.

"They had Unitas, Tom Matte, Earl Morrall, Bubba Smith," he recalled. "It was a veteran team. It was a great place to play. I loved the Colts."

Mauck also spent time playing minor-league football in Harrisburg, Pennsylvania, in the Atlantic Coast League. Harrisburg was affiliated with the Colts until 1968.

"I made about $100 a game and went both ways," Mauck said. "I played right guard and middle linebacker."

Mauck spent just one season with Baltimore but soon found himself with the Miami Dolphins when head coach Don Shula left the Colts for Florida.

"I started the last three games. We had to win them all to get into the playoffs and we did," Mauck said. "I got to start the playoff game too."

The following season, Mauck was traded to San Diego. During his three seasons with the Chargers, he accomplished a rarity for a center by scoring a touchdown. San Diego running back Sid Edwards fumbled the ball inside the five-yard line.

"Nobody knew where the ball was," Mauck remembered. "I fell on it and rolled and rolled into the end zone."

In 1975 Mauck was acquired in a trade by the Houston Oilers. He would spend seven productive seasons with Houston playing for head coach Bum Phillips, who became a lifelong friend.

Mauck also had the pleasure of blocking for Earl Campbell, the Heisman Trophy–winning back who would later be enshrined into the Pro Football Hall of Fame.

"Earl was the best, in my opinion," Mauck answered when asked how good Campbell was.

"People have asked me what it was like blocking for Earl Campbell," Mauck said. "Number one, when you heard him coming, you got out of his way. Number two, what did it sound like? Well, think about being 20 feet from the railroad track when it comes rumbling through. That's what it was like."

Campbell burst onto the NFL scene with a rare combination of speed and power. He won the NFL Offensive Player of the Year Award in 1979 and led the league in rushing his first three seasons.

"He imparted his will on the opposition," Mauck added. "Earl never said a word. He'd finally get brought down, and he'd just get up, get back to the huddle and play."

Riding the legs of Campbell, the Oilers fought their way into consecutive AFC title games in 1978 and '79. Both years, Houston fell to the powerful Pittsburgh Steelers.

"We came along at the wrong time," Mauck said. "Pittsburgh kept us from winning at least one Super Bowl."

Yet, rather than dwelling on those losses to Pittsburgh, Mauck remembers what followed.

"(After both losses), they took us into the Astrodome (where the Oilers played their home games)," Mauck recalled. "It was packed both times. It was packed for a team that had just lost. We loved the town, and they loved us. It was the whole Luv Ya Blue era. It took us three hours to get out of there."

When his 13-year NFL career ended in 1981, Mauck had played in 166 regular-season games. Remarkably, he played 156 of those games in a row.

He was about to begin his postplaying career by doing a show on Houston radio when he got a call from Phillips, then the head coach of the New Orleans Saints.

"It was right before the draft," Mauck said. "The regular offensive line coach had just had surgery and couldn't be on the field. Bum wanted me to run the meetings and be on the field."

Mauck wound up being on NFL fields for the next 24 years. His coaching résumé reads like a travelogue: New Orleans, Kansas City, Tampa Bay, San Diego, Arizona, Buffalo and Detroit.

Topping the list of coaching highlights is reaching the Super Bowl with the Chargers under head coach Bobby Ross.

"It took me 25 years to get into that game," Mauck said. "It was the third time I played for the AFC championship in Pittsburgh."

The third time proved to be the charm for Mauck, now the coach, rather than Mauck the player.

"I told my players before the game, '(Terry) Bradshaw ain't going to be on that field. Mean Joe Greene won't either,'" he said.

San Diego advanced to the Super Bowl by defeating the Steelers 17-13.

Though San Diego lost to the San Francisco 49ers ("They beat our ass; we couldn't stop them"), Mauck enjoyed his return to San Diego.

"We started 0-4 that first year and won 11 out of our last 12," Mauck noted. "The AFC West was pretty good in those days."

Mauck also enjoyed working with the likes of Phillips and Ross.

"You've seen that movie *The Natural*? Remember that scene when the two coaches are whistling songs and naming them? That's what Bum and I did sitting in the back of a plane. We were doing that with country songs the whole trip back."

Going back is something Mauck also did when his NFL coaching career ended in 2005. He spent the next two years as an SIU assistant under then head Saluki coach Jerry Kill.

"(Mauck is) the type of coach you would see depicted as being an offensive line coach if they made a TV show about football," said the Salukis' Bryan Boemer, the 2011 Rimington Award winner.

When Kill took the head coaching job at Northern Illinois University late in 2007, Mauck returned to Texas. He served as a volunteer coach at Argyle High School.

Everything you hear about Texas high school football is true. It is king.

"We were 12-1 this past year and made it to the third round of the state playoffs," he said. "Everything you hear about Texas high school football is true. It is king. Friday Night Lights, the band, the cheerleaders, all of it. It's a spectacle."

Carl Mauck should know: He's seen football on every level over the years. And he's seen it on far more than a 12-inch black-and-white TV.

FOUR DOWN TERRITORY

Favorite Football Movie—When I was a kid it was *Knute Rockne: All-American*. Now I'd say it's *Leatherheads*. That movie captures the essence of pro football in its infancy.

First Car—A 1962 Chevrolet black convertible that I bought for $700 in Baltimore, Maryland, when I was with the Colts. It had about 95,000 miles on it.

Worst Summer Job—I worked in the oil fields for a while. I pulled old pipe out of

Gary Smith was a longtime NFL scout who got his start at SIU. *Photo courtesy of Indiana University Archives (PO024568)*

GARY SMITH

Gary Smith spent two decades as an NFL scout for the Chicago Bears and the New York Jets. He helped coordinate the NFL Scouting Combine. Yet the seeds of his career were planted at SIU.

"I grew up in the little coal-mining, farming town of Virden, Illinois, which is about 20 miles south of Springfield," said Smith in the summer of 2014. "I played football and ran track. I didn't play basketball. I was a short guy anyway, and when I looked out there to see who was playing on our team, which happened to be pretty good, I decided to just lift (weights) and run and get myself ready for football season."

Smith said that as a high school athlete he was "probably 5-(foot)-7 and had a 28-inch waist. I was probably 160 pounds soaking wet."

He played every position "at some time or other on both sides of the ball" for the Virden Bulldogs, with the exception of holder, kicker and punter.

Upon graduation from high school Smith earned a music scholarship to SIU.

"The funny thing is that I never played in the band or orchestra (at SIU)," he said.

Smith also didn't play football his freshman year.

"I would have had to walk on to the team, plus I was 17 at the time," Smith recalled. "Another factor was that I had received a 1A classification for the (military) draft. At that time everything was going on, the Vietnam War, the drug scene. It was crazy."

In addition, there was a transition in coaching at SIU.

the ground. By the end of the day you'd be covered with oil and salt water. I made $2 an hour, which was pretty good money in those days. After about three weeks my mom made me quit because it was costing more to clean my clothes. After that, it was back to the hayfield.

Favorite Subject in School—Math.

"I wasn't even involved in football my first year, since the timing of everything wasn't right," he said.

Smith did walk on to the team his sophomore year.

"I got injured early on, but the coaching staff kept me on," he said. "At that time you could get grants. I had to work at the (athletic) arena at Southern Illinois. I handed out towels and other things like that."

Saluki head football coach Dick Towers took a liking to Smith.

"He said, 'Why don't you help us, since you're here? You're injured and you can't do a whole lot out there (on the field), but you can help us in here.' I helped break down film and some odd jobs. I was kind of like a graduate assistant, but I was a student assistant."

The position also came with a stipend. The following year, Smith again assumed the same duties along with a partial grant. He also gained Towers's trust.

"A lot of the stuff I was doing back then I was later doing when I was scouting," Smith explained. "I got a feel for the coaching side as well as the behind-the-scenes stuff, things like setting up for a recruiting weekend.

"Dick Towers was really good to me. He didn't have to do all that."

As graduation neared, Smith's future remained up in the air.

"I was waiting to see if I was going to be a 4F or a 1A for Vietnam," he said.

As fate would have it, Smith returned to his hometown and coached for three years. He made other high school coaching stops along the way: Lyons, Reavis, Crete-Monee.

"I got RIFed a few times, you know, reduction in force, the last one hired is the first one fired," Smith said. "I got to the point where I had to ask myself what I was doing. I wasn't advancing. I wasn't going anyplace."

Yet there were factors working in Smith's favor.

"I didn't have a wife or kids or pets or anything really holding me in place," he said. "I wasn't going to be a tree hugger. I was going to go out on a limb and see what happens."

Smith had also developed a friendship over the years with Joe Novak, Bill Mallory's defensive coordinator at Northern Illinois University.

Thus, in 1985, Smith joined Bill Mallory's staff at Indiana University. He would remain with the Hoosiers until 1991.

"For lack of a better term, I was director of football operations. One of my duties was handling the in-house recruiting. By doing so, without even really realizing it, I made a lot of contacts. Today you'd call it networking," he said.

As a result, Smith met a number of scouts, coaches, trainers and general managers at the professional level.

"One of the guys who came in was Jeff Schwiebert, who was with the Bears," Smith said. "Jeff recommended me to Bill Tobin, who was then the director of player personnel for Chicago."

Tobin phoned Mallory to discuss the matter. Mallory in turn called Smith into his office.

"After I went through an interview in Chicago, Coach Mallory called me and said, 'You know, you really need to look at this job. We only have so many slots here. There's only so much I can pay guys. This is probably a career move,'" Smith recalled.

Mallory also intimated that his retirement wasn't that far away (as well as the possibility of being fired).

"Coach Mallory added that when new coaches come in they always bring their guys along with them. Part of Coach Mallory's job was to help his own guys get jobs other places.

"I had hit that fork in the road. Did I want to stay in coaching or move on to something else? That's how I got involved in scouting," he said.

Smith never looked back. He spent seven years with the Bears before moving on to 13 with the Jets.

"Seventy-five percent of the time was spent sitting and watching tape or film (of players)," he said. "Every school was different, but every school was the same. There was a routine to it. You went to the pro days. You went to spring practice. You went into different schools in the fall."

With the exception of two seasons, Smith's time as a scout was based in the Midwest.

"I worked closely with Dick Haley when I was with the Jets," he said. "Dick was, next to Chuck Noll, the most instrumental in getting Pittsburgh all those great draft picks when the Steelers won those four Super Bowl championships. Dick went to the Jets after his time in Pittsburgh."

Smith also worked with Hall of Fame head coach Bill Parcells.

"He and Bill Belichick had come to Indiana when I was there to look at (Heisman Trophy runner-up) Anthony Thompson," Smith said.

Accurately or not, scouts are often viewed as men who find diamonds in the rough.

"One of those guys would be a kid named Joe Burger, who played at Michigan Tech. I remember he came to the Combine with his coach and the coach's daughter. He came into Indianapolis; well, you could have dropped him off in New York, Chicago, Indianapolis, it was all the same to him. Tall buildings, a lot of traffic. Joe was out of his element, that's for sure, but he hung on and played for Dallas," Smith said.

"There was another kid from the University of Illinois who we took in the sixth round when I was with the Jets (in 1999). (J. P.) Machado was his name. He hung around for quite a while. He was more of a backup, but he could play a number of positions. He later moved on and played for Bill (Parcells) in Dallas."

Who was the most impressive player Smith ever saw?

"He was also my favorite player, Curtis Martin. He was *the* leader. He would take guys aside and explain things to them. He and Jumbo Elliott, Vinnie Testaverde, Kevin Mawae were all great at that," Smith said.

Smith also maintained friendships with two former Salukis.

"Carl Mauck, of course. Carl is a Saluki through and through. His daughter actually worked for the Bears when I did. Carl is a great guy," Smith said.

"There is another guy, who went on to work for the FBI, by the name of Roger Kuba. He was a running back (at SIU). I'd known him through junior high, high school and four years at SIU," he added.

Smith retired from scouting in 2011. What does he miss the most?

"The people. That's what you miss the most when you get out of it," he said.

Yet Smith isn't completely removed from the scene. He helps coordinate the NFL Combine in Indianapolis each spring. He still attends meetings for National Football Scouting.

"It's like the third version of *The Godfather*. Just when you think you're out, they pull you back in again," he mused.

FOUR DOWN TERRITORY

Favorite Football Movies—I'll be honest with you; there aren't any really good football movies that I've seen. That's mainly because of all the dynamics that get thrown in there that don't really have anything to do with what really happens. I saw *Draft Day* and enjoyed watching it. It wasn't realistic. *Any Given Sunday* I liked but only because of Al Pacino. There are the old, old movies like *Knute Rockne: All-American*. When those come on I still watch them. They are so hokey and corny but still fun to watch.

First Car—We had a '98 Oldsmobile that my dad gave me when I was a junior in college. My dad went out and bought another one and said, 'Here, take this back to school.' Where I lived (Virden) you didn't need a car, you could walk everywhere. Not many of us had cars back in the early '60s. There might be five guys who had a car and everybody just jumped in theirs and we took off. Everybody put $2 in the pot and that took care of the gas.

Worst Summer Job—I worked for my dad on the milk route; he was a milkman. I'd do that in the summer, and I also worked construction. Most everything I did was heavy labor. Like most kids I bucked (hay) bales to make a couple bucks. Bucking bales was tough. It was always hot. Every guy that ever did it got hay fever. I remember the first time I did it I laid down in bed about two o'clock, and I didn't wake up until 10:30 that night. I was freaking exhausted.

> **I**t's like the third version of The Godfather. *Just when you think you're out, they pull you back in again.*

Favorite Subject in School—It would have been math in high school. Algebra, calculus, trig. In college I had an engineering course, which ended up my major. There was a design class at Southern at the time. We had a visiting professor by the name of R. Buckminster Fuller. He is the guy who popularized the geodesic dome and invented other things. There was also a visiting professor from NASA. That was the time when we were going to the moon. It was really fascinating. Those two guys were at the top of their art form of engineering. It was incredible. I was just amazed sitting in that class. I took another class with them the next semester. I couldn't get enough of those two guys. And people asked me, "What the hell are you doing in football?" I have an engineering degree, an education degree, but my passion was football, dating all the way back to high school. In fact, every year I go out to California and visit my high school football coach (Bud Grosner) and just have a great time.

TOM LAPUTKA

Tom Laputka defied the odds.

"In the 18 years of organized football—junior high, high school, college and pros—I played, I never had an athletic injury. Never," said Laputka years later.

Laputka lettered two seasons (1969 and 1970) as a Saluki. He attributed his durability to being prepared.

"You conditioned your body to be ready to reduce your chances of injury," he said. "(You) don't slow down. I never had my ankles taped. None of that."

Laputka hardened into a solid player while prepping at Bordentown Military Institute in New Jersey.

"It was a football factory," said the Pennsylvania native. "They recruited from all over the country. They found guys that needed a little boost in academics and a little boost in maturity, and they teach you football like no one else in the country."

Bordentown closed its doors in 1973, during the era in which America had grown weary of Vietnam. Nevertheless, the school produced its share of well-known athletes, including pro running back Floyd Little.

"At Bordentown everything was a scrimmage, and man was it ever rough and competitive. Even the guys on second string got (college) scholarships. If you survived it, you made it," Laputka said. "We played all college freshmen teams. The team went undefeated for 15 years."

Laputka thrived in the environment.

"I started lifting weights. You didn't see that back in those days from anybody," he said.

Laputka entered high school "at around 200 pounds."

"I left there about 265 and a 500-pound presser," he said. "I wasn't just a strong guy; I was a fast guy who could play several positions."

According to Laputka, he had offers from several Big 10 schools, including powerful Michigan State, then coached by the legendary Duffy Daugherty. Laputka enrolled at the University of Minnesota and began taking summer classes. Yet the defensive tackle soon changed his mind.

"I didn't want to redshirt. I asked (offensive line coach Mike) McGee if he knew anywhere I could go to play right away. You can't sit out. You have to play to keep your skills going," Laputka explained.

Since McGee's brother Jerry coached at SIU, the Minnesota assistant suggested Laputka transfer to Carbondale. The move benefited both player and SIU.

"We had a great team. Lionel Antoine played for us, and you know Lionel was (later) a first-round draft pick of Chicago," Laputka said. "Southern was a scrappy team. You don't get the depth of the larger schools, but the guys that play are good players. They could play on the field with anybody, but if there's an injury or they get worn out there's a major difference because you don't have the quality player to replace him."

The Salukis, coached by Dick Towers and his staff, opened the season with Louisville three straight years, beginning with a 33-10 loss to the Cardinals in 1968. Following a four-point loss the next year, SIU shocked Louisville 31-28 to begin the 1970 season.

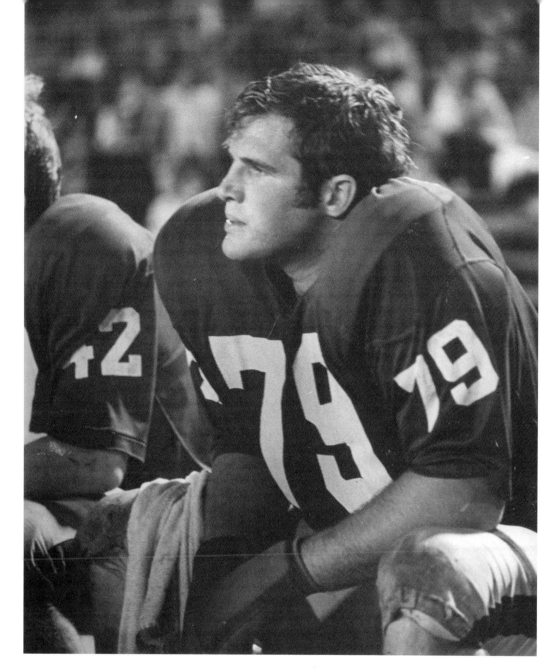

Tom Laputka was known for his toughness and strength in his playing days at SIU, as well as in the Canadian Football League and the World Football League.

"We just took it to them; we beat them good," Laputka said of the win.

The victory came off the heels of an abbreviated spring practice that was halted when SIU closed due to student rioting. The Salukis won their first six games of that '70 season, including routs of Illinois State and Bradley. SIU faltered down the stretch, however, dropping three straight road games to end the season.

Laputka earned All-America honors, playing both defensive tackle and blocking fullback in offensive goal line situations.

"What everyone from Southern remembers from those years is Little Grassy, our training camp," Laputka said. "Dick Towers took us to this large outdoor facility with cabins and a big lake. It was very remote, very isolated. They would take your car keys and put them in a box.

"You were out in the wilderness living in a cabin. Don't get me wrong, the facilities were nice, but you were there four or five weeks. The first week was three-a-day practices, and it was tough. Then it was two-a-days and scrimmages mixed in."

Laputka also remembered "large troughs of ice water" on the sidelines.

"They weren't for drinking. They were to put players in when they got so overheated that they stopped sweating," he said.

---

*Y*ou were out in the wilderness
living in a cabin.

Laputka also reminisced about the pioneering days of what has developed into a sideline staple of American sports.

"In those days Gatorade was just coming out. Powered Gatorade. It was awful," he said. "It was supposed to be the latest and greatest thing to replace what you were sweating out. Drink this stuff, they said. It was orange and it was awful. Water tasted better."

After his SIU days ended, Laputka played six seasons of professional football, five in the Canadian Football League.

Laputka said, "We were Monday Night Football in the CFL at the time. The contracts were very competitive (with those of the NFL)."

To prove his point, Laputka cited the fact that collegiate stars Joe Thiesmann (Notre Dame) and Jim Stillwagon (Oklahoma) chose to sign with Canadian teams. Despite being a draft choice of the San Francisco 49ers, Laputka stayed with Ottawa of the CFL.

"It was really good football (in the CFL). From a player's standpoint it couldn't get much better than that," he said.

Listed at 6-foot-3 and 255 pounds, Laputka enjoyed Ottawa's berth in the 1973 Grey Cup (the CFL's version of the Super Bowl).

A year later, Laputka jumped to the newly minted World Football League. He signed with the Philadelphia Bell of his home state.

"They paid me up front," Laputka said of the Philadelphia franchise. "I made twice what I made the year before. The CFL took them (WFL) to court. The players (who jumped leagues) had to go back (to Canada). I didn't have to go because Philadelphia bought my contract. I made about $140,000 that year."

After a year in the financially strapped WFL, Laputka returned to Canada to play his final two pro seasons with Edmonton. He was part of the Eskimos' 1975 Grey Cup team.

Always an avid weight lifter, Laputka began working for the Nautilus Corporation as his playing career wound down.

"I was involved with them early on," he said.

Laputka worked for Nautilus for many years, including a stint as the company's director for sales and marketing. That position landed him in the White House.

"I was the government sales coordinator," he said. "That put me in the White House a couple of times."

One of those times was to instruct President Ronald Reagan and Chief of Staff Ed Meese on how to use the Nautilus equipment during Reagan's recovery from a 1981 assassination attempt.

"I have a very fine portrait of the president hanging on my wall. It's a very rare piece because it's titled; in other words, it says 'To Tom and Gail,' who was my wife, 'Thank you for all your help.' And it's signed 'President Reagan.' Most of those pictures are just signed (not personalized)."

Perhaps inspired by Reagan, Laputka today serves as the mayor of Orange City, Florida. Yet SIU remains a firm fixture in his life.

"I was attending a funeral here in Orange City, and as I was coming up the circle driveway I noticed the letters *SIU*," Laputka said.

It turned out that the funeral home was owned by SIU alumnus Dennis Johnson.

"He went to Southern at the same time I was there, but we didn't know each other. We sure got to know each other that day, and he's been a dear friend (ever since)," Laputka said.

Then there was the time former SIU teammate Charley Tenelli called.

"He stopped by out of the blue. I hadn't seen him in over 40 years. We met up at a McDonald's at eight in the morning and were there until four in the afternoon. We didn't even touch our coffee."

Tom Laputka. Again, defying the odds.

FOUR DOWN TERRITORY

Favorite Football Movie—I used to read an author called R. J. Archibald, and he wrote novels for high school kids. I'd hide them in my textbook and read. They were all about football, different stories. The guy must have played football, because he really had a handle on it. I couldn't get enough of those books. I loved to read them. So, no, I don't have a particular movie in mind. In fact, I never saw the film of our '73 Grey Cup until 30 years later. Your memories are your highlight film. (As you remember it) you never got beat on a play. Then you see an old film clip and say, "Wow! That's not the way it happened!"

First Car—I had an old Army-issue jeep without a top, a little dicey in the rain and snow, but it was mine and it beat walking. It was an old 1940s-something jeep. It was a hand-me-down from my brother. My younger sister got it after I was done with it.

Worst Summer Job—Oh, mercy, I worked in a brick plant once. I didn't enjoy it. Clay bricks, and it was hard. We were the low guys on the totem pole. We were high school kids as summer help. You had to sort those bricks and put them on a pallet with straw between each row and then put the pallets on open truck carriers. Sorting in the morning, stacking in the afternoon. That was your day.

Favorite Subject in School—I liked ergonomics, the study of the body and work. I was a safety education major. They gave you a situation such as we're running a factory and we're wearing our people out, so what do we do? It's a science today, and it should be because it's directly associated with workmen's compensation. I was fascinated by it.

Pro football Hall of Fame member and former Chicago Bear Gale Sayers (*right*) led the SIU athletic department in the 1970s. He visits with Ernie Banks, baseball Hall of Famer from the Chicago Cubs.

1970s

LIONEL ANTOINE

Lionel Antoine is the highest NFL draft pick in SIU history. In fact, of all players in the state schools, only quarterback Jeff George of the University of Illinois, taken number-one overall in 1990, topped Antoine. Yet, for him, nothing measured higher than being on his roof during Hurricane Katrina.

"All of my childhood had been spent dealing with hurricanes, but Katrina was the worst hurricane in history," said the Biloxi, Mississippi, native.

Hurricane Camille had ravaged the Biloxi area—along with parts of Alabama and Louisiana—in 1969. Camille was one of three category 5 hurricanes to make landfall in the United States in the 20th century.

"But I missed that one," said Antoine. "I was at Southern."

When word came that Katrina was building into another catastrophic storm, Antoine, back living in Biloxi, let curiosity get the best of him.

"I wanted to see this bad rascal," he said.

Thus Antione sent his family away to the safety of nearby Alabama and settled in for the hurricane to hit.

Lionel Antoine stands as the highest NFL draft pick in SIU history. The Chicago Bears took Antoine with the third overall selection in the 1972 draft.

"My family called from Alabama and asked me if anything had happened yet. It hadn't, but no sooner did I get off the phone than it hit," he said.

And it hit hard.

"I was sitting in my den, and water started coming under the door," he said. "I moved to the living room because it's higher than the den. The water got up to my chest inside the house. At that point I started planning my escape route."

That escape route meant going onto the front porch, climbing an awning and getting onto the roof. Once on the roof, Antoine soon realized the situation he was in.

"I wanted to go, but I had nowhere to go," he said.

Antoine sat on the pitch of his roof and was buffeted by high winds and tumultuous rain. Meanwhile, he feared for his great-aunt who lived across the street.

"She was in her 80s and suffering from Alzheimer's," he said. "I looked over, and her house was under water."

Antoine said the water got "as high as the third row of shingles on my roof." Scanning the horizon for his next option, Antoine spotted a tree off in the distance.

"If the water kept climbing, I made up my mind that I would swim to that tree and climb it as high as I had to," he said. "But a tornado came along and completely blew that tree away. I wouldn't be here if I had gone to that tree. God has looked after me all my life."

Meanwhile, Katrina hovered over the area. Antoine was "soaked to the bone and frightened as you would imagine."

At one point, a puppy swam into view. Antoine called for the dog to join him on the roof.

"I'm not sure who was happier to see the other, me or that little puppy," he said.

Finally, after about three hours, the water began to subside.

"I heard voices coming down the street," he said.

Once he was off the roof, Antoine began to survey the damage.

"Some of my neighbors returned, and we found my great-aunt dead inside her house. The inside of my home was ruined. We went three days without water, food or power. There were dead bodies all around. Many of the bodies were unidentifiable."

Yet, through it all, Antoine maintained his faith.

"My sister always told me that my (deceased) mother was granting me my blessings. I understand what she meant now. I've read the passages in the Bible about Moses. I've got six kids and 20 grandchildren. I'm living for them now. That's my goal now. I'm blessed."

Antoine grew up in Biloxi as one of seven children born to Bertrand and Gertrude Antoine. He graduated from high school in 1968.

"I went to an all-black high school. I played football, basketball and a little semipro baseball," he said.

How good of an athlete was Antoine?

"I was drafted by the St. Louis Cardinals to play baseball, and LSU offered me a basketball scholarship," he said.

Football, however, remained his first love.

SIU athletic director Donald "Doc" Boydston was on his annual recruiting trip through the South, seeking future Saluki athletes. Boydston stopped at Picayune, Mississippi.

"They had a legendary school," Antoine said. "My high school team beat them for the first time in 10 years, and we won the conference my senior year."

When the Picayune head coach Marion Henley finished talking about his players, he told Boydston, "Look at this player over on film. You need to get over to Biloxi."

As a result, Boydston recruited Antoine to SIU.

"Once word got out, other schools came after me," Antoine said. "J. C. Caroline was on the University of Illinois staff, and he recruited me. So did the University of Wisconsin and Marshall University."

Ironically, had Antoine chosen Marshall, he would likely have perished when the Thundering Herd's plane crashed outside Huntington, West Virginia, in 1970.

"In all honesty I never had seriously thought of going there," he said.

Antoine was quick to point out that Wichita State experienced a similar crash the same year as Marshall. Thirty-one died in the crash.

"SIU was scheduled to play at Wichita State that year, but of course, that game wasn't played," he said.

Antoine played tight end, offensive line and defensive end for Dick Towers's Salukis.

"Coach Towers did a heck of a job recruiting," Antoine said. "He got us good players from all over."

Like many outstanding athletes, Antoine dwells on his failures as much as his successes.

"Louisville was on our schedule. They always won the Missouri Valley Conference. I remember lining up against (future NFL star) Tom Jackson. I was playing tight end, and he was playing linebacker. I was supposed to block Tom. He made one heckuva play on me. He put a spin move on me and was right in the hole when the running back came through. Those bad plays always stick out in your mind."

> **H**e put a spin move on me and was right in the hole when the running back came through. Those bad plays always stick out in your mind.

Antoine didn't make many bad plays in his time as a Saluki. In fact, the 6-foot-6, 262-pound Antoine quickly became a focal point for Towers's team. The Salukis raced to a 6-0 start in 1970.

"There was talk that we would make the first (major) bowl appearance in school history," he said.

However, with an important game looming, Antoine rushed out of class and into the locker room to prepare for practice.

"I didn't take the time to stretch like I should have," he said. "I ran out to the field and went out for a pass. I tore a hamstring."

Consequently, Antoine didn't play. SIU lost the game; the Salukis stumbled to a 6-3 finish.

Antoine, meanwhile, was named a 1971 *Time* magazine All-America honoree.

Antoine played in the College All-Star Game, the charity game played between the defending NFL champions and a team of star college seniors from the previous year. Antoine and his teammates lost to the Dallas Cowboys 20-7 at Chicago's Soldier Field.

They liked what they saw on film, but I didn't play enough for them to risk taking me.

"I played alongside (future Buffalo Bill) Reggie McKenzie," he said. "We had Franco Harris and Ahmad Rashad, of course, back when he was Bobby Moore out of Oregon."

When the 1972 NFL draft rolled around, Antoine was poised to be selected in the first round.

"I was rated as the number-one offensive tackle, the number-two tight end behind Riley Odoms (from the University of Houston) and the number-three defensive end," Antione said. "Buffalo had the first pick. They needed a defensive end. They took Walt Patulski out of Notre Dame. Word was that he dodged me (in college postseason all-star games) so that I wouldn't show him up and (make him) lose his draft spot."

According to Antoine, Cincinnati, holder of the second draft choice, considered taking him as a defensive end.

"They liked what they saw on film, but I didn't play enough for them to risk taking me," he said.

Accordingly, the Bengals made Sherman White of the University of California their selection. The New York Giants held the third pick.

"The Giants' staff had coached me at the Senior Bowl," he said.

Yet the Giants traded the third pick to the Chicago Bears, then under head coach Abe Gibron. Chicago selected Antoine.

"It was very surprising," Antoine said.

The Bears of that era were a miserable excuse for a football team.

"The organization was the pits," said Antoine. "Those first three years with the Bears were the worst of my life."

Tight-fisted management, inferior training camp facilities and an outdated medical staff were among the reasons cited by Antoine for the Bears' poor state of affairs.

"I got injured in an exhibition game in the Astrodome," Antoine said. "Since I was their first pick, the Bears wanted me to play."

Consequently, Antoine's cast was removed, and he played in the season's first game against Atlanta. But another injury soon followed.

"My shoe got stuck in the Astroturf and my knee went out," he said. "This time I had surgery, but again they rushed me back. I played the last three games of the season. I even played defensive end against the Eagles. I played in below-zero weather in Minnesota."

Antoine returned home to Biloxi for the holidays. Soon he was coughing up blood. He returned to Chicago to be examined.

"The Bears wouldn't tell me what was wrong with me," he said. "Some of my teammates turned up to see me. We went out and had a few beers. They tracked me down and said the Chicago police had been out searching for me. Turns out, I had a blood clot in my lungs. I could have died."

Things began to turn around when the Bears hired Jim Finks as their general manager. Talent began to show up in the form of draft choices Wally Chambers, Waymond Bryant and Walter Payton. Jack Pardee was hired as Chicago's head coach.

"Finks started spending George Halas's money," he said. "Things were looking up, and I was feeling good."

So good in fact that in 1976, Antoine earned second team All-NFC honors from United Press International.

"That was my breakout year," he said.

Yet, even during the brightest hour, darkness returned.

"I injured my knee in the last game of the season," he said.

According to Antoine, Dr. Theodore A. Fox, the Bears' physician for over 30 years, wrapped his swollen knee and sent him on his way. Antoine drove from Chicago to Biloxi.

"When I got there, I couldn't get out of the car. I had to fly back to Chicago," he said. "It continued to swell. It gave way when I tried to play."

The result was reconstructive surgery, still a dicey proposition in the 1970s.

"I would not let Dr. Fox operate on me," Antoine said. "His cure for everything was the needle. He'd shoot you up every time."

As a result, Antoine's surgery was performed by the Chicago Bulls' team doctor.

His rehabilitation was conducted by a downtown personal trainer rather than by the Bears' staff.

"The Bears were behind the times. They didn't expect me to play again," he said. "I worked my butt off and got back and played again."

However, the injuries took their collective toll. By 1979 the swollen knee became too much for Antoine.

"Neil Armstrong, then the Bears' head coach, told me that if I could just keep myself in shape and play on Sundays, I didn't have to hurt myself during the week of practice," Antoine said. "But I knew it was time to give it up. I have no regrets. I gave it my all. I played eight years. I have a lot of respect from my peers."

Antoine spent his post-NFL career working as a semipro football coach, liquor store owner and bail bondsman.

"I traveled the country as a bounty hunter, but when the crooks started shooting back, that was enough for me," he said.

These days, Antoine remains in Biloxi.

"I'm drawing retirement. I fish. I enjoy time with my family," he said. "I love Southern Illinois University. If I had to do it all over again, I'd go to Southern Illinois University all over again."

As for the next hurricane coming his way?

"No, thank you. This time I'm leaving town," he said.

FOUR DOWN TERRITORY

Favorite Football Movie—*North Dallas Forty.* The comedy is great, and it makes a lot of points that are realistic. Like when that player is injured and won't take the shot. Or when that receiver drags himself out of bed to get back to the game. I could relate to a lot of it.

First Car—It was a Buick Electra 225. When I signed with the Bears, they told me not to buy a Cadillac because the veterans on the team wouldn't like it. I kept that Buick for four years; then I got my Cadillac.

Worst Summer Job—John Hancock Insurance. I didn't like selling insurance at all. During my era you had to have a summer job during the off-season.

Favorite Subject in School—History. I still enjoy it today.

ANDRE HERRERA

Andre Herrera rushed for 2,346 yards, 21 touchdowns and a 5.2-yards-per-carry average during his SIU career. Yet he is probably best remembered for one sensational quarter against Northern Illinois in 1976.

Herrera, listed at 6 feet and 197 pounds, broke the NCAA record by rushing for 214 yards in the first quarter against the rival Huskies. The game, which was played in a driving rain at McAndrew Stadium, quickly turned into a 54-0 rout by the Salukis.

Herrera shattered the previous mark held by Mercury Morris of West Texas State. Morris later starred along with Larry Csonka and Jim Kiick in the Miami Dolphins' backfield.

In all, Herrera ran for 319 yards and six touchdowns that day. He finished the season with 1,588 yards.

SIU athletic director and Chicago Bears Hall of Fame running back Gale Sayers stood on the sidelines watching Herrera's record-setting performance that October day.

"Andre is a fine runner, and he's going to be even better in the National Football League," Sayers said that day. "His performance was absolutely outstanding. But the thing that impressed me the most is that he carried the ball 35 times in a downpour and didn't fumble once. To me, that's an even bigger feat than gaining 300 yards."

Sayers is often remembered for his six-touchdown performance in his NFL rookie season against the San Francisco 49ers on a muddy Wrigley Field turf in 1965.

SIU head coach Rey Dempsey removed Herrera from the game with 10 minutes left on the clock. After the game Dempsey said that he was unaware that Herrera was nearing the single-game rushing record of 350 yards set by Eric Allen of Michigan State in 1971.

"I really didn't know he was so close to the record when I took him out," said Dempsey, in his first season as SIU head coach. "But I promised myself a long time ago that I wouldn't run a tired and hurting player for a record when I had a game won.

"Andre was tired and hurting a bit, and we still had four games to go. I'm sorry that he didn't get the record, because he was fantastic."

Herrera's parents moved from Cuba to New York shortly before Andre was born. Herrera never played high school football but played at a junior college in Westchester, New York, before arriving in Carbondale.

Herrera's record-breaking day included runs of 85, 53 and 45 yards. Meanwhile, his

Andre Herrera rushed for an NCAA record 214 yards against Northern Illinois University in a 1976 game.

An outstanding baseball and football player, Kevin House
played eight seasons in the NFL during the 1980s.

touchdowns came on runs of 2, 2, 9, 13, 1 and 4 yards.

Herrera's record lasted until 1996, when Corey Dillon of the University of Washington rushed for 222 yards on 16 carries against San Jose State. Dillon later ran for more than 11,000 yards in the NFL while playing for Cincinnati and New England.

Herrera was inducted into the SIU Hall of Fame in 1994.

KEVIN HOUSE

Though he made his living catching passes in the NFL, Kevin House dreamed of playing center field for the St. Louis Cardinals as a child.

"Growing up in St. Louis I was an avid baseball fan," House said from his Florida home in the spring of 2014. "I started playing when I was nine. My favorite player growing up was Curt Flood. He was a center fielder; I was a center fielder. It was Curt Flood, closely followed by Lou Brock. Those were my two favorites, but Lou Brock was left-handed."

A gifted athlete, House soon took up the sport in which he would excel.

"I started playing football at age 11 over at Sherman Park (in St. Louis)," he said.

By high school, House had added basketball to the mix.

"I even ran a little track," he noted.

Coming out of high school, House had an offer to play football at Northeast Missouri State, a Division-II school in Kirksville.

"At the last minute my high school coach called Southern, and they made an offer. That's how I wound up signing with Southern

Illinois. Coach (Rey) Dempsey handled most of it. It was about an hour-and-a-half drive from St. Louis. It was the right choice."

At SIU, House played football and baseball.

"The only requirement (for me to play both sports) was that I had to play in the spring (football) game my freshman year. Other than that, Coach Dempsey was fine with me playing baseball."

Thus House played football for Dempsey and baseball for Richard "Itchy" Jones.

"The biggest challenge was academically. Being a two-sport athlete, you still had to find time to keep up with your studying."

In baseball, House was drafted by both the Cardinals and the Chicago White Sox while he was at SIU.

"I preferred baseball to football as a fan, but football seemed to come naturally to me. When I had a choice to make (to play professionally), I chose football," House said.

Among the highlights of his time as a Saluki, House and his baseball teammates qualified for the 1977 College World Series in Omaha. SIU won its first two games, defeating Temple and Arizona State. After losing a close game to South Carolina, the Salukis stayed alive in the double-elimination tournament with a victory over Cal State–Los Angeles.

"Then we ran into a buzz saw called Arizona State, led by Bob Horner at the time. We just couldn't get by those guys," said House of the Sun Devils' 10-0 triumph over SIU.

The 1977 team returned to Carbondale in the spring of 2014 for a reunion and for the dedication of the playing surface to honor Jones.

"I really enjoyed seeing everyone after all those years," House said.

Meanwhile, on the football field for the Salukis, House found early success.

House said in 2013, "The first time I stepped on the field as a Saluki: that was a thrill. It was during my freshman year. I got my chance against East Carolina, and I ended up with a few catches."

It's my belief that Kevin could have been an outstanding baseball player. He was used primarily as the stereotypical pinch runner.

House's totals rose each year, culminating with a 27-catch, five-touchdown senior season in 1979. He caught 71 passes for 1,524 yards and scored 11 touchdowns during his SIU career. He averaged 21.5 yards per catch.

"All I remember is they had to get the fire department to put the flames out as he ran down the field," said former Eastern Illinois defensive end Pete Catan. "Kevin is one of the fastest receivers I've ever seen."

Longtime SIU broadcaster Mike Reis noted, "He was a terrific receiver. I wish he could have played in a pass-oriented offense, but Rey Dempsey likes to run the ball. He was a likeable guy. I could not have forecast his time in the NFL. I knew that he would be terrific on kick returns, but we just didn't see him as a receiver all that much.

"It's my belief that Kevin could have been an outstanding baseball player. He was used primarily as the stereotypical pinch runner. If he had been given the chance and if he had concentrated on the game, he might be remembered as quite a baseball player."

With the Cardinals and White Sox each drafting him in different years, House did have both pro baseball and pro football as options.

"I was asked what it would take for me to sign to play baseball. Just off the top of my head I threw out a figure like $85,000. I never really heard much after that. The following year I got drafted by Chicago and never really heard much from them. I wasn't really looking forward to playing in the minor leagues. As I said earlier, football came naturally to me. It was pretty much a no-brainer."

The Tampa Bay Buccaneers selected House in the second round (49th overall pick) of the 1980 NFL draft. Things didn't start off exactly as House hoped.

"It's my first practice, and I hurt my shoulder going for a catch. If you know my history, I separated my shoulder my sophomore year at Southern. The next day I had surgery. They put a three-inch screw into my shoulder, which I still have to this day. I had flashbacks of that. I remember thinking, "Oh no, here we go again.'"

Fortunately, the preseason injury wasn't severe. Yet House soon realized the challenges of the NFL.

"Here I am, a 155-pound wide receiver. It was really intimidating at the beginning. It was a totally different world. The linebackers run like wide receivers. Speed kills in the NFL. You have to persevere. I had to have discipline to run the (pass) patterns. I had to work at it. You had to develop if you wanted to stick (with the team)."

Nevertheless, House soon saw success.

"My second year, that's when I really came into my own," he said.

House had 56 receptions for 1,176 yards and nine touchdowns for the Bucs that season. In 1984 House caught a career-high 76 passes.

Perhaps the best compliment came from an opponent, cornerback Lester Hayes of the Oakland Raiders.

"Lester the Molester, that's what he was called back then. He saw me and said, 'Dang, I didn't realize he was that fast,'" House remembered.

After seven years with Tampa Bay, House played his final two seasons with the Los Angeles Rams.

"Playing with the Rams you had guys like Eric Dickerson, Fred Dryer, Jack Youngblood. It was a veteran crew. You were treated first-class. It was very professional.

"In Tampa we were treated more like a college team. To give you an idea, if you were on the practice field and you wanted a new jockstrap, you had to turn in your old one before they'd give you a new one. That about sums it up."

House finished his NFL career with 299 receptions for 5,169 yards and 34 touchdowns.

In 1995 the Rams left Los Angeles and began playing as the St. Louis Rams. Asked if he is surprised that LA, the nation's second-largest city, has not had an NFL team since 1994, House didn't hesitate.

"Very surprised," he said. "When I was there the team was supported very well. The fans traveled very well. It's very surprising that LA does not have a professional football team. It has to be a political thing." Ironically, the Rams moved back to Los Angeles after the 2015 NFL season.

Following retirement from the NFL, House and his first wife ran a hair salon business for 10 years. He later worked as a recruiter for the Census Bureau as well as for a cell phone company. Moreover, House also has been active in the NFL Retired Players Association.

"We do a lot of charity events with our chapter. There are a lot of good causes out there," he said.

In 1991 House was added to the SIU Athletics Hall of Fame. In 2013 he was named to the Salukis' All-Century Football Team.

"That was a big honor. To be one of the top 50 players from the entire history of Southern Illinois Saluki football, I am honored. It was very exciting and very moving," House said.

FOUR DOWN TERRITORY

Favorite Football Movie—It would have to be *Brian's Song*, the movie with Gale Sayers. With him being the SIU A.D., I can relate. I always found that movie to be very captivating.

First Car—It was a white Firebird, I forget the year, but it was white. When I came to campus I was told that I had to get something safe. I was like, really? I was stubborn.

Worst Summer Job—I played in the Central Illinois Collegiate League. During the day I would cut grass, and at night I would play baseball.

Favorite Subject in School—It would have to be industrial arts. I like to work with my hands. I still use those things even today.

OYD CRADDOCK

"Oyd Craddock" is a name that resonates with Saluki fans of the 1970s for the player's on-the-field exploits. Yet his name resonates far more off the field in the Atlanta and New Orleans communities.

"Mr. Craddock has achieved the stability that was so sorely needed, and he has worked with the Board of Directors and the Josephites to create a strategic long-term vision that positions St. Augustine High School to compete as a school of excellence for future decades," board chairman Justin Augustine III told the *News Orleans Times-Picayune* in 2016.

Craddock, a 1976 St. Augustine graduate, had returned to his alma mater in 2013 to serve as president of the all-boys Roman Catholic high school in New Orleans' 7th Ward following a 31-year career at IBM.

According to the newspaper, Craddock "righted the ship after a tumultuous few years." In 2011 the Josephite order reassigned the school's president over a corporal punishment issue. The president who followed lasted less than a year. Enter Craddock.

"We owe Mr. Craddock a substantial debt of gratitude," Augustine said.

According to his SIU Hall of Fame biography Craddock started 43 of 44 games in his Saluki career. A three-time all-conference selection at defensive back, Craddock was a major factor in SIU's leading the Missouri Valley Conference in scoring defense during his final two seasons.

Craddock was named honorable mention All-American by the Associated Press in

Former Saluki Oyd Craddock made tremendous off-the-field contributions in the Atlanta and New Orleans communities following his playing days.

1979. His 426 career tackles rank second overall on the Saluki leader board. His 11 career interceptions land Craddock in a tie for seventh place on the all-time SIU list. An SIU Hall of Fame member, Craddock was named to the All-Century Team in 2013.

Upon his graduation from SIU, Craddock worked in sales, marketing, operations and management for IBM. He earned his MBA from Tulane University in 1995. After Craddock retired from IBM, he became an instructor at Morehouse College in Atlanta. He has also served as an advisement board member for SIU minority affairs.

Today Craddock is the president of DYO Management, Inc., where he provides management consulting and project management in the media, entertainment and technology industries.

September 13, 1980, was Mark Hemphill Day at McAndrew Stadium.

1980s

MARK HEMPHILL DAY

As expected, the day was emotional.

Mark Hemphill Day was the SIU home opener for 1980 at McAndrew Stadium. Hemphill, a former Saluki defensive back who had been paralyzed during the 1979 season, was to be honored at halftime.

Shortly before the intermission ceremony was about to begin, however, Hemphill became ill. No doubt the emotion of the day took hold, as well as temperatures reaching into triple digits.

The illness landed Hemphill in the hospital.

"The governor of Illinois (James Thompson) was there. Our slogan was 'Make a Mark for Mark,' or something like that," Fred Huff told Todd Hefferman years later. "When he came into the stadium in a wheelchair, that east side was jammed, and they started chanting, 'Mark! Mark! Mark!' I just remember chills going down my spine that day."

Hemphill waved to the crowd, estimated to be 17,150 that afternoon.

According to Hefferman's 2009 newspaper story Hemphill "could only muster a broken 'Thank you' when he attempted to address the crowd."

Gale Sayers, the former Chicago Bears Hall of Famer turned SIU athletic director, announced that no one would ever wear Hemphill's number 30 again for the Salukis.

SIU responded by holding off Eastern Illinois for a 37-35 victory. The Panthers were just two years removed from a Division-II national championship and would also play in the 1980 title game.

Hemphill, a sophomore, was injured diving for a fumble during the second quarter against Illinois State on October 6, 1979. He became a paraplegic and later died in a van he bought with money the university raised for him. SIU gave him a portion of their income from ticket and concession sales at the 1980 home opener. Those funds totaled nearly $35,000.

According to Hefferman's story, Hemphill froze to death three years later when the van's electrical system failed on a bitterly cold winter day. Hemphill was unable to get out of the van or sound the horn for assistance.

CHRIS LOCKWOOD

Offensive lineman might be the most overlooked position in all of sports.

Think about it: In baseball, each position player gets to bat. There are only five players on a basketball court for a team at one time. They all touch the ball at one point or another. The same goes for hockey players and the puck.

In football, defensive players get noticed by being in on tackles, forcing or recovering fumbles, defending or intercepting passes. The so-called "skill" players also run, pass or receive the ball. Television cameras focus on placekickers and punters.

But offensive linemen are an obscure bunch. Maybe it's because there aren't recognizable statistics the general public can identify with. Maybe it's because you don't see offensive linemen regularly appearing in commercials.

Maybe that's why the name Chris Lockwood may not be one immediately recognized by Southern Illinois fans. Yet, to those who coached and played with him, Chris Lockwood isn't likely to be forgotten.

He grew up in North Riverside. Lockwood moved after his freshman year in high school and attended Riverside-Brookfield, the same school that sent Tom Baugh to SIU and ultimately to the National Football League.

Lockwood played football all four years of high school, but he also wrestled.

"(I) took up the shot put my senior year instead of wrestling," he said in an e-mail. "Could care less about putting the shot. I went that route because the coach (Duane Buturusis) was on the cutting edge of weight training and I felt it would be good prep for college football."

Though Lockwood's college football would be played at SIU, the Salukis were late to the recruiting trail.

"I was mostly recruited by a handful of Big Ten (Iowa, Northwestern) and Big 8 (Kansas, Iowa State) schools, plus Virginia," Lockwood said. "Iowa and Northwestern showed the most interest."

SIU was the only other Illinois university, besides Northwestern, that took an interest in Lockwood.

"Mike Barry recruited me," Lockwood said. "(He) was my first position coach in college. He went on to coach for two national champs, Colorado and Tennessee."

SIU was also the only school that offered Lockwood a scholarship during his visits.

He said, "I felt quite at home at SIU, fell in love with the area and felt I had a good chance of playing early.

"With offer in hand and not knowing if the other schools would come through, I jumped on the opportunity. It was the right choice."

As is the case for most college football players, the experience flew by.

"There is so much to remember, and the overall experience was great," Lockwood noted.

His senior season stands out most clearly in his mind.

"We were coming off a lousy 3-8 season that wasn't much fun," he said. "We were expected to be even worse in '81."

Things appeared that way as the Salukis stumbled to a 0-3 start, which included a

loss to a Tennessee State team featuring future Chicago Bears defensive end Richard Dent.

Next on the schedule was a road game at Tulsa. Moreover, it was homecoming for the Golden Hurricane.

"They were 0-3 as well but had lost to Kansas, Arkansas and Oklahoma State (all by slim margins)," Lockwood said. "After that schedule, Tulsa was eager to feast on us."

Yet SIU was the team to relish the victory. The Salukis rode out of Tulsa with a 36-34 win.

"Walter Poole lit them up for about 260 rushing yards," Lockwood said. "We then went on a six-game winning streak before losing what was essentially the conference championship game."

That contest against Drake was played in front of what was then the second-largest crowd in McAndrew Stadium history.

"We were just too banged up and had too many key players missing," he said.

SIU wrapped up the season with a win against New Mexico State to finish with a 7–4 record.

"We also beat Fresno State in their new stadium that year," Lockwood said.

He took pride in ending his collegiate playing days on such a high note.

Chris Lockwood (67) is joined on the cover of the 1981 SIU media guide by running back Walter Poole.

"The turnaround from the previous year despite all of the negative projections was a very rewarding experience," Lockwood said. "It was a very tight team with a wonderful group of guys that never gave up."

Lockwood also saw the season as a building block in the 1983 national championship Saluki team.

"A lot of guys on that ('81) team participated on the '83 team as well," he said, citing Baugh, quarterback Rick Johnson and defensive back Terry Taylor.

Lockwood also remembered a variety of coaches who added to his SIU experience. Lockwood listed, in addition to Barry, future NFL head coach Jim Caldwell, Florida State offensive line coach Rick Trickett and SIU head coach Rey Dempsey.

"(Caldwell) was a grad assistant at Iowa when I made my visit there," Lockwood said. "He drove me around campus a little bit. SIU was his first full-time college coaching position, and it was fun to run into him when I arrived on campus for my freshman year. Great coach, even better person."

Trickett served as Lockwood's position coach during his junior and senior years.

"There's not enough time to type all of the Rick Trickett stories, but suffice to say, the mold was broken after he was born," he said. "Most either loved him or hated him. I loved him.

"He's a character in so many ways, and he is widely regarded as the premier O-line coach in the college ranks."

As for Dempsey, Lockwood called the former SIU head man "a firm disciplinarian and task master, workaholic and great recruiter."

He added, "Coach Dempsey did things his way, and it wasn't until we spoke with players from other schools that we found out that Coach Dempsey ran things much differently than what was done in most programs."

Today, Lockwood realizes the impact all four of the coaches he listed had on his life.

"Hardly a day goes by where I don't think about one (or) all of the coaches," he said. "Furthermore, hardly a day goes by where I don't put their teachings and lessons into play in my own life, business and personal."

That life led Lockwood to Colorado in the late summer of 1983.

"I've been in the equipment rental/leasing business with a focus on trucking equipment and power generation equipment virtually the entire time I've been here," he said. "(I'm) married, (have) three kids and (am) loving life in a beautiful state."

FOUR DOWN TERRITORY

Favorite Football Movie—*Remember the Titans*, because it reminded me of how our team in my senior season overcame adversity, grew close together with bonds that exist to this day and succeeded against all odds. Otherwise, any football movie with Rick Johnson making an appearance.

First Car—A green '72 Torino. Bought it for $50 and had to replace the transmission and exhaust system to make it run. Then it got stolen, and it cost me $36 to get it out of the impound lot after it was recovered.

Worst Summer Job—Tuck Tape factory in Carbondale, summer of 1981. Hot and nasty environment, and just a depressing and crappy job.

Favorite Subject in School—Biology.

1983 SIU NATIONAL CHAMPIONS

Michael Jackson wasn't the only one producing a thriller in 1983.

The Southern Illinois Salukis gave their fans the ultimate thrill with a Division I-AA national championship.

Almost to a man, SIU players point to their second game of the regular season as the springboard. In that September 10 game, the Salukis slipped past Eastern Illinois 17-14 at McAndrew Stadium.

In that tide-turning contest, future NFL defensive back Terry Taylor blocked a short field goal attempt that, if successful, would have tied the game in the waning seconds.

"That game really got us over the hump and gave us confidence," said quarterback Rick Johnson.

Taylor agreed and noted "that game got us rolling."

More than a quarter century later, the 12-year NFL veteran still remembered the play.

"I saw the (Eastern) center squeezing the ball, and I took off," Taylor said in 2010. "In fact, I almost ran past the ball. I came in from the right side and had to pull my hands back to get the kick."

SIU ran through the regular season with 10 straight victories. The Salukis lost the final game of the regular season at Wichita State 28-6.

"Wichita State should not have even been on the same field with us," Taylor said. "They didn't even throw the ball. They ran the option all game. That loss bugged me for a long time."

Yet some good did come from the defeat.

The 1983 national championship plaque.

"It got us focused (going into the playoffs)," Taylor said.

To Johnson, the Saluki success started with the defense.

"Our defense was like the '85 Bears in its dominance," said Johnson. "We had Terry Taylor and Donnell Daniel. They were two shutdown cornerbacks. That meant we could bring everyone else on the rush. You can do so much on defense with two shutdown corners."

Taylor pointed out that things began up front.

"Our defensive line was so good," said Taylor. "They made it easy for us. There were games when they were sacking the quarterback seven, eight times. I would get selfish and say, 'Let them get a pass off so I can intercept one!'"

Daniel said the defense was more than playoff ready.

"Not to be arrogant, but as the playoffs started, the defensive mindset was that if they don't score, we win, and that was our mission, to lay a bagel (shutout) on each opponent," he said.

While Johnson is quick to credit the defense, SIU head coach Rey Dempsey cited his quarterback as a difference maker.

"His teammates knew he worked hard and would do anything to win," Dempsey told Luis Medina of the *Daily Egyptian* in a 2009 article. "He was a real general out there. He exuded confidence, and they admired him and knew they had something good."

Johnson was a fifth-year senior due to a redshirt season as a freshman.

Offensive lineman Tom Baugh saw first-hand Johnson's abilities.

"Ricky had the respect of his teammates," said Baugh.

The late-season loss to Wichita State didn't affect the Salukis once the playoffs began. SIU breezed past Indiana State 23-7 in the quarterfinal round.

The 1983 team celebrates with Coach Rey Dempsey.

Saluki fans who made the trip to the national championship game were rewarded with a 43-7 SIU victory.

"It was a downpour, but we dismissed them," Daniel said. "Their seven (points) came after an interception and return inside our five-yard line."

A week later, the Salukis knocked off Nevada-Reno by the same score.

"Reno had the nation's number-one rushing attack," said Daniel. "The defense crushed the Wolfpack and stifled their so-called running game."

The semifinal victory earned SIU a berth in the I-AA championship game against Western Carolina. The December 17 showdown in Charleston, South Carolina, saw the Salukis romp 43-7.

"It was kind of anticlimactic," Johnson said.

Terry Taylor (21) turned the fortunes of the 1983 season by blocking a field goal attempt to preserve a win over rival Eastern Illinois.

SIU led 10-0 at the half before blowing the game wide open with a 23-point third quarter.

The Saluki defense dominated the game, intercepting seven passes by Western Carolina quarterback Jeff Gilbert. Greg Shipp led the way with a record-setting four interceptions.

With the game safely in hand in the fourth quarter, play was stopped for an injury. One of the Western Carolina players stood alongside Johnson and mumbled some trash talk.

"That's when it really hit me," Johnson said. "I told him where he could go. We were the (national) champions!"

Johnson finished the day with 213 passing yards and two touchdown throws.

The game was carried on national television.

"Keith Jackson and Frank Broyles did the game," said Johnson.

Daniel recalled, "I remember Terry Taylor and I getting excessive press coverage all week long, doing multiple interviews with Keith Jackson and his signature, 'Whooaaaa Nelly!' In our final interview Jackson pulled a five-dollar bill out of his pocket, autographed it and gave it to me. I still have the old five-dollar bill, and I manage a smile every time I look upon it."

Roger Lipe, the Salukis' team chaplain since 1994, was working in a retail store during the game.

"I was carrying a little radio around with me that afternoon," he said.

Meanwhile, the broadcast wasn't just for viewers or listeners in Carbondale.

"I was already living in Colorado," said Chris Lockwood, an offensive lineman whose Saluki career ended in 1981. "I had on my SIU jersey as I watched the championship game on my black-and-white TV in my Fort Collins apartment. And it was really fun to watch so many guys I knew performing on national TV.

"And, of course, a lot of pride comes with knowing so many of the players on that team, pride for being associated with SIU, and a lot of pride knowing that my fellow teammates probably had a positive impact on a lot of guys on the (championship) team that maybe, just maybe, helped them win all of those games. And, of course, I was very happy for Coach Dempsey."

Mike Reis, the Salukis' longtime broadcaster, was a student when Dempsey arrived at SIU in 1976.

"Dempsey's first team was 7-4. (The Salukis were) 3-18-1 (in) the previous two seasons. Same players in '76 as '75. Likely the best one-season coaching job done by any Saluki football coach," Reis said.

Baugh also carried an appreciation for Dempsey.

"Obviously Rey Dempsey had everyone's respect," Baugh said. "My most memorable moment with him was when I awoke from unconsciousness after a motorcycle wreck my junior year.

"He was standing over me with Carl Angelo praying in tongues. He's a follower of Jesus and a good man. When I first arrived at SIU I heard all kinds of stuff about him parting the skies for practice and mysterious activities during meetings. All I can tell you is the man loves Jesus with a passion."

Shortly after leading SIU to the I-AA title, Dempsey left the school to accept the head coaching job at Memphis State. On-field success would not follow him. Dempsey went 7-12-3 in his two seasons at the Tiger helm. He then became a full-time minister in Ohio.

"The thrill of winning was short-lived," Lipe said. "When Dempsey left for Memphis State, it took all of the air out of the balloon."

"Some people didn't take it lightly because they felt I shouldn't go, but most of the players accepted it," Dempsey told Medina. "I've always held SIU deep in my heart."

It's a feeling most SIU players and fans would reciprocate. So what if he couldn't moonwalk. Rey Dempsey proved to be a thriller in his own right.

TOM BAUGH

Over the years, college football coaches have used all sorts of methods to land prized recruits.

Some use flashy video presentations. Others hang a uniform affixed with the prospect's name and preferred number in a neatly staged locker. Many bring in high-profile alumni to hawk the virtues of the program. There are also pretty girls called Dazzlers or Sparklers to escort the recruit around town.

For Tom Baugh, none of that happened.

In fact, part of the pitch of then Southern Illinois offensive line coach Rick Trickett included the cult classic TV show *The Love Boat*.

"Rick Trickett, now the offensive coordinator at Florida State, was the O-Line coach at SIU and did the majority of the recruiting at my house. He was a small guy but had everyone's respect for being a Vietnam marine. He was a regular (weekly) visitor during recruiting season. He would come by and watch *The Love Boat* with me and my girlfriend at the time (now my wife)," Baugh stated in a 2009 e-mail.

In the end it wasn't Captain Merrill Stubing, yeoman-purser Gopher Smith, cruise director Julie McCoy or even bartender Isaac Washington that got Baugh to commit to SIU. It was Trickett.

"Every week like clockwork he was there. He ended up being the main reason I went to SIU," Baugh said.

Baugh was also persuaded by Trickett's honesty.

"After all the hubbub, I asked him one simple question. 'Will you promise to be there (at SIUC) for my four years?' His answer was 'No, I can't promise that.' I respected the truthfulness of his answer. I believed that I could trust him," Baugh said.

Baugh wasn't an easy person to sway. Born in Chicago, Baugh moved first to Cicero and then to North Riverside for his school years.

He attended Riverside-Brookfield High School, where he starred on both sides of the ball.

"I began on the offense and defensive lines, but my senior year I was so frustrated by the linebackers not filling the holes that I asked to play linebacker in practice. I made nine tackles on 10 plays and played middle linebacker from then on," Baugh recalled.

He also tasted success in track and field.

"I was a four-time all-state shot-putter and discus thrower and still hold the (conference) indoor shot put record. I played basketball until junior year and then concentrated on indoor track," he said.

Yet it was football that Baugh played on the next level.

"I visited Michigan State and Indiana State, had a trip set up to go to Wyoming but never took it after I committed to SIU," he noted.

Once in Carbondale, Baugh and his teammates set their minds and bodies on developing into a dependable offensive line.

"We had a good tradition of hard work ethic," Baugh said. "(We were) nicknamed 'the Labor Gang' by Rick Trickett. We took pride in starting our workday before everyone and ending it after everyone."

The typical postpractice workout would include 50 to 100 push-ups and sit-ups followed by as many as 10 quarter-mile sprints.

"That was every day," he said. "It was more than work. It was team building, reliance on each other, a lesson in life. I had a lot of respect for the guys that preceded me. We worked hard, and we played hard. We knew that we had each other's back, and we still do today.

"After 25-plus years there isn't a guy from that group in 1981–85 O-Line that wouldn't do what he could for the other. One aspect of our team, which may be unique, is that we held each other accountable. Nobody felt sorry for anyone who got hurt, nobody sympathized with injuries and taking the easy way out. We all realized that everyone was important and if anyone wasn't giving his all they were cheating the team."

The collective effort wasn't without some social consciousness.

"Everyone was hurting during workouts; that was part of getting better and we accepted that. For the most part, our teams

Tom Baugh (59), a member of the Saluki All-Century Team, was a fourth-round NFL draft choice of the Kansas City Chiefs in 1986.

were comprised of working-class guys from homes with working-class parents (when parents were in the picture). Guys from wealthy or noticeably affluent families were teased and had to earn everyone's respect by working even harder. Hard work was the key to approval," Baugh said.

It was also the key to winning. His sophomore year, Baugh anchored the offensive line from his center position as SIU won the 1983 NCAA Division I-AA national championship.

Yet the title game isn't necessarily the contest that proved to be the most memorable.

While the national championship was special, we dominated the game so it wasn't that special.

"While the national championship was special, we dominated the game so it wasn't that special," Baugh said of the Salukis' 43-7 thrashing of Western Carolina.

Instead, Baugh mentioned a 17-14 victory over state rival Eastern Illinois earlier that '83 season.

"Terry Taylor had to block a field goal for us to win; that was more memorable," he said.

Yet a game from his senior season stands out above the rest. SIU lost a heartbreaking 28-25 decision to the University of Illinois at Champaign's Memorial Stadium.

"Our field goal kicker missed a short kick," Baugh recalled. "We dominated them on the line of scrimmage, and even their coaches (Mike White among them) acknowledged it after the game. We had a couple hundred yards rushing."

When asked to name the toughest defensive player he went against in college, Baugh didn't cite an opponent.

"I practiced against the best nose guard in practice every day: Sterling Haywood," Baugh said. "'Quick Stud' could take a great deal of credit for helping me to become a professional center. Sterling was stocky, quick and powerful. He practiced hard and made me work hard to get better."

Baugh noted that Haywood was an all-conference selection and a Saluki captain.

"(He was) truly better than some of the guys I played in postseason bowl games from 'Big Name U,'" Baugh said. "So that you don't think I'm slighting other schools, there was a fellow from Indiana State that was pretty good back then. I don't remember his name though."

Baugh also credits Trickett, the man who recruited him, with his development.

"Rick Trickett was my first line coach and probably had the single biggest effect on my technical abilities," Baugh said. "He was the one that converted me from tackle to center and provided the leadership I needed as a young man.

"He wasn't necessarily the best example, but he didn't put on a face. He was real, authentic and a man of his word."

Whatever the factors, Baugh blossomed into a pro prospect. The Kansas City Chiefs took him with their fourth-round selection in the 1986 National Football League draft.

"I had a pretty good idea that I was going to get drafted," he said. "After playing well in the Blue-Gray Classic and the East-West Shrine Game against so-called better competition, I was informed that I would probably be drafted somewhere between (rounds) three and six, but I really didn't know by whom."

Baugh had a pretty good idea, however, when Carl Mauck, another SIU great who played in the NFL, called during the second round to inform him the Chiefs were interested. Mauck eventually became Baugh's line coach in Kansas City. Baugh was the second center taken in the '86 draft.

Baugh played four seasons in the NFL, three with Kansas City and his final year with Cleveland.

"I remember my first real action against the Bears," Baugh said. "Rick Donnelly, the starting center, got injured. The Saluki marching band was playing at halftime, and I got my first 'real action' on offense. I played in all the prior games as long snapper for punts and field goals. But I was at home and somehow was meant to play in that game."

Being a member of the Chiefs also meant clashing twice a year against the Raiders, Kansas City's long-time rival dating back to American Football League days.

"Chiefs and Raiders don't mix," Baugh explained. "Back then we had fights in every game. I was fined for fighting in every game I played against the Raiders."

Baugh also relayed a story that he has frequently told over the years about one of those Chiefs-Raiders wars.

"Mark Adickes was playing guard for us, and Howie (Long) was lining up (for the Raiders) in the C-G gap. So every time we passed, we would temporarily double team. Then one of us, usually me, would release to pick up a blitz if needed. If nobody was blitzing I would come back and cut block Howie.

"Of course cut blocking while a guard was engaged (chop block) was illegal, and Howie was complaining to (referee) Ben Dreith all day. So Ben comes to the line and says, 'I'm watching you, 58.' The same series of events happens, I release to check for blitz, Mark locks onto Howie, and I come running back in and cut him. We were all lying in a pile when Howie says, 'Ben, did you see it? They did it again.' Ben waddled over and said, 'Yeah, I saw it, Howie. It was legal; now shut up and play football.' He just wanted Howie to quit complaining."

Baugh was inducted into the SIU Hall of Fame in 2001.

"I remember walking the halls of the student center and looking at pictures of Carl Mauck, Jim Hart, but never really thought of being among those pictures," Baugh said. "After having played in the pros, I had a hunch I would make it someday. I guess that's an advantage of being from a smaller school. We don't have six to ten draftees each year so if you make it, you're a big fish. As an offensive lineman, with almost no statistics to back your candidacy, the probability of getting in is less. I'm very thankful to all of my teammates for pushing me to become the best I could, and to that extent I owe each of them."

When his NFL days were over, Baugh returned to the Chicago area. He took some classes to earn a teaching certificate from Chicago State University and helped coach football and track at Riverside-Brookfield, his alma mater.

"I've had an interesting life. After 15 concussions and a release from the Detroit Lions, I returned to my old stomping grounds," Baugh said.

He taught and coached at RBHS from 1990 to 1993.

"We had a good run at the playoffs a couple of times with Otto Zeman. I also coached the throws in track with Gary Johnson. I had a couple of good throwers. One of them eventually was a state champion in the shot put."

Baugh was then hired at Elmhurst's York High School, where he coached track with the legendary Joe Newton.

"I had continued success with the throwers, having one discus thrower take second place in the state meet and ultimately ended up becoming an all-American hammer thrower at (the) University of Iowa," he said.

Baugh, however, left education to return to the Kansas City area.

"Jeannie, my wife of 23 years, and I always loved KC, so we ultimately returned here to raise our family," Baugh said. "I have been involved in a construction company; I graduated from SIU in construction technology and real estate management."

But do they ever find themselves watching *The Love Boat* reruns and reminiscing?

"No love boat for us anymore," Baugh said in 2009. "Twenty-three years of wedded bliss, two great college-age children. Life is good."

FOUR DOWN TERRITORY

Favorite Football Movie—I like *Rudy* for its "anyone can live the dream" message, and I also like the movie *Radio* for its message of accepting everyone for who they are. *Jerry McGuire* is a good movie too. Ricky Johnson, our SIU quarterback, plays a part in that one.
First Car—I actually had a motorcycle first. A Yamaha 250 Enduro. But next was a 1969 Chevy Impala, which I was given by a family friend. All I had to do was make it run. It cost me about $75 in used parts in 1979. It used about two quarts of oil for every tank of gas.
Worst Summer Job—One summer at SIU I had a job which I walked five miles to work for one hour (maximum time allowed by homeowner) pulling weeds in a beautiful garden for $5 an hour. Later, the "Tommy Baugh rule" was enacted by the SIU coaching staff for summer work. If an athlete had a job that was less than five miles away the athlete had to find his own transportation. "If it was good enough for Tommy Baugh . . . it's good enough for you. I never once complained. . . . I just did my job."
Favorite Subject in School—I had an industrial technology class called Time and Motion Study. I remember it being very challenging and informative. It encompassed real-life planning of developing a product from start to finish utilizing industrial standards, sort of like engineering I suppose.

DONNELL DANIEL

Donnell Daniel vividly remembers his key moment of the Salukis' 1983 national championship season. In fact, he compared it to Joe Montana's famous drive against the Cincinnati Bengals in Super Bowl XXIII.

"It was like when Joe looked into the stands and told his teammates, 'Look, there's John Candy,' and it relaxed the team and they won with a long drive," Daniel said in an e-mail. "As I dropped back for the first punt return of the game I happened to look in the stands and in the sea of all the people I see my younger brother, Wilbert Daniel Jr."

What so amazed Daniel, then a senior at SIU, was that he didn't expect to see his brother at all.

"He was in the United States Army," Daniel said. "I had no idea he was coming to the game. It was a complete surprise, and moreover, how I was able to locate him in the stands amongst the sea of all the people in the crowd.

"In that moment everything seemed to just slow down. I had laser-like focus, and I knew that it was over for the Catamounts of Western Carolina. All that was left to determine was how much we'd destroy them by, and that we as a defense (were) to drop a bagel on them (shut them out)."

While SIU didn't shut out Western Carolina, the Salukis indeed steamrolled to a 43-7 rout in the I-AA championship game.

The game capped the SIU Hall of Fame career for Daniel. Carbondale, however, isn't necessarily where he pictured himself during his prep days at Larkin High School in Elgin.

"I played basketball and was the starting point guard for the Larkin Royals," Daniel recalled. "Larkin made tournament runs my junior and senior seasons under Coach Ken Johnson, who later went on to coach college basketball for the University of Wisconsin Badgers."

During those days on the hard court, Daniel squared off against the likes of Isiah Thomas, Glenn "Doc" Rivers and Terry Cummings.

"I relished the challenge and opportunity to compete against the country's best," he said.

Donnell Daniel (4) was a key member of the Salukis' 1983 defensive backfield. He played two seasons in the United States Football League.

Daniel also competed against future SIU teammate Tony Adams, who starred for Larkin's archrival, Elgin High School.

"I wasn't recruited heavily out of high school in football or basketball, and the oddity was that I was far more talented in baseball," Daniel said.

Baseball, however, didn't hold his attention.

"It came too easily," he said. "There were just too many lulls in baseball, and I lost interest."

Daniel did draw interest for football and basketball from Division II and III schools in Illinois, along with a host of junior colleges in California, Oklahoma and Kansas.

Daniel settled on Fort Scott Community College in Kansas.

"Although at the time I was very disappointed in the lack of offers I felt I had earned coming out of high school, it was a blessing in disguise," he said.

Daniel cited the Kansas Junior Community College Conference as the primary reason.

"(It was the) top junior college football conference in the country (with) national JUCO powers like Coffeyville, Butler County and Garden City. I played football and (ran) track against (future) Heisman Trophy winner Mike Rozier and Mel Gray of the Detroit Lions."

The competition paid off, as scholarship offers came Daniel's way from the likes of Kansas, Kansas State, Missouri, Iowa State, Oklahoma State, Arkansas State, Tulsa and several I-AA schools.

"It was during that time that I realized I was good enough to play at any level and felt vindicated for not being recruited heavily out of high school," he said.

Yet it was Adams, his former high school rival, that helped bring Daniel to SIU.

"Tony constantly encouraged me to just accept an official visit to SIU and at least see what SIU had to offer," Daniel said. "Tony talked about the tremendous athletes SIU had, and Southern was only a player or two away from winning a national championship."

Though Daniel initially had no interest in SIU, he soon warmed up to the idea of becoming a Saluki.

"I had matured greatly during my time at Fort Scott and realized that I wanted my family to be a part of any future success I attained. I understood that from the very beginning, it was the love, dedication and sacrifice by my family that were the foundation of my athletic career," he said.

Those sentiments soon mixed with simple geography.

"When making a choice for the next phase of my college career I had to reflect on how it would affect my family and their ability to see me play. I thought about how my dad would leave work on Friday evenings from Geneva, Illinois, and drive to Fort Scott, Kansas, and be there for the opening kickoff on Saturday afternoon," he said.

Enter SIU head coach Rey Dempsey, his coaching staff and the Saluki community.

"I never expected to attend SIU. It wasn't until I went there on my recruiting trip that I was hooked and knew this is where I wanted to be," he said. "During my visit it was totally awesome. I bonded immediately with the players and coaches, the campus, students, and the city of Carbondale was totally bananas.

"The nail in the coffin, so to speak, that sealed the deal for me was my one-on-one meeting with Coach Dempsey, defensive back coach Fred Manuel and a heart-to-heart with my closest friend and homeboy Tony Adams."

In the meeting with Dempsey, the head coach didn't begin with football.

"The first words out of his mouth were his faith and his relationship with Jesus Christ," Daniel recalled. "Coach wasn't forcing his beliefs on me; he simply shared how Christ was at work in his life and that he viewed himself as a willing, humble, but flawed servant of Jesus Christ."

Dempsey spoke of life beyond football and urged Daniel to focus on how he could become a better person and asset to his community and society as a whole.

"Coach spent the entire time sharing his life experiences and asking me about mine. He was focused on me the person, not the athlete," Daniel said.

The meeting ended with Dempsey looking Daniel in the eye.

"He said to me, 'It doesn't matter where you go if you don't use the talents God gave. You have to make those around you better and love your family as Christ loves (you),'" Daniel said.

Meanwhile, Manuel's approach was more conventional for a football coach.

"He said to me, 'If you can't play man-to-man defense from one end of the football field to the next without help from the safety, you can't play for me and you can't play for the Salukis,'" Daniel said. "I was

sold on Salukis football at that very moment."

If there were any lingering doubts, Adams dismissed them and delivered Daniel into the SIU fold.

"TA reminded (me) since we were in elementary school together and rivals throughout high school we had talked about playing college football together and winning a championship in our home state," Daniel said.

The transfer didn't view the moment as happenstance.

I became a Saluki, and the rest is history and the best decision I ever made.

"TA asked me one question and said if I was able to answer 'Yes,' then SIU isn't the right place. He asked me, 'Is there anything about SIU that doesn't feel like home to you?' My response was simply, 'No.' I became a Saluki, and the rest is history and the best decision I ever made."

That history includes the Salukis' national championship. It also includes being named Associated Press All-American and Missouri Valley Conference Defensive Player of the Year in 1983.

Those honors came on the merits of seven interceptions, three of which were returned for touchdowns. Daniel also returned a punt 85 yards for a touchdown.

Yet those awards aren't what Daniel dwells on. Instead, his memories, he said, focus on "my relationship with Jesus Christ and how Christ was not only the cornerstone of my life, but (also) the lives of my teammates, coaches and the foundation of our football team."

Like many athletes in team sports, Daniel recalls the relationships with his teammates and coaches.

"It was special and unique. We had had young men from all walks of life that came together through Christ for a single-minded purpose and goal, a championship," he said.

His memories include the break of the defensive huddle before every play.

"It's hard to describe, and words seem to fail. It's one of those things you have to experience," he said. "On defense, we were 11 rolled into one, looking into the eyes of one another in that huddle. There was a trust, an unshakeable confidence. We knew that with the sound in unison of the 'ready, break' there wasn't anything we couldn't do."

That feeling started from the opening game of the '83 season against rival Western Illinois.

"After all the hard work, studying, film sessions and practices, Coach Manuel came to me right before kickoff and said, 'Sweets, we go as you go.' I knew at that time I had arrived. My attitude was that I was the straw that would stir the drink for a championship," he said.

Daniel excelled in the game against WIU; he was named MVC Player of the Week from his performance.

"It was the catalyst that led to my All-American season and Hall of Fame career at SIU," he said.

Following his days at SIU, Daniel was drafted by the Chicago Blitz of the United States Football League. When the Blitz disbanded after the 1984 season, however, he joined the New Jersey Generals as part of the league's dispersal draft. Daniel played two years with New Jersey and Los Angeles.

Yet professional football proved to be quite different from Daniel's collegiate experience.

"It was a business, all the college fanfare and camaraderie of the students, alums and fans were gone. (There was) no stopping off at the local burger joint after beating your archrival at State U. It was strictly business," he said. "Secondly, the speed of the game and you add in the fact you had bigger, faster, stronger and smarter athletes at every position."

When his playing career ended, Daniel spent three years in the U.S. Air Force. He later served as the athletic director at the U.S. naval base at Guantanamo Bay, Cuba.

In 2005 Daniel was inducted into the Saluki Hall of Fame. He also returned for the 25th anniversary reunion of the national championship team.

Though it has now been more than three decades since he stood waiting for that first punt of the '83 I-AA title game, Daniel still remains a Saluki.

"I check the ESPN ticker every Saturday to see how the Salukis fared," he said.

Most likely, that ticker slows down ever so slightly as the SIU score scrolls across Daniel's TV screen. After all, moments like those tend to grab his focus.

FOUR DOWN TERRITORY

Favorite Football Movie—*Brian's Song*, because I was raised to be proud of my heritage, my people, my culture and the struggle those before us overcame to give us the freedoms I now enjoy. More important, I was raised to be color-blind and judge men and women on the contents of their character and not by the color of their skin. *Brian's Song* epitomizes that: two men vying for the same position on the football team and yet the love they had and shared for each other conquered all. Their love for one another was based on the character of each other, and that love transcended race, creed and color.

First Car—The very first car I purchased was a 1984 BMW 318i M.

Worst Summer Job—Working at Kentucky Fried Chicken; it lasted all of two days. It was filthy, greasy, sweaty and a downright horrible experience.

Favorite Subject in School—Economics. I enjoyed the way my high school teachers were able to relate the course subject matter to real-life business and caused us to think and not just fill dots on a scoresheet.

RICK JOHNSON

When you wind up breaking the Southern Illinois career passing record held by the legendary Jim Hart and lead your team to the national championship, how many people would guess you nearly gave it all up and walked away before it began?

Yet that's precisely what happened to Rick Johnson.

Johnson came from a long line of star quarterbacks at Wheaton North High School.

"I was the starter when a guy named Chuck Long was a sophomore," Johnson said. "Kent Graham came along after us."

Long, of course, later finished as the runner-up to Bo Jackson in the closest Heisman trophy race in history. After originally signing with Notre Dame, Graham transferred to Ohio State and later played in the NFL.

"There were three schools recruiting me," Johnson recalled. "Oklahoma State, Indiana State and Southern Illinois."

Johnson most likely would have gone to Oklahoma State, but the entire staff got fired.

> **J**immy Johnson, who later coached at Miami and with the Dallas Cowboys, came in and he didn't recruit me.

"Jimmy Johnson, who later coached at Miami and with the Dallas Cowboys, came in and he didn't recruit me," Rick Johnson said.

That left rivals Indiana State and Southern to battle over the quarterback. SIU won out due to the strong-arm tactics of head coach Rey Dempsey.

"He basically said, 'Why would you consider going anywhere else when I've recruited you?'" Johnson said.

After signing with the Salukis, however, Johnson soon regretted his decision.

"I thought it was a huge mistake at first," he explained. "I wasn't even the best player on my high school team, but I was pretty good. To go from that to being a peon was tough."

Dempsey made it even tougher.

"Coach Dempsey ran things much like the military in that he would break people down first and then build them back up," Johnson said.

Johnson almost immediately called his father with his concerns.

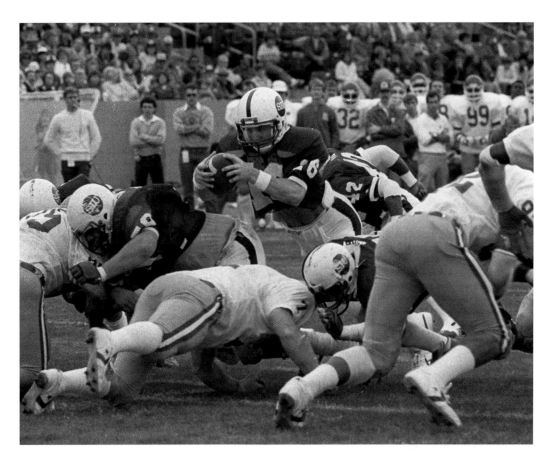

Quarterback Rick Johnson broke Jim Hart's SIU career passing record and led the Salukis to the 1983 NCAA I-AA national championship.

"My dad was always supportive. He didn't push me one way or another," Johnson said. "The decision was mine."

For a time, he considered going to Northern Illinois.

"Two of the guys from my high school team were there," he said. "But the Northern coaches weren't really interested."

Johnson spent his freshman year on the scout team. He vividly recalls running a bootleg and throwing an incomplete pass in practice.

"The defensive coordinator was screaming at me," Johnson said. "He had helped to recruit me. Anyway, he was yelling that he couldn't believe he ever saw anything in me on film. He said, 'You ain't got it!'"

Thoughts of quitting ran through Johnson's mind, but he kept those to himself.

"If the coaching staff knew, they probably would have encouraged me to do so," he said.

Things began to turn, however, during his sophomore year. While the Salukis were struggling on the field, the SIU coaching staff was banking on another sophomore named Arthur Williams for the future.

"There were two seniors (at quarterback), but one got hurt," Johnson said. "They had Arthur Williams on the shelf. He was the future."

Though Johnson got three starts down the stretch of a losing Saluki season his sophomore year, the quarterback battle was set for spring ball.

"Arthur and I went toe-to-toe," Johnson said. "Coach Dempsey wanted it that way. He put tremendous pressure on us. One day, Arthur snapped and ran off the practice field. To this day, I've never seen a guy throw better than Arthur Williams."

Strong arm or not, Williams was gone from the Saluki roster. Rick Johnson was in as the SIU starting quarterback.

"The last two years were more like I envisioned it," he said. "I was given more freedom. I was able to call plays. Coach Dempsey was now building me up."

This continued no matter the circumstances.

"I developed this bad habit after throwing an interception of getting down on myself," Johnson said. "One day, Coach Dempsey runs up to me and yells, 'Don't worry about it!' I liked that."

Not only didn't Johnson worry about the interceptions, there were fewer of them.

"I had confidence," he said simply.

That confidence ballooned in 1983, the season SIU captured the Division I-AA national championship.

Johnson cited numerous factors in what he termed "the magical season."

First, there was a key 17-14 victory over Eastern Illinois on September 10.

"Terry Taylor blocked a field goal that would have tied the game at the end," Johnson recalled. "That's the game when we all really started to believe."

Johnson noted that he didn't even play in the game or in the next two due to an injury. Still, the victory over Eastern propelled SIU forward.

"For whatever reason, we hadn't been able to beat them before that," Johnson said. "But that win really got us going."

While the Saluki offense finished the year averaging nearly 33 points per game, Johnson singled out the defense as a major factor in SIU's title.

"They really gave us good field position to work with nearly every possession," he noted.

The third factor Johnson cited was the team concept.

"When I was a freshman there were two buses to transport the team. I got on one of the buses and saw it was filled with black players. Someone shouted out, 'You're on the wrong bus, rookie.'

"(By 1983) there was none of that. There were no race issues. We were all one big family."

In the national championship game, Johnson and the Salukis overwhelmed Western Carolina 43-7. Johnson went 19-for-25 for 213 yards and two touchdowns in the title game rout.

In the fourth quarter, there was a timeout for an injury.

"It dawned on me all of the sudden, we're national champions!" Johnson said.

During his collegiate career, Johnson broke the all-time SIU record for passing yards by moving past a mark by Hart that had stood since the 1960s.

"Jim Hart was one of my heroes," Johnson said. "I had his NFL posters all over my dorm room. It really meant a lot to me."

When Johnson moved past Hart and into the SIU record book, the former Saluki great was on hand for the milestone.

"They stopped the game and he handed me the game ball," Johnson said.

The moment hasn't lost its luster over the years.

"You've got to understand, I was an overachiever," Johnson explained. "I wanted success so badly. I would have done anything for it. I wasn't the best quarterback in high school. Don Stockton, a kid from West Chicago, got a scholarship to Purdue. I couldn't run fast. I did have a quick release and a pretty strong arm, but boy did I ever want to win."

You've got to understand, I was an overachiever. I wanted success so badly. I would have done anything for it.

Johnson finished his SIU career with 5,804 yards. The mark stood for 22 years until Joel Sambursky passed it in 2005.

A national championship helped bring interest from pro football.

"I started to get some letters," Johnson said. "One was from the 49ers. The Colts, maybe, also sent one. I began to think I had a shot (at playing professionally)."

Former Saluki teammate and 12-year NFL cornerback Terry Taylor remembered Johnson's quick release.

"His hair was long enough to hang out the back of his helmet," Taylor said. "When Ricky J got rid of the ball, his hair would flip up. He was very accurate."

When the upstart United States Football League held its annual draft, however, Johnson's name wasn't called.

"I kind of panicked," he said. "If the USFL didn't draft me, what were the odds the NFL was going to? Coach Dempsey was gone to Memphis State at that point, so I called my high school coach."

Soon, Johnson was put in touch with Ray Odom, a Chicago-based agent. Though the USFL rosters were set, he received an invitation to try out for the Oklahoma Outlaws.

"I had to pay my own way and pay for my hotel," Johnson said. "My dad helped me out and got me to Tampa, where the camp was being held."

Not everyone in the Outlaws front office, however, was aware of Johnson's tryout.

"I was told that the roster was full. They didn't have any room for me; it was time to go home," Johnson said.

Soon thereafter, though, the Outlaws reconsidered and decided to give Johnson a shot.

"It was a two-day minicamp of just quarterbacks and wide receivers," Johnson said. "I was one of 11 quarterbacks."

With starter and former NFL veteran Doug Williams fully entrenched as the starter, the remaining 10 were left to compete with each other.

"We were lined up to throw passes to the receivers," Johnson said. "Well, I started jumping in and throwing every third one. The other quarterbacks were getting ticked, but I figured that was my shot."

Johnson's brash move paid off. He wound up landing the job as Williams's backup.

"I got something like $40,000 and maybe a $5,000 or $10,000 bonus. That was pretty good money coming out of college," he said.

When Williams went down with injuries, Johnson got four starts over the course of the next two USFL seasons. Next up was the NFL supplemental draft of USFL players.

"I was taken in the second round by the (Los Angeles) Rams. I think I was the second quarterback taken after Steve Young," he said.

The Rams, however, offered Johnson less money than he'd been making in the USFL. With five quarterbacks already on the Rams' roster, Johnson saw the handwriting on the wall.

"They all had NFL experience," he said. "I tried to go back to the Outlaws, but their player personnel guy had been with the Rams. He knew what was going on. So they pulled their original offer. They offered me less than the Rams were willing to give. I had lost all my leverage."

Then an offer came from the Canadian Football League. Bud Riley, the father of Oregon State head coach Mike Riley, called.

"He was with Calgary at the time," Johnson said. "He told me they were 0-4 and to come up and finish out the season there."

Johnson wound up staying five seasons in the CFL.

"My second year up there was a gas," Johnson said. "I got to call my own plays. I had great wide receivers. I threw for over 4,300 yards. I played a bit like Brett Favre. I'd get back and wing it. Sure, I threw interceptions, but it was the most fun I had."

That 1986 season saw Johnson lead the CFL in passes (604), completions (302) and yards (4,379). He also threw 31 touchdown passes and was named to both the West and All-Canadian All-Star teams.

Injuries, however, soon began to hamper Johnson's play. In fact, he briefly lost feeling in his arm after the '86 season. The remainder of his CFL career was riddled with injury. Johnson noted that he suffered eight concussions.

"When your arm hurts, that's one thing, but when you're talking about your brain, that's a whole different situation," he said.

Yet Johnson did return to Los Angeles in 1990 for one more shot with the Rams. There he was reunited with Long, his former high school teammate.

"That was the year Jim Everett took the Rams to the NFC championship game against the 49ers," Johnson said. "But many people will tell you that they'd have been better off with Chuck Long.

"The NFL is not much on coaching technique. It's more about scheming. Jim Everett threw off his back foot all season long."

Football soon ended for Johnson, a prospect he wasn't prepared for.

"One of my biggest regrets is that I didn't take my studies very seriously," he said. "It was all about football. I knew that I didn't want to be a coach."

Johnson then came up with an idea.

"I'd always loved movies," he said. "I go see a movie and then go back and see it again and again. I'd watch the actors. I'd watch the camera angles and directions. I'd look at things from all the different aspects of the movie industry."

Johnson signed up for an acting class. The bug bit him hard.

"I knew this is what I wanted to do," he said.

Johnson appeared in bit parts both on TV and in the movies, including roles in the football flicks *Jerry Maguire* and *Any Given Sunday*.

He also began directing and producing. In 2001 Johnson directed a movie called *Rustin*.

"It's very loosely based on my own life," he said. "It's about a former player who has to grow up and change his ways."

Though the movie was well received by critics and was honored by the Method Fest Independent Film Festival, it didn't do well at the box office.

"The movie business is tough," Johnson said.

While seeking funding for his second movie venture, Johnson decided to take a job with First Trust Portfolios.

"I was kind of hesitant because it signaled the end of my film career," Johnson said. "But, for the first time, I had a consistent, steady paycheck."

Today, he is based in the San Francisco area.

"I make financial presentations," he said. "That satisfies the performance bug for me."

And Rick Johnson, national championship quarterback, knows a little something about performing.

FOUR DOWN TERRITORY

Favorite Football Movie: *Jerry Maguire*. I don't want to sound conceited, because I was in the movie, but it's a very good movie. It captured the NFL experience accurately. The NFL is a business; I learned that fast. I was proud to be in this movie.

First Car: A Mazda RX-7.

Worst Summer Job: In high school I worked for a friend's brother's concrete business. You talk about hard work. I made $5 an hour in 1978, which was great money, but that was a grind.

Favorite Subject in School: Kinesiology.

TERRY TAYLOR

Some have compared being a cornerback in the National Football League to being alone on an island. Terry Taylor offered a different analogy.

"I'm an only child," said Taylor from his home in North Carolina. "I'm the loneliest person in the world. You're out there guessing, and then it's up to your athletic instincts."

Taylor used those instincts for 12 seasons in the NFL. He finished his career with 25 interceptions and two touchdowns.

"Football to me was a fight," he said. "That's the way I approached the game."

Taylor learned the game growing up in Youngstown, Ohio. He competed in football, basketball and track as a high school standout.

"I was all state in every one," he noted. "My first love was basketball."

Football coaches, however, came after him from the likes of Kent State, Akron and Indiana State. In the end, Southern Illinois won out.

"Coach (Rey) Dempsey was one of the main reasons (I chose SIU)," Taylor said. "My parents knew of him already from his days as an assistant at Youngstown State."

Taylor never regretted his decision to come to Carbondale.

Defensive star Terry Taylor (21) was the first-round pick of the Seattle Seahawks in the 1984 NFL Draft.

"Other than having my kids, college was the best four years," he said. "Man, did I ever enjoy it!"

That enjoyment reached its apex his senior season when SIU captured the 1983 Division I-AA national championship.

Taylor helped get the steamroller moving by blocking a potential game-tying field goal to preserve a 17-14 home victory over Eastern Illinois in the second week of the season.

"I had messed up something earlier in the game," he said. "I can't remember if it was a fumble or a mental mistake or what, but when it came down to the last seconds I knew I had to do something to win the game."

> **I** *had messed up something earlier in the game. . . . When it came down to the last seconds I knew I had to do something to win the game.*

The block and subsequent victory ignited the Salukis.

"That told us just how good we were," Taylor said.

Indeed. SIU finished the regular season with a 10-1 record and entered the I-AA playoffs knowing it had a real shot to capture the national championship.

"I remember it was so cold, freezing cold, for those first two playoff games," Taylor recalled.

Taylor warmed things up, however, with an interception in the Salukis' 23-7 quarterfinal win over Indiana State.

A week later, Taylor grabbed two Nevada-Reno passes as SIU again won 23-7.

"I had two interceptions within about 12 seconds," he said. "I took the second one back for a touchdown."

The triumph sent Taylor and his teammates into the national championship game against Western Carolina.

"Coach Dempsey had us prepared," Taylor said. "We watched so much film. It was all strictly business. I was filmed out! We didn't have any time for leisure activities. The (assistant) coaches were tired of it too. I complained to (assistant coach) Carl Angelo. He told me, 'Go tell the head man (Dempsey).'

"So, the last day before the game, Coach Dempsey is all set to show us more film. Well, I had enough. I went up to him and said, 'We've got them. We've *got* this game.'"

Taylor proved to be prophetic. SIU trounced Western Carolina 43-7 and stood at the top of the I-AA football world.

A starter since his freshmen year, Taylor began to realize his potential to play at the next level.

"Coach Dempsey told me I was going to be his first number-one draft choice," Taylor said. "As time went on, I understood why."

That understanding grew when he attended NFL combines following his senior season.

"I went to Indianapolis, Seattle, New Orleans and New York," Taylor said. "I ran 4.3 (in the 40-yard dash) at all of them."

The Seattle Seahawks made Taylor their first-round draft choice, the 22nd overall selection.

"Seattle was the best place I could have gone," Taylor said. "(Head coach) Chuck

Knox wanted me there. The Seahawks had guys like Kenny Easley, Dave Brown and Keith Simpson in the secondary. Those guys taught me how to be a professional and gave me what it took to last 12 years in the NFL."

Taylor made an impact as a rookie, recording three interceptions. Seattle won three of its last four games and grabbed the Seahawks' first-ever playoff berth.

Rick Johnson, SIU's record-setting quarterback of the '83 national champions, wasn't surprised by Taylor's success.

"(He's) flat out the best athlete I've ever seen or known," Johnson said. "No question. I don't know what else I can really add to that."

Donnell Daniel played the cornerback position opposite Taylor.

"Terry is the most gifted athlete I've ever seen," said Daniel, who played two seasons in the USFL. "Terry could wake up at 3 a.m. and run a 4.3 40-yard dash, start at guard for any number of Division I basketball teams and was a member of the SIU Olympic-qualifying track team."

Taylor, however, soon realized the NFL was a business.

"Once you start getting paid, the fun is over," he said.

In the years that followed, the Seahawks traded away the likes of Easley and Brown.

"I was upset and bent out of shape," he said. "If they could get rid of those guys, then what were they going to do with *me*?"

What the Seahawks did was trade Taylor as well. After five seasons in Seattle, the team shipped him to Detroit for running back James Jones.

"I wanted to go to the Raiders," he said. "I couldn't stand Detroit. When I landed at the airport nobody was even there to meet me. I had to get a cab from the Detroit airport all the way out to Pontiac. It was over an hour ride."

To illustrate his point, Taylor cited examples showing why Detroit was such a poor organization from a player's standpoint.

"You were only allowed two towels after practice, and you had to pay for your own shoes," he said.

Yet Taylor did enjoy his time playing for Lions head coach Wayne Fontes.

"Wayne, his brother Lenny and Frank Ganz, those were guys I loved playing for," he said. "They stuck up for their players."

Taylor spent three seasons with the Lions. Then, in 1992, he joined the Cleveland Browns.

"I loved it because I got to play at home in front of friends and family," he said.

Taylor spent two years with the Browns before returning to Seattle for one season. In 1995 he played his final season in the NFL with Atlanta.

"(Falcons head coach) June Jones had been an assistant coach in Detroit," Taylor said. "He called me up and asked me to come and teach his cornerbacks how to play the position. He also offered me a bonus."

Taylor wound up starting four games for the Falcons and finished the season with three interceptions.

"Al Davis called me after the season and wanted me to play for the Raiders," Taylor said. "I told him, 'Thanks, but no thanks.' I was done playing."

One of the reasons Taylor was ready to give up the game was the person he had become.

"I did not enjoy being me," he said. "To get up for the games mentally, you had to really become something that was against your personality. On the way to games I'd get into arguments, heated arguments, with my wife. I was a mean, angry person. I was not a pleasant person to be around."

Pro football also took its toll on him physically.

> **T**his is a violent game; it's a game you have to play when you're hurting. They really took the fun out of the game.

"You had to play hurt; they'd want to shoot you up with pain killers," he said. "I wasn't any shot taker. The first five or six years were fine. But those next few years, I was really suffering. After games, I'd just lie in bed with ice all over my body. It really is like being in a car wreck."

Reflecting on his career, Taylor singled out quarterbacks as the difference makers in the passing game.

"All the receivers are good," he said. "It's the quarterbacks that make teams something more. Joe Montana was good. Dan Marino was good. If you give even somebody as talented as Jerry Rice a quarterback like Dave Krieg, he's not going to have the same success."

Asked to name the best quarterback he went against, Taylor chose John Elway.

"I really feared him," he said. "He was the best because he could run a 4.5. He was big. You'd think he was running out of bounds and he'd run over you. And then he'd throw the ball 60 yards in the air. Elway could beat you running or throwing.

"Those types of quarterbacks were always tough to play against. Steve Young was another one."

Since retiring from the game, Taylor rarely tunes into the NFL.

"I might start watching a game on TV, but pretty soon I'm outside doing something else," he said. "The game had changed. You've got wide receivers running their mouths. Kenny Easley would have knocked them all out. You get fined for nearly every hit. This is a violent game; it's a game you have to play when you're hurting. They really took the fun out of the game."

Still, Taylor said he would like to play in today's NFL.

"There's no telling what I'd make today, probably around $3 million (a season)," he said. "They're giving rookies who have never played a down $10 million. That's crazy."

At his financial peak, Taylor made "around $750,000 or $800,000."

With his playing days behind him, Taylor has served as an assistant high school football coach.

"I coached in Seattle," he said. "We won a couple of state championships."

He later coached in his native Ohio and then in North Carolina.

"It's the next best thing to playing," he said. "I get out there and show them how to do things. As a coach you can't just run your mouth; you've got to show them how to play the game."

Taylor also found time to work on his golf game.

"That's what's great about North Carolina," he said. "The weather is better down here."

Ironically, Dempsey lives in nearby Charlotte.

"Yes, we still talk," Taylor said.

And no matter how the conversation starts, you can be sure it eventually gets around to that national championship fall of 1983.

FOUR DOWN TERRITORY

Favorite Football Movie—*Jerry Maguire*; Ricky Johnson is in that movie. I'd recognize that round head and blond hair of his anywhere.

First Car—It was a 1984 Park Avenue. I got that toward the end of college.

Worst Summer Job—Washing cars. That got old real fast.

Favorite Subject in School—Science. I always liked biology.

Yonel Jourdain (39) breaks through the line during action from the 1990s.

1990s

JUSTIN ROEBUCK

Justin Roebuck played all over the field at Chicago's Whitney Young High School in the late 1980s.

"I played football and ran track. I played quarterback, wide receiver, free safety and cornerback," Roebuck said in 2016.

Such versatility brought Roebuck multiple scholarship opportunities.

"(My) offers were mostly (from) MAC (Mid-American Conference) schools and Illinois State. Illinois wanted me to walk on," he said.

Roebuck chose SIU because he felt it was the best chance to play as a freshman. Saluki head coach Bob Smith and his staff also made the decision to use Roebuck as a receiver. That choice proved to be wise, as Roebuck led SIU in receptions in 1991 and 1992.

Roebuck caught 42 balls for 647 yards as a junior. He was joined by teammates Doug Amaya (tight end), Yonel Jourdain (running back), and Tom Roth (tackle) as All–Gateway Conference second team honorees.

Yet what stands out in his memory most about that season was the Salukis' 21-20 upset of fifth-ranked Northern Iowa. A week later, SIU knocked off number-19 Illinois State.

Roebuck repeated as all-conference second team with a 46-catch, 645-yard senior season. The 5-foot-9, 180-pound receiver also matched his junior season with four touchdown receptions.

"Becoming the all-time leading receiver in the history of the school is what I remember

Justin Roebuck was an All–Gateway Conference receiver in 1991 and 1992.

most," he said. "All-time leading receivers in catches and yards really speaks to my consistency and work ethic. I wasn't the biggest or fastest, but I showed up to work every day."

As of 2016, Roebuck ranks eighth with 120 career catches at SIU. His 1,809 yards put him fourth on the all-time list. Roebuck hauled in 10 touchdown receptions, placing him 12th in Saluki history.

Roebuck may have fashioned more impressive numbers his senior season, but SIU often used him to draw the defense away from other Saluki weapons.

"It was successful because Justin Roebuck, SIU's all-time receiving leader, was running a decoy pass route to the right corner of the end zone," read one newspaper account of a teammate's touchdown play.

Roebuck talked of the on-field chemistry he had with quarterback Scott Gabbert.

"Just when the defenses were in Cover 2 (pass defense) Gabby and I had a known circle-out route that we would run without him having to audible, and we always would get key first downs with that route," said the receiver.

Roebuck noted that the friendships he made last as much as any records or victories the Salukis attained during his days at McAndrew Stadium. He cited Gabbert, Billy Swain, Greg Brown, Wes Yates, JJ Chaney, and Ken and Kevin Cater as his closest teammates.

"Coach Smith and my receiver coach, Sam Venuto, (also will always stand out)," he noted.

Roebuck especially connected with Swain, his fellow talented receiver, and Gabbert, his quarterback.

"(Gabbert) was always relaxed and a hell of a competitor. Billy helped me learn how to get off the line better; I helped him with route running, reading the defense and catching in traffic."

When his days at SIU ended, Roebuck continued to play football, albeit not in the way he had dreamed.

"Playing in the NFL was always the goal," Roebuck said.

When that plan didn't work out, he gave Arena football a chance.

"(I) didn't like Arena," he said; "tried out . . . small field and no loot equals time to start working in the real world."

That led Roebuck to his current line of work. Yet he didn't completely give up football.

"I played competitive flag (football) about eight years post SIU," he said. "(I'm) director of business analysis at Amerisure Insurance Company and raising my kids, Lauren and Jordan," he said. "The future for me is watching my kids grow, traveling with my lovely wife Marlo and playing as much golf as I can."

FOUR DOWN TERRITORY

Favorite Football Movie—*Friday Night Lights*, because it's about overcoming adversity.

First Car—Plymouth Sundance.

Worst Summer Job—Selling knives.

Favorite Subject in School—Calculus.

DAMON JONES

Damon Jones easily ranks as one of the greatest players to ever don a Saluki uniform.

His record speaks for itself. Jones was the only tight end named when the SIU All-Century Team was revealed in 2013. Listed at 6-foot-5 and 270 pounds, Jones played five seasons for the Jacksonville Jaguars of the NFL.

"Getting drafted (as the) first (tight end) in franchise history will always be special," Jones said in 2015 from his home in Florida.

Jones originally attended the University of Michigan after excelling at Evanston Township High School. He arrived in Ann Arbor as the nation's number-two-rated tight end upon his 1992 high school graduation. Things didn't work out with the Wolverines, however, and he transferred to SIU after his freshman year.

According to a 1997 *Chicago Tribune* story by Scott Merkin, Jones admitted that then-head Saluki coach Shawn Watson and SIU "received a more mature and polished

Damon Jones (*left*), who transferred to SIU from the University of Michigan, was the first tight end ever drafted by the Jacksonville Jaguars.

version than what appeared at Michigan. His first two years, Jones suffered from homesickness in Ann Arbor and had troubled adjusting to playing behind Mark Burkholder and eventually Pierre Cooper at tight end on the Wolverines' depth chart."

Watson told Merkin, "We knew about Damon's problems at Michigan when he came here, and I laid it on the line for him that this was his last chance. But I could tell Damon was a good person, a young man with a big heart. My two sons (ages 10 and 8) literally think he hung the moon. I could also tell this was someone who loved playing football."

According to a 1997 *Chicago Tribune* article by Teddy Greenstein, Jones pleaded guilty to a three-count felony for placing and manufacturing bombs in his dormitory while at Michigan in 1992. Two years later, Jones was arrested—along with Wolverine basketball players Jimmy King and Ray Jackson—and charged with shoplifting beer from an Ann Arbor convenience store.

Jones told Greenstein, "There was a girl working in the store. She told me I could take whatever I wanted without paying. It wasn't like I went in there with a gun and a mask and shot at the cash register."

Jones was acquitted but, according to Greenstein, "felt that people on campus saw him as a guilty man, so he left for Carbondale to resurrect his career."

At SIU, Watson twice suspended Jones, for one game each in 1995 and 1996 for disciplinary reasons.

"Damon had his days, but fewer of them as he continued to grow up," Watson told Greenstein.

In 2015 a retrospective Jones said he experienced personal growth during his time at SIU.

"(It) taught me a lot about being a leader and (about) patience. I wasn't the best at (those things) and had some struggles, but it helped me mature over time," he said. "I chose to go to SIU based on my relationship with wide receiver coach TJ Wrist. He was a graduate assistant at Michigan."

Watson's gamble paid off on the field. In his three seasons with the Salukis, Jones caught 104 passes for 1,500 yards and nine touchdowns. He was an All-American and a First-Team All–Gateway Conference choice.

"On the field he was a man among boys, but he behaved like a boy among men. He looked like a Big 10 athlete playing in I-AA ball," said Mike Reis, the longtime Voice of the Salukis.

Certainly there were adjustments to make with Jones's transition from the Big 10 to Division I-AA football.

"One difference was the stadiums and crowds. Playing on TV wasn't weekly like at Michigan," Jones said. "The equipment was different. As a redshirt freshman at Michigan I had all kinds of stuff. As a starter at SIU I asked for wrist bands and was given the top of socks (that were) cut off. Guys told me I had to get my own. Only starters got gloves.

"(As far as) competition, some guys were still at the high school level. That made it tough to gauge (where I was at in my development for the pros)."

Like many I-AA athletes, Jones also experienced some of the downside of playing at a school many view as a stepping stone to more lucrative positions.

"It was hard to keep some of our best coaches," he said. "Other administration stuff held football back."

Despite this disadvantage, Jones relished his time at Southern.

"Each year at SIU was special and taught me a lot about being in shape," he said.

"(My) second season I had my best stats because I was in shape, and I had to study defenses from success from the first year."

Indeed. After seeing on the field and on videotape what Jones could do, opponents often designed defensive schemes to stop him.

"I was seeing different (defensive) coverages to take me out of the passing game," Jones said. "Northern Iowa was probably the best at defending me with a triangle of a defensive end, a linebacker and a strong safety.

"I had to deal with coaches and defenses that were designed to keep me out of the passing game. That year helped with my blocking."

Jones is quick to credit his SIU coaches for his transformation from a little-used player at Michigan into an NFL draft pick.

"Coach Wrist would always talk to me and keep it 100 percent about playing at the next level," he said.

So what was his biggest on-field growth as a Saluki?

"Running routes and getting open in space is what most improved," he said.

Jones had all the attributes of a big-time pro tight end, and his speed caught the attention of NFL staffs. In a workout with the New York Jets, Jones was timed at 4.62 seconds in the 40-yard dash.

Questions remained, however. Greenstein quoted an NFL player personnel director as saying, "When he wants to play, he's outstanding. Other times he stands around and looks like a pole."

Yet Jones impressed during the Senior Bowl by catching three passes for 87 yards and earning praise for his run-blocking.

I *always still watch the sports ticker for the SIU score and (follow former) Salukis in the (National Football) league.*

Thus Jones found himself in the NFL after the expansion Jaguars made him the 147th overall pick in the 1997 draft. Jones played 50 regular-season NFL games. He caught 41 passes for 550 yards and 11 touchdowns. He added another three catches in three playoff games.

"I wish I had gotten more time to play, but injuries got me. But (at least) my son and his kids can say (that I played in the NFL)," he noted.

In recent years, Jones spent some time coaching at Seacoast Christian Academy in Jacksonville. Today, Jones often appears at Jaguars events.

"I'm still part of the Jaguars alumni. (I'm) actually going to sign some autographs at the scrimmage tonight," he said during the 2015 NFL training camp.

No matter where life may take Jones, his mind often returns to Carbondale.

"I always still watch the sports ticker for the SIU score and (follow former) Salukis in the (National Football) League," Jones said.

Favorite Football Movie—*Remember the Titans*, because it showed how locker rooms get rid of racial bigotry and depend on the man next to them regardless of color, race, sexual orientation.
First Car—1980 Chevy Impala.
Worst Summer Job—A lesson learned not to mess up the opportunity to play football and attend college on a scholarship. Working for the forestry department for the city of Evanston the summer between transferring from Michigan to SIU.
Favorite Subject in School—Math.

KARLTON CARPENTER

SIU fans and players of the 1990s can easily picture the running gait of Karlton Carpenter.

"He was something to watch, that's for sure," said teammate Cornell Craig.

When he finished his SIU career in 1998, Carpenter was the Gateway Conference's Offensive Player of the Year as well as the Salukis' all-time leading rusher with 3,181 yards.

Yet it could have been so much more. Coming off a season in which the Chicago native rushed for 1,892 yards, Carpenter sent an inquiry to the NFL regarding his draft status. Carpenter ultimately made the decision to stay for another year in Carbondale, but things soon unraveled after that.

Carpenter was arrested July 2, 1999, by Carbondale police for allegedly attempting to burglarize a parked car. A warrant was issued after he failed to appear in court 20 days later. That warrant was overturned, however, after his attorney learned Carpenter was in a Chicago-area hospital at the time of his scheduled court appearance.

Nevertheless, Carpenter's legal woes continued as he also faced misdemeanor charges for allegedly fleeing state police and improperly using traffic lanes.

In an August 1999 *Daily Egyptian* story, then–SIU head coach Jan Quarless was quoted as saying, "I'm really interested in seeing that he is a member of our football team. And we're going to take him back with open arms when he returns."

That reunion never took place, as Carpenter never again played for the Salukis.

Carpenter came to SIU out of Chicago's Dunbar High School, where he led the Mighty Men into the 1994 city championship game. Carpenter rushed for 190 yards and two touchdowns, along with a two-point conversion, in the semifinals. A week later, Carpenter rushed for 88 yards, as Dunbar won its first Chicago Public League championship since 1967.

Carpenter had an immediate impact for the Salukis. As a freshman in 1995, he scored two touchdowns in the fourth quarter as SIU rallied past Western Kentucky 30-28 at McAndrew Stadium. Carpenter's four-yard touchdown run with 2:26 remaining proved to be the winning score.

As the leaves changed color each fall thereafter, Carpenter provided SIU with power and speed. By 1998, opponents tried—usually in vain—to thwart Carpenter's running. For 10 straight games he rushed for 100 yards. He found the end zone 16 times.

Running back Karlton Carpenter came out of Chicago to land on the Saluki All-Century Team.

"He's really risen to the occasion," said Illinois State head coach Todd Berry after Carpenter rushed for 190 yards against the Redbirds. "He's quite a load to handle. He's extremely durable. From that, I would have to say he's the top back in the league. With their offensive game plan, it's truly amazing."

Carpenter surpassed Burnell Quinn as the Salukis' all-time leading rusher in the third quarter of a game against Southwest Missouri State. Carpenter ripped his way into the SIU record book with a 37-yard run, erasing Quinn's 19-year-old mark.

"The career (record) means a lot," Carpenter said afterward. "Just to be on top of everyone else says a lot. It feels good and everything. . . . I just don't know what to say."

Carpenter finished that day with 189 yards on 35 carries, all the while playing with a thigh bruise sustained earlier in the year.

In fact, the injury kept him out of practice in the week leading up to the game. Carpenter also felt it kept him from scoring on the historic run.

"I'm not supposed to get caught like that even with a bad leg," Carpenter said in reference to being tackled on the 37-yard run. "I had a bad leg, and I was supposed to have way more yards than that."

Opponents continued to marvel at Carpenter.

Indiana State head coach Tim McGuire said, "He hurts you when you tackle him. He's like the Energizer Bunny. He just keeps running and running. Our players had a lot of respect for him after the game."

Though Carpenter fell short in his bid for 2,000 yards in 1998, he remains one of the all-time greats in SIU and Gateway/Missouri Valley Football Conference history.

"He's the best I've seen in a while," said Southeast Missouri head coach John Mumford after Carpenter rushed for 206 yards and three touchdowns in the season finale at McAndrew Stadium.

CORNELL CRAIG

Cornell Craig left SIU as the Salukis' most prolific receiver. But for those who saw him play, Craig left more of an impression than just raw statistics.

"SIU has (had) no one like him at wide receiver for at least 25 years," said Salukis' broadcaster Mike Reis in 2015. "Tall, and could go up for the ball and catch it over a defender. Surprised his record lasted as long as it did. That a wide receiver hasn't broken it (MyCole Pruitt was a tight end) is a testament to Craig, a high-quality individual."

Craig grew up in Louisville, Kentucky, and arrived in Carbondale in 1996. By the time his collegiate career ended in 1999, the 6-foot-1 receiver held virtually every major receiving record at SIU.

"I played every sport as a kid but by high school had settled on football, baseball, and track," Craig said. "I played basketball in high school until my sophomore year but decided to focus on football more. Louisville is a big basketball area, and by the time football season was over the (basketball) team was pretty much set. They had played in the summer leagues together, and I figured I didn't have that much time to dedicate to basketball. I was better in football anyway."

Though his high school team's offensive plays mostly called for runs, college recruiters did notice Craig. Though there were offers to walk on at Division-I universities and proffered scholarships from Division-II schools, Miami of Ohio came after the lanky receiver hard.

"They wanted me to commit right away, but I wanted to see what else was available for me," Craig said.

After making the rounds, Craig came back to Miami.

"I verbally committed to Miami of Ohio, but by that time they had decided to give another player an offer before they moved forward with me. They didn't think he was going to come to them, because he was being recruited by Missouri. But he ended up choosing Miami of Ohio, so they pulled back their scholarship to me because they only wanted one receiver that year."

Nevertheless good fortune was about to shine on Craig. SIU head coach Shawn Watson had spent time as an assistant at Miami, so "they made contact for me."

Craig arrived in Carbondale for his campus visit.

"I really liked the environment. I really liked the university. I had a good time, and it looked like a good college for me. It was a chance to go to a new state and experience something different," he said.

Though the Saluki staff probably didn't fully realize it at the time, it had just landed a difference maker. Even Craig wasn't sure himself—at first, anyway.

"I was a late bloomer. I was always pretty good but never the star growing up. I always had talent. I always had skills, but I wasn't the homecoming king type. I was a good player, but not the best," Craig said.

After going against him in practice, veteran SIU players assured Craig he was ready for the college game.

"They gave me confidence," Craig said. "After that, things went really fast."

Craig's fast start was apparent from the get-go in the 1996 opener versus Central Arkansas.

"I didn't start the game, but I was in the rotation, the third or fourth receiver," he recalled.

"My first catch was a touchdown pass. It was a slant. The sports page of the *Daily Egyptian* ran a picture of me of going into the end zone. I was like, 'Wow, this is amazing!' It was more than I could have imagined."

Between his freshman and sophomore year, Craig noticed something.

"I was always one to look through the history and statistics of things," he said. "I noticed that no receiver had caught 1,000 yards worth of passes (in a single season) in SIU history. I remember saying, 'How is that?!'"

Craig experienced what he called "my breakout game" in 1997 against Murray State.

"I had something like six catches for 185 yards. That game really stands out. I believed in myself, and I knew I had talent," he said.

Meanwhile, the reactions from his teammates and others was different.

"Everybody was shocked," Craig said. "I remember thinking to myself that when I have a game like that (again) it's not going

Cornell Craig, who played from 1996 to 1999 and left SIU as the school's most prolific receiver, was named to the Saluki All-Century Team

to be a surprise. I want that kind of game to be the standard.

"I always thought of myself as a piece of the puzzle, not a major cog, but that year was the start of me being a major piece of the offensive puzzle."

That kind of game did become a standard for Craig. He added three more 100-plus-yard performances that season, including a 219-yard act against rival Illinois State.

Craig also credited the addition of Dan Enos to the SIU coaching staff.

"We really had a connection as player to coach," Craig said. "He put in this new (pass) route. It was a post-corner-post route."

The play worked just as the coaching staff had drawn it up.

"Our completion percentage and our yards per completion (with that play) were amazing. It was always open, and we were always able to connect on it," he said.

As a junior, Craig topped the 100-yard plateau four times. A year later, he doubled his output with eight such performances.

Craig was the first SIU receiver to earn First Team All-American honors (1999). He was also selected as the Gateway Conference Offensive Player of the Year and Division I-AA Player of the Year. A three-time all-conference choice, Craig racked up over 2,000 all-purpose yards as a senior.

Does Craig place more value on one award compared with the others?

"It's tough to put one above any of the others," he said, "but my first time being acknowledged by the Gateway Conference as a member of the all-rookie, all-newcomer team was big for me. Ultimately being recognized as a consensus All-American was huge. That was never a goal of mine. It was a hope or a wish, but it was never a goal. It was never something I worked toward. Everything has to fall in place for that. The team had to be right, the plays had to be called, the preparation had to be together. It's something where everything had to come together to work out for you."

Craig also took tremendous pride in leading the nation in receiving yards as a senior.

"I got a plaque as a statistical leader from the NCAA; that was big. My freshman year our punter Mark Gagliano got one for leading the nation. I remember thinking, 'Wow, that would be amazing to do.' It was a wonderful award, but it wasn't just what I did. It was what the team did," he said.

In his Saluki career, Craig caught 207 passes for 3,508 yards and 37 touchdowns. He held the school's single-game records for receptions (13), yards (219) and touchdowns (3). Craig also held the single-season record for receptions (77), yards (1,419) and touchdowns (15).

Upon graduation with a radio/television degree from SIU, Craig signed a professional contract with the Montreal Alouettes of the Canadian Football League.

"I really hoped to get some invitations to NFL training camps, but that didn't happen for me, but I got an opportunity when Montreal opened up for me. It was a good experience," Craig remembered.

Unfortunately, a partial tear in his quad muscle cut short his plans. The structure of CFL rosters also proved to be a factor.

"You're competing against all the other Americans on the team, because there are limits on non-Canadians on each roster," he said.

Yet Craig refused to hold any grudges or have any regrets.

"I enjoyed the city of Montreal. I enjoyed the guys on the team. I enjoyed the opportunity," he said.

After his injury, Craig gave football one more shot by signing with the Peoria Pirates in Arena Football 2.

Craig said, "We won the league championship, and then I went back to Montreal again. I was hoping that would open up some opportunities for me to play. I had a window of about three years that I was going to play, and if it didn't work out I was going to move on with my life.

"I definitely have no complaints. There was a time when I was disappointed, but no blame to be placed anywhere. Overall, the access and the opportunity I've been given I wouldn't trade for anything. I had no major injuries. I had no significant surgeries. The focus now is concussions, and I had no significant concussions. I had the opportunity to get an education and memories that will last me a lifetime."

Though his pro football career never developed further, Craig completed his master's in business administration at Bellarmine University in Louisville.

"During that time I began working at the university. I worked in the admission office," Craig said. "I really got interested in the student affairs aspect of the university. I also got involved in diversity. Diversity has always been important to me. That was one of the things that attracted me to SIU. There was always diversity. I got my minor in black American studies. Things came together when I finished my master's and I became director of university affairs. I helped that office."

Football still remained a part of his life, although not in the same capacity that it once had.

"I did a little moonlighting working with the football team at my high school. I helped out coaching the kids there and really enjoyed it," he said.

Today, Craig is the director of multicultural affairs and diversity programs at Pace University in New York City. He even worked briefly with the wide receivers on the school's football team.

"Again, I really enjoyed it, but my time constraints just don't allow for that now," he said.

Craig was inducted into the SIU Athletics Hall of Fame in 2008 and was also placed on the Missouri Valley Football Conference 25th Anniversary Team and the SIU All-Century Team.

FOUR DOWN TERRITORY

Favorite Football Movies—*The Program*; it came out when I was in high school. That movie connected with me at a formative age. It looked at college and college football, and it really stands out in my memory.

First Car—I had a '79 Volkswagen Rabbit. I bought it for like $500.

Worst Summer Job—At the YMCA, handing out towels and that sort of thing.

Favorite Subjects in School—I really liked philosophy. I wanted to go into premed when I got to SIU, but then I came across a few hurdles in math and decided to change my major. I thought about philosophy, but when I called to tell my parents, they asked, "What are you going to do with philosophy? Are you going to become a college professor?" I said, "Of course not." They responded and said, "Then you aren't majoring in philosophy." I didn't major in it, but I really enjoyed the subject. I like thinking about thinking, I like thinking about your behavior. I like looking at things from various angles. I think perspective and context are very important. I enjoy looking at things from a critical perspective and breaking things down. That really attracted me to philosophy.

Chris Dieker had a 20-9 record as a three-year starter for the Salukis (2008–10). He finished
his career ranked third in SIU history with 5,237 passing yards and 41 touchdown passes

2000s

JERRY KILL

Jerry Kill knows the value of hard work, commitment and loyalty. He learned it at an early age while growing up in Cheney, Kansas.

"I wouldn't trade it for the world," said the man who revitalized SIU football and took it to sustained heights of success. "I grew up on a farm outside of town. I was out there working at an early age."

Cheney, a town of approximately 2,000 people, is about 25 miles west of Wichita.

Though he strung together a successful coaching career that lasted over three decades, Kill is still very much a product of his formative years. His father, Jim, worked two jobs while his mother, Sonja, ran the household.

"I was fortunate to have two parents growing up," he said. "I was the first one in my family to get a college education, but those two uneducated people taught me more than I'll ever know about life."

Many of those lessons came from long hours of work. Beginning at age 14, Kill worked on farms, in factories and at grocery stores.

In his spare time, he played whatever sport was in season.

"It was football and basketball during the school year and baseball in the summer. I played them all because it got me out of work," Kill joked. "Back in the day you didn't have any fancy uniforms. You played in blue jeans and cleats you got from K-Mart. The sponsor gave you a cap and t-shirt to wear."

Kill easily recalls the names of his high school coaches.

"Jack Thomas, Ken Disken and Roger Hilton," he said. "Being at a small school, those three did it all."

For Kill, one of the highlights of the 2009 football season was having Disken attend a Northern Illinois game.

"That was very special," Kill said of his then 80-year-old former coach.

As a high school football player, Kill worked his way into the starting lineup and eventually made the all-conference team. A two-time captain, he was named the team's most inspirational player as a senior.

With graduation fast approaching, Kill desired to keep playing.

"I maybe thought about baseball a little, but I was smart enough to look around and

Jerry Kill left a lasting legacy in southern Illinois far beyond his coaching.

see that there were 22 players out on the football field, so my chances were better," he said.

Kill landed at Southwestern College, an NAIA school in Winfield, Kansas. He met his future wife, Rebecca, and married her there. He also played outside linebacker for coaches Phil Hower and Dennis Franchione, the latter of whom would later coach at Texas Christian University, Alabama and Texas A&M.

"(Southwestern) was his first job," Kill said.

With a teaching degree in hand, Kill set out to begin his postcollege life.

"We're in a different era today (with coaching careers)," he said. "All I wanted to do was get a job."

That opportunity came at Midwest City High School in Oklahoma. Mike Gundy, the future Oklahoma State head football coach, was the school's quarterback.

"I was making $20,000, my wife and I had a great apartment and I remember thinking, 'We're rich!'" Kill said.

Those feelings were short-lived when Franchione called to offer him an assistant coaching position at Pittsburg State, a Division-II school in Kansas.

"I made about $250 a month," Kill said.

What he lacked in money Kill soon more than made up for with experience.

"(Franchione) was tremendously organized," Kill said. "He always had a plan. He was classy, but he was very demanding."

Kill earned his way to offensive coordinator at Pittsburg State. In 1991 the Gorillas won the Division II national championship.

By 1994 Kill landed his first head coaching job at Saginaw Valley State in Michigan. His teams turned in five straight winning seasons, including consecutive 9-2 teams in 1997 and '98. Those final two teams also led Division II in rushing. In addition, Kill served as the school's athletic director.

All that changed when his father passed away from liver cancer in 1999. Kill and his family made the decision to accept the head coaching job at Emporia State in Kansas.

"It gave me the opportunity to come back toward home," he said.

While it also meant a $20,000 cut in pay and trading in a nationally ranked program for a losing one, Kill thought it more important to be closer to his grieving mother.

He coached at Emporia State for two seasons before the Southern Illinois job became open.

Saluki athletic director Paul Kowalczyk told Kill, "I'm looking for a guy who can turn the program around."

SIU had gone nine years without a winning record. During that period, the Salukis averaged fewer than four wins per season. SIU had not finished better than fourth in the Gateway Conference.

Kowalczyk took Kill on a tour of the SIU campus and facilities.

"It was dark, but I could see that the facilities weren't in too good of shape," Kill said. "I had some doubts (about taking the job)."

To help make his decision, Kill contacted Franchione and Gary Patterson, another trusted friend in the coaching profession.

"They both said you're not going to get a good job (to begin with)," Kill recalled.

When weighing whether to take an assistant coaching position elsewhere as another option, Kill was reminded that "as a head coach, you always control your own destiny."

Thus Kill accepted the SIU offer. Things didn't start easy for him.

"I thought it would take at least five years to turn things around," he said, "but it was worse than I thought."

Kill's first Saluki team won only a single game in 2001. Unaccustomed to losing, Kill placed a phone call to Northern Illinois head coach Joe Novak, a man who had endured the hardships of winning just three games in his first three years as the Huskies head coach.

It took time, but you've got to make kids realize it's not always about the game.

"I didn't know him very well," Novak said. "He called me about his struggles and asked for some advice. I told him, 'You don't need my advice; you've had success.' Stay with what you're doing."

Thus Kill stayed the course.

"He held three-a-day practices. He ran (the program) like a boot camp to get things going his way," said Mike Reis, the SIU radio play-by-play broadcaster.

Soon Kill was coaching an improving team. His second year at SIU brought a 4-8 record. Kill continued putting to use the old-fashioned work ethic he had learned growing up.

He was instrumental in reaching a deal with the local electrical union to install lights at McAndrew Stadium so the Salukis could again play night football. He and his team did community service work.

"I try to treat people like I want to be treated," he said. "It took time, but you've got to make kids realize it's not always about the game."

By the third year, it all came together. The biggest crowds in a decade flocked to see the new-look Salukis. SIU rolled to a 10-2 season, tied for the conference title and earned a trip to the Division I-AA playoffs.

Things were just getting started. Before Kill arrived in Carbondale, SIU had never worn the Gateway crown. Starting in 2003, the Salukis captured the conference championship three straight seasons.

By 2005 the Salukis qualified for the playoffs a third consecutive year. Kill, however, suffered a series of seizures. He was diagnosed with kidney cancer. Following the season, Kill had surgery to remove the cancerous tumor.

While being treated, Kill met other southern Illinois residents battling the same illness. Realizing many of them did not have the same financial resources he did, the Coach Kill Cancer Fund foundation was created.

"Because I have seen firsthand what others have faced, I would like to give something back. I think the hardest moments in dealing with this disease are when I see children, middle-aged individuals and the elderly who may not have the opportunity to see another day," reads a Kill quote on the foundation's website.

The 2005 playoffs also marked a turning point for SIU. The Salukis weren't just glad to make the tournament field, they wanted victory. That goal became a reality when SIU defeated Eastern Illinois 21-6 in the first round.

Thus SIU earned the right to take on perennial power Appalachian State in the quarterfinals. Though Kill's team lost to the eventual champions 38-24, the stage was set for even more Saluki success.

Despite slipping to fourth place in conference play in 2006, SIU again advanced to the playoff quarterfinals, where Southern's season came to an end with a 20-3 loss to perennial power Montana.

A year later, SIU won 12 games, the most since the Salukis' 1983 national championship. This time around, Kill's team made it all the way to the national semifinals before falling 20-17 to the Delaware Blue Hens in a game played at McAndrew Stadium. Delaware was quarterbacked by Joe Flacco, who would later win a Super Bowl with the Baltimore Ravens.

"Jerry Kill saved the program," said Mike Reis, the longtime Voice of the Salukis. "He achieved what nobody thought he could for two reasons: No one knew him, and Southern hadn't won (for many years). No one expected it."

Reis again pointed to Kill's three-a-day practices.

"He ran it like a boot camp to get things his way," Reis said. "He mirrored the program on what Bill Snyder did at Kansas State."

Along the way, Kill's SIU teams caught the attention of the administration at Northern Illinois University. In 2004 Kill made the decision to gamble on a two-point conversion that would have pulled off an upset at Huskie Stadium. While the decision failed and SIU lost 23-22, an impression was made.

Three years later, SIU returned to DeKalb and claimed a 34-31 victory. A season earlier, the Salukis had shocked Indiana University of the Big Ten with a 35-28 victory.

When SIU's 2007 season ended, Northern Illinois came calling—literally.

"(NIU athletic director) Jim Phillips called me on his way down to Carbondale," Kill said. "I can't remember if he was halfway there or how far into the trip he was, but he had (retiring head coach) Joe Novak and Tim McMurry with him."

When the NIU contingent met with Kill, it wasn't just the coach who came away with a good feeling.

"My wife was really impressed with Jim Phillips," Kill said. "He's a pretty persuasive guy. In the end, it was a family decision. (Staying in Illinois) also allowed me to still be active with my cancer fund organization."

Thus Kill took over the NIU reins from Novak on December 13, 2007. He finished with an impressive 55-32 record at Southern. His teams went to the playoffs five straight seasons. Twice he was selected as I-AA Coach of the Year and won the Eddie Robinson Award in 2004.

"I was fortunate to be around good players," Kill said. "You also have to give credit to your coaching staff."

Former NIU assistant coach Mike Sabock knows a Kill-coached team when he sees it.

"Jerry Kill's teams just don't give up, they don't quit," Sabock said. "I remember one time when he was at Southern Illinois, we had them down 28-7. They scored, recovered two onside kicks and the next thing you know they had us beat."

Later an assistant at Mid-American Conference rival Western Michigan, Sabock faced the Kill-led NIU Huskies.

"I told my guys they better come ready to play for 60 minutes," he said. "It doesn't matter if you're up by three points or down by seven, Coach Kill's teams will just keep coming at you."

Jack Pheanis has been around NIU athletics since 1950. He played football and later coached football and golf for the Huskies. He ranks Kill among the best coaches he has ever seen.

"He is tremendous," said Pheanis during Kill's days at NIU. "I see the things he does with his team firsthand. I would have loved to have been an assistant under Jerry Kill."

NIU play-by-play broadcaster Bill Baker shares similar sentiments.

"Jerry is a class act," Baker said. "He is so level-headed. He has a sense of humor and a sense of business about him. The two never cross. He can be having fun one minute, but when it's time to get down to his job, Coach Kill is serious about what he does."

Veteran Chicago radio and TV personality David Kaplan was immediately impressed with Kill.

"I'm a huge fan," Kaplan said. "Jerry Kill is as honest as the day is long."

Like Kill, Kaplan has dealt with threats to his personal health.

"Everything is in perspective with Jerry," Kaplan said. "Sure, he wants to win and is as intense as anyone. But he realizes that fourth-and-inches isn't the same as life and death."

Kill knew his work was cut out for him. Phillips and Novak warned him that the team he was inheriting might win only three or four games. In addition, Phillips left NIU to take the director of athletics position at Northwestern University in February 2008.

"I was very disappointed when he left," Kill said.

As a cancer survivor, Kill knew that life continues. NIU turned in a 6-6 regular season and landed in the Independence Bowl.

"I was in shock to be able to go to a bowl game that first year after all I'd heard," he said.

Yet Kill had his past coaching experience to guide him.

"Coaching is coaching," he said. "You're fighting your life off. Being at a mid-major really isn't all that different from being in I-AA. The BCS (Bowl Championship Series) schools have the resources. That's why they're the big boys. You're fighting your life off."

The Huskies continued fighting and returned to the postseason in 2009. Following a seven-win regular season, NIU accepted an invitation to the International Bowl, played in Toronto.

Though the Huskies lost to South Florida, NIU had made school history by going to bowl games in back-to-back seasons.

In 2010 the Huskies won the MAC West title and played in the Humanitarian Bowl. The same day NIU accepted its bowl bid, however, word leaked out that Kill was leaving DeKalb to become the head coach at the University of Minnesota, the very same Big Ten team his Huskies had knocked off during the season.

"Jerry was very disappointed the way it played out," said one NIU insider. "He wanted to tell his players first. It just worked out that it was the same day as the team's awards dinner. With the way the instantaneous news cycle works today, word got out before Jerry could tell the players. It was a lousy way for things to end."

Kill left NIU after compiling a 23-16 record in his three seasons. He was the first Huskies coach to post two wins over Big Ten teams. In addition, all three of his NIU teams played in bowl games.

At Minnesota, Kill's pattern continued. After winning just three games in his first year, Kill and his staff took the Golden Gophers to bowl games three consecutive seasons.

Unfortunately, his health issues again returned. He suffered two seizures during the 2011 season, followed by one each the following two years. After the 2013 seizure, Kill took a leave of absence to address his illness, which finally forced him into retirement during the fall of 2015. Longtime assistant Tracy Claeys was hired as Kill's successor by Minnesota. Kill accepted an associate athletic director position at Kansas State in May 2016. He returned to coaching when he was hired as the offensive coordinator at Rutgers University in December 2016.

Kill also wrote an autobiography with author Jim Bruton titled *Chasing Dreams: Living My Life One Yard at a Time.*

"I don't think I've met anybody that has had as much impact and influence on people as Jerry Kill," Bruton said.

No matter what comes his way, Kill realizes the past has made him the person and coach he is.

"You are who brought you up," he said. "I've also learned things along the way. It's harder to be a coach now than ever before with all the shit that's going on today. There's no discipline in our society. We're headed in a bad direction. And it's not the kids' fault. Some of them really don't know any better. They don't know the difference in right and wrong."

And coaches like Jerry Kill are just the sort of men to help them learn. Just like his parents did for him all those years ago in rural America.

FOUR DOWN TERRITORY

Favorite Football Movies—*Remember the Titans* and *Brian's Song.*
First Car—It was a Mustang, a 1967 that was blue. I paid around $800 and got it used.
Worst Summer Job—I don't know if I'd say any of them were the worst. I can tell you the hardest and the hottest. It was being up in the loft of a barn. You're the guy who's picking up all the bales of hay and stacking them. It's about 105 degrees up there. If I had my whole team out in that barn, there probably wouldn't be but two of them left.
Favorite Subject in School—Biology.

BART SCOTT

An apple doesn't just keep the doctor away; it also provides Bart Scott with daily motivation.

An apple was a key prop during Scott's junior year, when he was suspended by Southern Illinois head coach Jan Quarless.

"I don't know all the specifics of what happened," said Jerry Kill, the man who replaced Quarless as the Salukis' head coach. "I only remember that after our first team meeting we had a divided team. People were yelling at one another."

According to a 2001 story by Steve Cunningham in the *Southern Illinoisan,*

Quarless offered little insight to the situation. The result was that Scott didn't play a down afterward.

"I definitely wasn't happy with not playing for six games," Scott told Cunningham.

The story points out that Scott was hit with numerous personal foul penalties, including hitting opponents signaling for fair catches on punts several times during the season's first five games.

"I took all that negative energy I had and applied it wrong," Scott said.

According to Cunningham's account, Scott and Kill claimed to never having discussed the incident that got him suspended.

Kill said that after his first meeting with his 2001 SIU team, he and Scott talked.

"This kid was waiting for me (after the meeting ended). He was pretty emotional. He told me that he had been dismissed from the team for eating an apple at halftime," recalled Kill.

Whether the apple was the forbidden fruit or there's more to the story, Scott nearly lost his football future.

"I remember when I got suspended my junior year of college, and I thought football was going to be taken away from me," Scott told Greg Bishop of the *New York Times* in 2009. "And I vowed that if I ever got another opportunity to play football that I would never take a play off, that I would give it everything I had."

Scott got that opportunity with Kill.

"I told him that we'd see what he could do," Kill said.

Scott did plenty. He played linebacker, free safety and cornerback for the Salukis. What's more is that he held true to his promise.

"He was phenomenal for me," said Kill. "To this day he's still good to me."

Scott, a three-year starter at SIU, earned First-Team All–Gateway Conference recognition as a senior in 2001. He finished his collegiate career with 352 tackles. In 2009 Scott was selected for the Gateway/Missouri Valley Conference Silver Anniversary Team.

Tom Matukewicz was Scott's position coach at SIU.

"First off, he was really talented," Matukewicz said. "He had a big-time motor, just like he talks. That was his best attribute.

"He was a hitter. When he hit the pile, he moved it. Bart had speed. He could go sideline to sideline, and he could rush the passer too."

Asked to recall Scott's best game, Matukewicz paused and replied, "We played at Baylor (in 2001). Even though we lost, Bart really dominated that game."

The Detroit native came to SIU after a stellar prep career at Southeastern High School. Scott starred on both defense and offense. He racked up 76 tackles and three fumble recoveries while rushing for a team-high 635 yards and five touchdowns. Southeastern officially retired his jersey in 2008.

Following his SIU days, Scott signed with the Baltimore Ravens as an undrafted free agent in 2002. He made an immediate impact, playing in all 16 games as a rookie. In storybook fashion, Scott preserved a 13-12 Baltimore victory when he intercepted Steve McNair in the end zone in his NFL debut.

Throughout his NFL career, Scott was been an integral part of his team's success. He played seven years with the Ravens, earning a Pro Bowl appearance in 2006. That

Given an opportunity by Jerry Kill, Bart Scott made the most of his second chance. Scott developed into an NFL Pro Bowl player before becoming a TV analyst.

same season Scott earned second-team All-Pro status.

In his time with Baltimore, only future Hall of Famer Ray Lewis produced more consecutive seasons with 100 or more tackles.

In 2009 Scott left the Ravens to sign with the New York Jets as an unrestricted free agent. Madbacker.net, his official website, proclaimed, "With an explosive combination of speed, strength, quickness, and intensity, Scott has blossomed into one of the most feared defenders in the NFL."

"It's a great story," said Kill of Scott's success.

It's also a story that's been optioned as a movie, according to Scott's agent, Harold Lewis.

"Bart is one of my favorite people," said Lewis.

Scott's story features the strength of a number of important people in his development. First, there's his grandmother, Gwendolyn Pippen Osborne.

"She's the boss of the city," Scott told Bishop. "She definitely runs the block. When I think about my grandmother, I think about a person that sacrificed her quality of life for the family and really set an example that family is important. Right now, she's raising my cousin, William, who was her brother's son's kid. For her to still be raising kids at her age just shows how important family is to her. And I think that reflects in how close our family is."

Another is his mother, Dorita Adams.

"I think (she's) the single greatest mom in the world," Scott said. "A lot of people say that (about their own moms), but I think I may not be the only person in the world with that opinion about my mother. There may be other people (who are) not even related to me that believe the same thing. It wasn't until I had my own children that I could understand where she was coming from, why she protected me, why she worked so hard."

Kill agreed.

"An impressive woman," the coach said.

Scott also spoke of his father, Bart Capers, and his advice.

"If you want to go back to Yoda, man, it's either do or do not," Scott recalled the words. "Try isn't an option. You either do or you do not. Man, I won't allow anything to hold me back, no matter how bleak the odds may look, no matter how daunting the task may seem. I learnt that from him. And that's what he instilled in me all the time."

Those lessons weren't just applied on the field. Scott returned to SIU during the off-season and graduated with a degree in economics in 2005. That same year he provided uniforms and other equipment for the Southeastern High School football program. Scott has also purchased land near his grandmother's house to be turned into a neighborhood playground.

In 2006 Scott established his charity, which he titled A Son Never Forgets Foundation. It aimed to assist those suffering with paralysis after a random shooting left his cousin in that condition.

In 2008 Baltimore-area congressman Elijah Cummings honored Scott at the "Legends among Us" fund-raiser that recognized community service.

First and foremost, however, Scott remains a football player.

"I play this game not for Pro Bowls, not for popularity contests," Scott said, "I play this game so that one day when . . . those people that played football are sitting down, and they're having a drink with their buddies, they can be like, 'Hey, you know who was a hell of a football player, man? He knocked the hell out of me one day in that game. Man, Bart Scott was a beast.'"

A close look also reveals a key prop from yesteryear.

"He always keep apples in his locker," said Kill. "He says it keeps him motivated."

Today, you can see Scott on TV doing work as a studio analyst.

In the fall of 2014 Scott returned to the SIU campus.

"It was terrific having him back on campus," said team chaplain Roger Lipe.

TOM KOUTSOS

Already SIU's career rushing leader as a junior, Tom Koutsos found something that could stop him from gaining more yards—injury.

After scoring six touchdowns in his first two games of the 2002 season, "Touchdown Tommy" broke his wrist on the Salukis' second play from scrimmage against Murray State. Thus his season came to an abrupt end.

Yet the 5-foot-11, 220-pounder had established himself as one of the all-time greats in SIU football history. He had rushed for a record 3,747 yards. In fact, he broke Karlton Carpenter's school mark midway through his junior year in just his 28th collegiate game. He rushed for more than 1,000 yards in each of three seasons and is the only player in school history to record multiple 1,000-yard seasons. Koutsos accumulated 18 100-yard rushing games at SIU. He was the school record holder with 38 career touchdowns.

Oddly, Koutsos drew little recruiting interest during his prep years at Marmion Academy in Aurora, Illinois.

Paul Murphy, his high school coach, said, "Tom was one of the best running backs I ever coached. He had tremendous vision, he could outrun defenses as well as lower his shoulder and run a defender over. It usually took more than one defender to tackle him. Tom also caught the ball out of the backfield very well."

Despite Koutsos's skills, Murphy said that most colleges were looking for bigger backs. Murphy added, "He was getting lukewarm interest from the D-I schools mostly because of his size; he was 5-10, 195 pounds.

"Northern Illinois wanted him as a walk-on during most of the recruiting period. Jerry Kill was at Saginaw Valley State and was ready to offer a scholarship but then took the job at Emporia State."

Not to be deterred, Murphy and Koutsos sent a video to SIU.

"Once they saw Tom's video, they offered him an official visit. While (Tom was) visiting, SIU offered him a full scholarship, which was his dream. Tom accepted the scholarship offer before he came back to Aurora," Murphy said.

Though NIU called Murphy to offer a partial scholarship, Koutsos stayed with SIU.

"The rest, as they say, is history," said Murphy.

Tom Koutsos overcame injury to establish himself as one of the greatest running backs in SIU history.

Ironically, Kill was hired by SIU as Koutsos was preparing for his sophomore season as a Saluki.

"So as fate would have it, he was reunited with a coach who was recruiting him out of high school," said Murphy.

Together, Kill and Koutsos saw success. When Koutsos arrived in 1999, SIU was coming off a 3-8 season. By 2003 the Salukis were 10-2 and had reached the playoffs for the first time in 20 years.

"He was on track to be one of the few NCAA running backs to gain 4,000 yards in the four years he was in school," Murphy said. "Unfortunately, Tom broke his arm."

In 2010 SIU named Koutsos to its Hall of Fame.

"There are under 300 people in the entire SIU Hall of Fame, and to be one of them, and to be only 29 (years old), it was a huge honor for me," Koutsos told Dave Oberhelman of the *Arlington Heights Daily Herald* at the time.

Following graduation, Koutsos spent time coaching running backs at Nicholls State in Louisiana and Scottsdale Community College in Arizona. He also spent time as an athletic trainer and in business. Today, Koutsos is an office manager in the Chicago area.

Saluki broadcaster Mike Reis said, "Have never been happier for a player to finally achieve success than (for) him. That he stuck with the team after Jerry Kill replaced Jan Quarless as the team's coach was critical to 'Touchdown Tommy' and to Kill. He could've transferred to a number of MAC schools, but they wanted (him) to play (defensive back) or (linebacker). Kill kept him at

(running back). He couldn't believe SIU won the conference in 2003, and in undefeated fashion. He had a tear in his eye when he got off the team bus in Delaware for the 2003 playoff game. He looked at me and said, 'Reis, we finally made it.' Most outgoing SIU player I've ever covered. Worked hard. Played hard. On and off the field. Dramatic. Bombastic. Bark was worse than his bite off the field but not on the field."

BRANDON JACOBS

Though he played just one season at Southern Illinois, Brandon Jacobs left a lasting impact.

"He's a freak, someone who comes along once in a lifetime," said head coach Jerry Kill. "He was about 6-(foot)-4, 267 pounds and ran a legitimate 4.5 for the NFL (combine)."

Jacobs starred at Assumption High School in Napoleonville, Louisiana. He ran for a state-best 3,302 yards in 2000. Averaging 215 yards per game and racking up 35 touchdowns, Jacobs was lauded as Class 4A Offensive Player of the Year.

Jacobs began his college career at Coffeyville Community College in Kansas. As a freshman he rushed for 1,349 yards and 17 touchdowns to grab team Most Valuable Player honors. Jacobs was even better as a sophomore, running for 1,896 yards and 20 TDs. Averaging 7.1 yards per carry, Jacobs was named a junior college All-American.

Jacobs then transferred to Auburn University. The Tigers boasted a collection of future NFL draft picks, including running backs Carnell "Cadillac" Williams and Ronnie Brown.

However, with the handwriting firmly on the wall, Jacobs decided to transfer for his final year of eligibility. Thus he arrived at SIU.

Jacobs fit in immediately with the Salukis.

"I really love it here," Jacobs told sports reporter Scott Mees in the 2004 preseason. "You've got a lot of great people here in southern Illinois. I love Coach Kill to death because he'd do anything for you."

The Saluki fans soon loved Jacobs. He led the team with 992 yards. Though he played only one year, SIU recognized his 6.6-yards-per-carry average as its career record. In addition, Jacobs scored 19 touchdowns, one less than the school's all-time leader, Muhammad Abdulqaadir, another former Coffeyville running back.

Despite a 166-yard, four-touchdown performance by Jacobs, the Salukis fell 35-31 in their opening-round playoff game against Eastern Washington.

The Gateway Conference recognized Jacobs as its Newcomer of the Year following the season.

Jacobs came to the attention of NFL scouts and coaches in the East-West Shrine Game. He led all rushers with 102 yards and 11 carries. Jacobs scored his second touchdown late in the third quarter when he turned the corner and sprinted 52 yards into the end zone.

The New York Giants chose Jacobs with their fourth-round pick in the 2005 NFL draft.

"It's just an honor to be able to come to New York and put on that blue uniform and go to work," Jacobs said in a press release posted on the Giants' website.

Brandon Jacobs transferred to SIU from Auburn and later won a Super Bowl with the New York Giants.

"He was stuck behind those two great running backs they had down there," said Kill.

Though he was listed as the third-string back on the Auburn roster, Jacobs still managed to run for 446 yards and two touchdowns for the Tigers in 2003.

Longtime NFL general manager Ernie Accorsi explained the Giants' decision.

"It's important to understand that this is a running back, not a fullback," Accorsi said. "His specialty is short yardage, but he's a halfback. That's what he was drafted as."

Jacobs joined veteran Tiki Barber, the Giants' career rushing leader, on the roster.

"I was just talking to someone and they said, 'The Giants haven't been able to get a third-and-one in a long time.' So this will stop finally because I will not be denied one yard," Jacobs predicted.

"When I know it's short yardage I don't pitter-patter behind the line of scrimmage. I know the down and distance. I know where I have to go, so I get the rock and I barrel down, and I just get in. Just one person won't stop me from getting what I want. It's going to be a couple people.

"I'm going to surprise a lot of people when they only ask for one yard and I take it the distance," he added.

Entering the 2006 season, Jacobs said he studied film of power running back Eddie George, the former Heisman Trophy winner from Ohio State who starred for the Tennessee Titans, in an effort to refine his own style.

The work paid off, as Jacobs ran for 423 yards and nine touchdowns. He averaged 4.4 yards a carry.

When Barber retired, Jacobs took over as the starter for the 2007 season. Though he injured his knee in the season opener, Jacobs returned to the lineup a month later with a 100-yard game against the New York Jets.

Despite missing two games later in the season with a hamstring injury, Jacobs still managed to become a 1,000-yard rusher. More important, he proved to be a key in the Giants' run to the Super Bowl XLII crown.

When ESPN produced a documentary-style special about the famed 1958 NFL championship game between the Giants and the Baltimore Colts, 11 players from the '58 title tilt were paired with coaches and players from each franchise's 2007 roster. The pairings screened the '58 game and talked about life in pro football during the two eras. Jacobs was one of the Giants chosen.

After rushing for over 1,000 yards for a second straight season, Jacobs was tagged as the Giants' franchise player in February 2009. A week later, New York signed him to a four-year, $25 million contract.

Jacobs' fifth NFL season proved to be a disappointment. A knee injury ended his season after 11 games. He finished the year with 683 rushing yards. In addition, his yards-per-carry average slipped to just 3.9.

After a brief stint with the San Francisco 49ers, Jacobs officially retired as a Giant in 2014.

No matter his NFL performance, Kill will always remember his one-year running back for more than just his football prowess.

"He's a great kid who has become a great person," Kill said.

ELMER MCDANIEL

Today, as an airplane mechanic in Tulsa, Oklahoma, Elmer McDaniel is used to fixing things and providing support. As an offensive lineman in the early 2000s, McDaniel solved plenty of problems for SIU's offense.

"My job is kind of similar to football in the aspect that it takes a lot of teamwork for us to get our product," McDaniel said. "We gotta depend on everybody so we can achieve our goal."

Listed by SIU as 5-foot-11 and 305 pounds, McDaniel was lauded by coaches as the team's best offensive lineman of the era.

"I grew up in Muskogee, Oklahoma," McDaniel said, "so, yeah, I'm an Okie from Muskogee (laugh). I attended Muskogee High School, where I played football and threw the shot put on the track team."

The odds of continuing his playing days beyond high school seemed against McDaniel.

"I didn't have many offers except from junior colleges and small NAIA schools. So I ended up going to junior college to better my stock in schools," he said.

That plan worked out well for him. McDaniel earned honorable mention all-conference honors at guard his freshman season for Northeast Oklahoma A&M College in 2002. Additionally, his team posted an 11-1 record and won its conference title and a junior-college bowl game.

"I got recruited to SIU out of junior college, and I had never heard of the school until Coach Kill came to my college. I had a great recruitment trip to SIU, except for all the snow on the ground," McDaniel remembered.

However, SIU didn't initially offer McDaniel a scholarship.

"There was another lineman on my recruiting trip, so they said they were going to choose between us," he said.

Thus McDaniel took a trip to Louisiana, where Nicholls State University was also recruiting him.

"I had a great visit there, so I had my mind set on going there because I really didn't have any other offers I was interested in," McDaniel said.

Whether it was fate, fortune or some other outside force, the situation soon cleared up for both the player and the Salukis.

"On Christmas Eve I got a call from Coach Kill, and he gave me the best Christmas present ever and offered me a full scholarship to SIU," McDaniel said.

McDaniel more than earned that scholarship.

"What a player he turned out to be," said Kill years later.

McDaniel earned Gateway Conference Offensive Lineman of the Week accolades for October 15, 2003. The official SIU news release lauded his performance as grading "out at 80 percent on his blocking assignments against Illinois State on Saturday with an effort grade of 100 percent." The Salukis rushed for 358 yards and piled up 506 yards of total offense in the game.

"I felt like I had a great career at SIU even though it was only two years, but I had a lot of fun and made some great friends through the years," McDaniel said. "The competition was tough coming in, but I worked my way up to starting and made the best of it. We had good chemistry on our team, and everybody gelled together so our records reflected it."

McDaniel listed being named All-American two consecutive years as one of his greatest accomplishments.

"My favorite game would have to be my senior year (in 2004) against Western Kentucky. Coach (Matt) Limegrover took me aside and told me that this is probably the best defensive lineman I would face that year and that he needed me to step it up, so I took that as a challenge. I prepared hard for that game and had the best game of my life," McDaniel said.

McDaniel was rewarded with his second career conference lineman-of-the-week award after the Salukis rushed for 310 yards against the number-three-ranked scoring defense in the nation and throttled WKU 38-10.

"My offensive line really moved some Hill-toppers off the ball," said star running back Brandon Jacobs after the game. "They work hard all week, and I commend them for it. They did a great job."

Junior quarterback Joel Sambursky broke the school record for most career offensive yards in the game.

"It is an honor, and it shows how great the guys around me are," Sambursky said afterward.

Elmer McDaniel was one of those great guys. The irony is that a quarterback gets the glory while the linemen plod on. Sort of like an airplane pilot and his mechanics.

FOUR DOWN TERRITORY

Favorite Football Movie—*The Program*, because it reminds me a little bit of playing college football.

First Car—A two-door white Cutlass Oldsmobile.

Worst Summer Job—It was right after high school; I was trying to make a little extra money, so I got this job at a juice factory. Worst job ever, plus they wouldn't hardly give me any hours.

Favorite Subject in School—English; I was always fascinated by it for some reason.

ARKEE WHITLOCK

Mike Reis may have paid the ultimate compliment to Arkee Whitlock.

Elmer McDaniel's SIU biography states, "Powerful player with quick feet . . . loves to finish blocks . . . high-effort player."

Arkee Whitlock played in the Canadian Football League after being a standout for the Salukis.

"When you guys had the biggest games, you personally showed up," Reis told Whitlock at his 2013 Hall of Fame induction. "You had a good game when you played the best teams, and I think that's how you judge the best players. What do they do when they play the best teams?"

Reis proved his point by citing Whitlock's 207-yard, three-touchdown performance in a Saluki win over then-number-one-ranked Western Kentucky in 2005.

"It was the first (televised) game my family back home (in South Carolina) could see," Whitlock said of the ESPNU broadcast.

To Whitlock, those were the games that he used to build his legacy.

"I wanted to ring bells," Whitlock told Reis. "People don't remember the guys that don't step up in those big type of games."

Whitlock grew up in Rock Hill, South Carolina. He began playing Pop Warner football as a six-year-old. By high school, Whitlock was a star running back and linebacker.

Whitlock played a season of junior college football in Coffeyville, Kansas, before landing at SIU under head coach Jerry Kill. Though he entered a crowded Saluki backfield, Whitlock still stood out.

"At one point we had Arkee Whitlock, Brandon Jacobs and Terry Jackson in our backfield. Of the three, Arkee had the most upside," said former SIU quarterback Joel Sambursky.

Whitlock twice rushed for over 1,000 yards and was a two-time All-American, garnering first-team honors in 2006.

"By far '06 was my most productive year stats-wise," Whitlock told Reis. "For me it was an easier year than years before. It felt like I had (done) everything before. Every game felt like a game I had played before. The game slowed down because I had a lot of snaps early (in my SIU career)."

Whitlock rushed for 1,828 yards that season. He broke the SIU career record for all-purpose yards (5,599). He set single-season school records for points (125) and rushing touchdowns (25). Whitlock finished third in the Walter Payton Award balloting. Seven years later, Whitlock still feels he should have won the honor annually given to the best player in Football Championship Subdivision ball.

"It ate me up inside. Everybody is supposed to feel like they are capable of winning the award. I felt like I was very capable. . . . I think I meant more to my team than the other contestants meant to their teams," Whitlock told Reis.

"Arkee Whitlock is the best football player I played with," said quarterback Nick Hill, who roomed with the running back for a year.

Though he had dreams of playing in the NFL, Whitlock went undrafted.

"When I didn't get drafted, I didn't get rattled or lose my focus," he told the *Rock Hill Herald.*

Instead he signed a free agent contract with the Minnesota Vikings. The Minnesota backfield, however, featured Adrian Peterson.

"It's hard to say what my chances are," Whitlock said at the time. "My goal is to put good things on film for the front office to see. They are the ones who make the decisions."

The Vikings' decision was to release Whitlock. San Francisco picked him up briefly before also cutting him. Whitlock returned to Minnesota as a member of the Vikings' practice squad.

In 2009 Whitlock gave the Canadian Football League a try. Signing as a free agent, Whitlock made the Edmonton Eskimos' roster as a kick returner and backup running back.

An injury to starter Jesse Lumsden threw Whitlock into the CFL fire. His first start proved to be rocky. Whitlock dropped a pair of sure touchdown passes and also had another thrown his way get returned for a touchdown.

"I never gave up, though," he said.

Whitlock's persistence paid off. The rookie led Edmonton in rushing with 1,293 yards, good for third best among CFL leaders. He accumulated 1,685 all-purpose yards and scored 12 touchdowns. The Eskimos nominated Whitlock for Most Outstanding Rookie.

"He's dynamic as a runner," center Aaron Fiacconi told Dean Bennett of the Canadian Press. "He's got great vision of the field, allows us to set our blocks up. When we get on our man, he's great at making a cut, too, makes us look good."

Edmonton general manager Danny Maciocia said, "He's got tremendous vision and feet. He can make people miss in a phone booth."

Quarterback Ricky Ray spoke of Whitlock's elusiveness as a deciding factor in a victory over Toronto.

"We had a run play that he broke for a touchdown," said Ray. "We couldn't block the back side end and it was 1-on-1 with (Whitlock) and he made the guy miss.

He's got the ability to turn losses into gains for us."

Unfortunately, injuries soon began to unravel Whitlock's career. He suffered a season-ending foot injury in the CFL's Labour Day Classic. A hamstring injury delayed his 2011 debut. When he was finally activated, Whitlock rushed for 92 yards on 17 attempts. He caught two passes for nine yards and returned five kickoffs for 93 yards. The Eskimos, however, made the decision to release him.

"Parting ways with a player of Arkee's ability is never an easy decision, but we're pleased with the play of our other running backs," said Edmonton head coach Kavis Reed in a team statement afterward.

Thus Whitlock finished his CFL career with 2,074 yards and 16 touchdowns on 246 carries. He also had 58 catches for 479 yards and two touchdowns and returned 19 kickoffs for 290 yards.

Despite what he accomplished in pro football, Whitlock takes pride in his SIU career and induction into the Saluki Hall of Fame.

"I feel honored and blessed," Whitlock told Reis. "I always felt like the success I had was the success we needed to win."

JOEL SAMBURSKY

Joel Sambursky's place in SIU football history isn't lost on Mike Reis.

"Joel Sambursky has the biggest single impact on the program of anybody I've seen," said Reis, who has broadcast SIU football since 1978. "Nobody has lived, breathed and executed Southern Illinois football more than Joel. SIU football matters to him. It matters what people think about Southern football."

Sambursky, along with Jerry Kill and his coaching staff, turned around the fortunes of Saluki football.

"When I came to Southern, I didn't look like a football player," said Sambursky. "I was around 6-foot and 165 pounds and a long-haired hippie as Coach Kill referred to me. I would sit in lecture class, and the professors would joke about Saluki football. Nobody on campus went to the games."

It was a far cry from Sambursky's high school experiences in Liberty, Missouri, near Kansas City.

Sambursky was a gifted athlete at Liberty, starting at quarterback since his sophomore season. He refined his speed and quickness by competing in sprints, relays and the triple jump for his prep track team.

"Our weight room at Liberty was five times bigger than at Southern. We had huge crowds at our games. At Liberty our goal was to win by 50 points. At Southern, the team had only two winning seasons in the last 17 years. The culture and the environment from my high school experience was so different. I went from a perennial winner to a perennial loser," he said.

Sambursky almost didn't wind up at SIU. He had offers from a number of smaller schools, including Division-II powerhouse Northwest Missouri State, a program in which Sambursky's father had wrestled.

However, a visit from Matt Limegrover, one of Kill's assistants, changed things.

"Coach Limegrover was the offensive coordinator for Coach Kill at Emporia State. There really was no way I was going to Emporia State," Sambursky said.

While the Division-II school in Kansas wasn't appealing to Sambursky, SIU soon became an option—mainly because of the recruiting strategy of legendary Northwest Missouri State head coach Mel Tjeerdsma.

"Coach Tjeerdsma brought in three quarterbacks from the Kansas City metro area," Sambursky said. "He had us each work out back-to-back-to-back. He told us the scholarship offer was going to be for X amount of money and that the first two players to commit would get the scholarships. That's the business side of recruiting."

Limegrover contacted Sambursky again, this time as a member of Kill's newly formed Saluki staff. Wavering in his decision to enroll at Northwest Missouri State, Sambursky agreed to visit SIU.

"I literally had never heard of Southern Illinois University," he said. "A number of people told me that I owed it to myself to take the visit. I figured it wouldn't hurt to go and see Southern."

Before making his visit, however, the 18-year-old Sambursky played hardball with Kill.

"I told him I wouldn't come on the visit unless there was a full scholarship waiting," he said. "He called me back a short time later and agreed. Frankly, Coach Kill didn't have many options. I didn't know Coach Kill very well then. I would never talk to him like that now!"

Perhaps it was Sambursky's brashness; perhaps it was Kill's desperation to turn around a thin roster of talent, but whatever the reason, Joel Sambursky chose SIU.

Like Kill and his staff, Sambursky had something to prove.

Quarterback Joel Sambursky was key to the revitalization of SIU football under Jerry Kill.

"I definitely came to SIU with a chip on my shoulder. (Kansas coach) Terry Allen had told me I was too small. Missouri State said the same thing. I had something to prove. Both Coach Kill and I were in the same spot. That's what probably forged us together," he said.

But before Saluki success, there were still hard times to endure. Kill's first SIU team won only a single game.

"That was the hardest year," Sambursky said. "I was second-guessing everything. It was 18 months (into my time at SIU) before I saw a student wearing a Saluki football shirt. I remember thinking, 'Wow! Somebody is actually showing support for the team!'"

Kill's staff spent the off-season "working us to death." There was plenty of running, sometimes five days of it.

"Coach Kill knew there were some players who didn't belong. He talked about giving them an apple and a road map. In the end, he got rid of 10 or 15 guys. It was the most intense off-season program I've ever been a part of," Sambursky said.

While the extreme conditioning may have prevented players like Sambursky from gaining much-needed weight, it boosted the team in other ways.

"By running us to death and running off the guys who weren't fully committed, he made us a team. We were mentally tougher," Sambursky said. "Coach Kill now had the guys he was ready to go to war with."

In 2002, Sambursky's redshirt freshman season, that group improved its record from 1-10 to 4-8. According to the quarterback, an October victory over Western Illinois proved to be the springboard for future Saluki success.

"It had been 18 years since SIU beat them. Western was ranked number eight in the country. Coach Kill had guaranteed a victory at a pep rally," Sambursky said.

The Salukis outslugged the Leathernecks 54-52 in a contest decided when Sambursky lofted the game-winning touchdown pass to Brandon Robinson in the corner of the end zone.

"For the first time we truly began to believe. We began to think that our crazy bald-headed coach knew what he was talking about and what he was doing," Sambursky said.

The Salukis beat Northern Iowa the next week and boosted their record to 4-3. Injuries began to take their toll, however, and SIU lost its final five games.

"I'm not trying to make excuses, but we were down to our fourth- or fifth-string running back," Sambursky said. "Still, that win over Western pointed us in the right direction."

Whichever direction the Salukis came out of for the 2003 season, no one expected them to win 10 straight games and a share of the Gateway Conference crown.

"Every week we were snapping a streak of sorts. We were everybody's Homecoming opponent. You know how schools always bring in somebody they can beat for Homecoming? Well, we were winning those games," Sambursky said. "Suddenly people who had been only interested in tailgating were leaving their parties and coming into the games. The professors who had cracked jokes about SIU football were now supporting us. It was the greatest season of my life."

However, when the playoffs opened, SIU was sent on the road to perpetual powerhouse Delaware. The Blue Hens routed the Salukis 48-7 en route to winning the national championship.

"In all honesty, we were just happy to be there (in the playoffs). We weren't in the same class as Delaware. They blew us out big time," he said.

For the only time in his career, Sambursky was knocked unconscious and left the field on a stretcher.

A season later, SIU duplicated its 10-win season. Only a one-point loss at Division I-A Northern Illinois kept the Salukis from a perfect regular season. SIU won the Gateway title outright and entered the playoff field ranked number one. The team featured future pros Brandon Jacobs and Arkee Whitlock in the same backfield.

Yet the Salukis were upset 35-31 by Eastern Washington in an opening-round home game of the playoffs. Eastern Washington scored what proved to be the game-winning touchdown with 1:49 left. The Salukis' final drive ended as a Sambursky pass was knocked down at the Eagles' 20-yard line as time expired.

"We played a very good football team today, and we knew that going in. We didn't take them lightly or anything like that," Kill said afterward.

"We played hard, but the ball just didn't roll our way," said Jacobs, who ran for 166 yards and four touchdowns. "We made it down to the end zone; we just didn't hook up like we're used to doing."

Sambursky, the Gateway Player of the Year, threw for 163 yards and ran for another 51 during the game.

Sambursky wrapped up his Saluki career with another conference championship the next year. Moreover, he left SIU as the school's all-time leader in touchdown passes and completion percentage. He also rushed for a school-record 1,075 career yards.

"By my senior year there was a group of veteran guys, like myself, that had seen the extremes of the 1-10 season to the conference championships and national playoffs," Sambursky said. "As seniors we really felt (increased) expectations. We had put together back-to-back winning seasons. We weren't a fluke. We had put Saluki football back on the map.

"That was also the time when people found out that Coach Kill had cancer," Sambursky recalled. "It was a rocky time for the program, but fortunately Coach beat it."

> **W**e weren't a fluke. We had put Saluki football back on the map.

Despite the added pressure and Kill's medical concerns, the Salukis returned to the playoffs. Shaking off the postseason disappointment from a year earlier, Sambursky and SIU defeated Eastern Illinois 21-6 in the 2005 opening round.

However, for the second time in three years, the Salukis lost to the eventual national champion, as Appalachian State downed SIU 38-24 in the quarterfinals. Sambursky threw for 220 yards and two touchdowns. He wrapped up his career with 4,929 passing yards and a 41-to-14 touchdown-to-interception ratio.

With his college career over, Sambursky wasn't blinded with visions of NFL grandeur.

"I'll never be the old man saying, 'I blew my knee out or I could have played in the NFL,'" he said. "I realized that I was a good, successful college quarterback, but I wasn't an NFL quarterback. I just wasn't. That doesn't mean that I didn't play hard or study the game enough or that I wasn't talented. I put up some good numbers, but I'm about 6-foot and 190 pounds and my arm is subpar (by NFL standards). In the NFL they want guys who are 6-foot-5, 230 pounds that can throw the ball 70 yards into the wind. That's not me, and I knew it."

Sambursky was also worn down by playing a then-record 49 consecutive games as a Saluki starter.

"By the end of my senior year when I walked off the field at Appalachian State I physically didn't have anything left," he said. "I'm a guy, looking back 10 years later, who knows I gave it everything I had—physically, mentally, emotionally. I had opportunities for things like Arena football, but I was done.

"We all have a shelf life, whether you're Dan Marino or Joel Sambursky. Everybody's got to hang it up eventually. I know people who say things like 'I should have worked harder or studied more,' and those things haunt them. Well, they don't haunt me. I gave everything I had to Coach Kill and the Salukis, and I wouldn't want it any other way."

Sambursky's teammates appreciated his efforts. Four straight years he was voted "Toughest Saluki" by his peers.

"There's no question there were tougher guys on the team than me. If you were going to get into a bar fight, you weren't looking for my help," Sambursky said, "but it shows my teammates respected my toughness.

"The thing about my career touchdowns or some of the other records, you could hire a coach like Mike Leach or Art Briles and with his offense, those records would be broken in two years, but when your teammates voted you for something, that stays with you and means something special."

A year later Sambursky—the Salukis' all-time passing leader—joined Reis and Gene Green on the SIU broadcast team. Though he was listed as the sideline reporter, Reis doesn't see it that way.

"It's really a three-man booth, because Joel's mike is always live for good reason," said Reis. "His insight is invaluable."

For the former quarterback, the assignment places him back in the action.

"I love it there. I can see the coach's reaction, and as a former player, that's what I'm used to watching," he said.

Off the field, Sambursky uses the MBA he earned from SIU as a financial adviser based in Carbondale.

In 2012 Sambursky was voted into the SIU Hall of Fame as a first-ballot nominee. Kill was among those who returned for the event.

As time goes by, Sambursky realizes the decision he made as an 18-year-old was the right choice. Passing up the chance to play for a national power and instead opting for the unknowns of a struggling program, Sambursky has no regrets. Moreover, being called a Saluki is the ultimate compliment.

"It means more than probably I could explain," he said. "As part of that decision-making process I wanted to be a part of the turnaround story. The appeal of jumping into a program that was rebuilding something from the ground up was so overwhelming that I decided to forego my commitment to Northwest, a place that's only an hour away from (my childhood home) and that was my father's alma mater. Instead, I decided to jump in with this crazy bald-headed coach who acted like he could turn around programs. At the time, Southern Illinois was arguably the worst I-AA program in the country, facility-wise with a stadium falling down and a team that was pretty close to matching.

"But it all worked out. It really propelled Jerry Kill's career. In 10 years he went from SIU to Northern Illinois to the head coach at a Big 10 school. Together, as a group, we forged a relationship, stared at the impossible and put SIU football back on the map."

FOUR DOWN TERRITORY

Favorite Football Movie—*Remember the Titans.* When I first came to SIU, everyone called me "Sunshine" because I was a long-haired quarterback like in the movie. *Remember the Titans* is a great movie for many reasons.

First Car—I drove a Honda del Sol with the hardtop you can just take off. It was the two-seater. It was the only thing I could afford. I got a really cheap deal on it.

Worst Summer Job—The first year I came up to Southern I worked for Chartwell's, the catering service. It was horrible. I also worked on some farms, doing things like clearing brush in 90-degree weather. But, really, I didn't work much because I was so involved in sports year-round.

Favorite Subject in School—I'd have to say finance. Those early courses opened up a whole new world for me. It was math that had real-world applications. I see it as useful math, not something abstract that I wondered when I would use it.

NICK HILL, THE PLAYER

Nick Hill grew up in a football town, but his heart belonged to basketball—or so he thought.

"The whole town turned out for games," said the Du Quoin native. "I really enjoyed basketball. Football was just something to do for fun. I didn't want to be left out."

Hill excelled, being named first team all-state in both sports. As a three-year starting quarterback, Hill became the first 4,000-yard passer at Du Quoin since former major league baseball pitcher Don Stanhouse in 1968. Hill and DHS reached the Illinois High School Association 3A championship game his senior season. He threw for 19 touchdowns while being intercepted just once.

On the basketball court, meanwhile, Hill finished eighth in the voting for the state's Mr. Basketball. He averaged 22.7 points, 7.7 rebounds, 5.7 assists and three steals per game as Du Quoin finished 28-5 his final year.

Basketball seemed to be in his blood. In fact, Hill signed an early letter of intent to play hoops at Western Kentucky.

"I signed before football season my senior year," he said. "I had offers to play (basketball) at Southern and other Missouri Valley schools, including Illinois State, but Western Kentucky is where I wanted to be."

Du Quoin native Nick Hill gave up basketball to quarterback the Salukis to record-setting success.

However, before he left for the Bluegrass State, SIU football coach Jerry Kill let it be known that if Hill should ever want to reconsider, the Salukis would be interested.

Hill appeared in 23 games for Western Kentucky as a freshman during the 2002–3 season. However, Dennis Felton left the Hilltopper program and became the head coach at the University of Georgia.

"I really liked Coach Felton, but when he left, the new coaching staff wasn't as interested in me," Hill said. "I had a gut feeling that I wasn't going to be maybe even an all-conference-level player. I've always had a drive to be the best at whatever I did."

Hill also discovered something during his time at Western Kentucky.

"I realized that I missed football," he said.

That realization, along with other factors, brought Hill back to his home area.

"I had grown up during the down years of Saluki football," said the 6-foot-3, 210-pound Hill. "But, being 20 miles from SIU, I was comfortable."

More than anything else, Hill was comfortable with Kill.

"I took a leap of faith with Coach Kill. Everyone needs someone who believes in him, and for me, that someone was Coach Kill," he said.

Hill found himself competing with four other quarterbacks, including starter Joel Sambursky.

Hill not only returned to his roots; he also returned to something he knew well—hard work.

"I worked my way up the depth chart," he said.

"We had Joel Sambursky for four years, and then Nick came along for the next regime," said Kill. "I was blessed to get two quarterbacks like that. Nick came along at a great time. The basketball coaches were cooperative. Nick is an excellent young man. I got to be very close to his family.

"As a player, Nick is very smart. He throws a good, accurate ball."

After redshirting the 2004 season following his transfer, Hill showed flashes of the future when he relieved Sambursky four times in 2005. The mobile left-hander completed 16 of 20 passes for three touchdowns and no interceptions. He also ran for 102 yards on nine carries with one touchdown.

A year later, Hill burst onto the scene as the Saluki starter. He ranked second in the conference and seventh in the nation in passing efficiency (156.7 rating). He passed for 15 touchdowns and threw only four interceptions. In fact, Hill threw 103 consecutive passes before throwing his first career pick. He was also SIU's third-leading rusher.

"The first game I started was against a Division II school (Lock Haven), and we won easily (49-0), but the second game is the one I really remember," he said.

That game was against Big 10 foe Indiana. Hill threw touchdown passes to four different receivers as the Salukis stunned the Hoosiers 35-28 in Bloomington.

"The postgame was incredible. I remember our fans celebrating in a small corner of the end zone," Hill said.

The Salukis qualified for the I-AA playoffs. SIU won its opening-round game 36-30 over Tennessee-Martin of the Ohio Valley Conference. The Salukis' season ended a week later on the road against perennial power Montana.

Hill and SIU were even better in 2007. Hill rewrote the school record book as the Salukis rolled to a 12-2 season. The senior earned First Team All–Gateway Conference honors as he set SIU single-season records for passing in yards (3,175), touchdowns (28), completions (258) and attempts (361). Hill threw for an SIU-best 436 yards against archrival Northern Iowa. He finished sixth in the voting for the Walter Payton Award, annually given to the top offensive player in FCS football.

More important to Hill, the Salukis again qualified for the playoffs. SIU defeated Eastern Illinois and Massachusetts in the first two rounds. In the national semifinals, Hill and the Salukis squared off against future NFL quarterback Joe Flacco and the Delaware Blue Hens.

Despite jumping out to a 10-0 lead in the first quarter, SIU fell 20-17 to Delaware.

While Flacco passed for 243 yards and two touchdowns, Hill threw for 106 yards and was intercepted twice.

"It's not a game I like to even talk about," Hill said. "I haven't watched the entire thing on film to this day. We should have won. We had a lot of missed opportunities."

Among those missed opportunities were two big pass plays (one a touchdown) that were called back for penalties.

"It was a rainy, nasty day in southern Illinois," Hill recalled of the December game in which the official box score reported the game time temperature at 41 degrees with a seven-mile-an-hour wind.

The box score listed the official McAndrew Stadium attendance as 11,503.

"It was the loudest I'd ever heard McAndrew, and it wasn't even our biggest crowd," Hill said.

It's not a game I like to even talk about. I haven't watched the entire thing on film to this day. We should have won.

The loss ended Hill's collegiate career and left Saluki fans wanting more.

"I wish that Nick could have played one more year of football. He came here with the intention of being a basketball player. It took him a year to adjust to (Jerry) Kill. His 2007 season was worlds better than 2006," said Mike Reis, the longtime radio voice of SIU athletics.

As a starter, Hill led SIU to a 21-6 record, and his name fills the Saluki record book. Hill played in the Texas versus the Nation All-Star Bowl.

"Nick is the stereotypical quarterback. He fit the mold as a pocket quarterback. He was deceptively fast and stronger than people thought. Nick was especially good about reading opposing defenses. He could also communicate it well to his teammates," said Reis.

However, it's not just his athletic ability that remains with people.

"Nick Hill is one of the highest-caliber people who ever played here," said Reis.

Though not selected in the 2008 NFL draft, Hill signed as a free agent with the Chicago Bears. However, he was waived in late July.

"I had a tryout with the Colts, but that didn't work out either," Hill said.

Consequently, he completed his education degree from SIU and began coaching high school football. Hill had plans to play for the Orlando Predators of the Arena Football League.

"But that's when the AFL went bankrupt," he said.

After mulling his next decision, Hill joined af2, a secondary-level professional arena league. He played for the Rio Grande Valley Dorados.

"I made $200 a game," he said.

When the AFL returned for the 2010 season, Hill was again on the Orlando Predators roster. By midseason, he became the starter. Hill led the AFL in total offense with 321.8 yards per game.

"My pro career has been a wild ride, but one I feel so blessed to have had," he said at the time.

Hill's AFL success led to his signing as a free agent with the Green Bay Packers in 2012.

"(Playing in the AFL) got me a little recognition with the games being on the NFL Network. It gave me another shot at the NFL," he said.

Meanwhile, Hill continued coaching high school football in the Orlando area as well as running football camps and a local quarterback school.

"If pro football doesn't work out, I have my education degree. Eventually I would like to be a coach. I've been a coordinator down in Orlando and really enjoyed it," he said in 2012.

Coaching brought Hill back to his roots. He spent the 2013 season as the head coach at Carbondale High School. Next he returned to his alma mater when Dale Lennon added Hill to his SIU staff. Hill quickly rose up the ladder and became co–offensive coordinator in 2014. After Lennon was dismissed following the 2015 season, Hill was named first interim head coach and then was hired as Lennon's successor.

His official SIU biography calls Hill "one of the most decorated quarterbacks in Saluki Football history." Despite playing just two seasons as a Saluki, Hill ranks fifth in career passing yards (5,184), second in touchdown passes (46) and first in completion percentage (68.3). In 2013 Hill was voted to the Saluki Football All-Century Team.

Hill had a long history of enjoying athletics.

Tim Lee coached Oakwood-Fithian High School basketball in the late 1990s and early 2000s. His oldest son, Logan, attended SIU. His other sons, Cameron and Parker, later played football at Illinois State.

"We were down there (in the Du Quoin area) over a summer weekend to play some basketball games," Lee remembered.

Lee also remembered Hill, then a high school freshman.

"He talked my leg off," said Lee, adding Hill was an "inquisitive, talkative, polite freshman."

"Yeah, I remember when those teams came down," said Hill. "They stayed in some of the houses in town."

Just a few short years later, Lee was sitting in his house watching a preseason Bears game with his sons. Lo and behold, that "inquisitive, talkative, polite freshman" showed up again, this time on Lee's TV screen as a camp quarterback with the Bears.

Not bad for a kid whose heart was set on basketball.

FOUR DOWN TERRITORY

Favorite Football Movie—I watched all of them, *Rudy, Remember the Titans.* I'm a sports fan, so I've seen all of the sports movies. They all get me going.

First Car—It was a 1993 Chevy Blazer, a two-door one that was green.

Worst Summer Job—I can honestly say I've never had a bad job. I like to work, and I like to make money. We have a fairgrounds in Du Quoin. I worked maintenance there. I did all sorts of jobs from mowing the grass to putting things up. I even worked those jobs when I was back from Arena ball. I enjoy the people that I worked with.

Favorite Subject in School—Business classes in high school. I liked learning how things operate. Someday I'd like to be an entrepreneur. I'd like to own a business.

DEJI KARIM

Deji Karim almost gave up his dream.

Following a devastating knee injury that forced him to the sidelines for the entire 2008 season, the tailback nearly quit football.

The injury occurred during spring practice. Karim set up to pass block, only to have his left foot get stuck in the stadium turf. The result was a tear in the patella tendon.

"Deji, along with Larry Warner, was going to be in our backfield," Southern Illinois head coach Dale Lennon said. "Unfortunately, his knee never got better."

Lennon added that it's often difficult for a running back emotionally to bounce back from an injury.

Those words held truth, for Karim strongly considered not coming back to the game he had played for so long. However, an October meeting with Saluki trainer Lee Land changed his mind.

"I was about to hang it up," Karim said. "He told me that we would get through it."

Together, Land and Karim endured the rigors of rehabilitation.

"Deji wanted to quit because his body didn't appear to have the same passion for football as his heart and mind did," Land wrote in an e-mail. "When he came into my office and expressed that frustration and fear and feeling like he was going through this alone, I let him know that he was not going through this alone. The coaching staff and I and the rest of the medical staff were going through this with him at the same time, that same questioning, frustrating, maddening response to his injury was working on all of us."

Encouragement also came from another source, his mother, Tai.

"When I told her (about giving up football), she said, 'That's not my son talking,'" Karim said.

After redshirting the 2008 season, Karim returned with a vengeance when granted a fifth year of eligibility.

"I learned a lot about myself (during that time)," Karim said. "It taught me patience."

The hard work paid off once the 2009 Saluki season got under way. In the second game of the year, Karim returned the opening kickoff 82 yards for a touchdown. He finished that game with 310 all-purpose yards (210 of those rushing).

Karim proved to be a vital part of SIU's attack. The Salukis plowed their way to an 11-game winning streak, the Missouri Valley Conference championship and a seventh consecutive playoff appearance.

Karim rushed for 1,694 yards and 19 touchdowns that included four runs for 70 or more yards. His 2,339 all-purpose yards broke the school record. Karim racked up a career-best 273 yards in a conference win over Illinois State.

"I was just out there running," he said. "I didn't even realize it. The game was close. I just stayed focused and played."

Lennon said afterward, "Deji is pretty impressive. It's just one of those things that when you have a player like that offensively, it makes it difficult to defend."

Saluki quarterback Paul McIntosh said, "Obviously, he's a game changer. He can be in the end zone any time he touches the ball."

All of this combined for Karim's spectacular senior season. He finished third in the balloting for the coveted Walter Payton Award as the nation's top FCS player.

"To be mentioned in the same breath as Walter Payton is special," he said.

At the awards ceremony held in Chattanooga, Tennessee, Lennon said, "I'm very proud of Deji, and there is yet another chapter for him to write and I look forward to watching him."

Deji Karim overcame injury to enjoy stellar success with the Salukis. Karim later returned a kickoff for a touchdown in an NFL playoff game.

Karim was also selected as the MVC Offensive Player of the Year. In addition, he was invited to play in the fourth annual Pro Football Hall of Fame Texas versus the Nation Challenge held in El Paso.

"All of these honors I've gotten are team awards in my mind," said Karim. "You don't do these things by yourself."

None of this surprised his Oklahoma high school coach.

"We've been known to have some great tailbacks here at North," Putnam City North head coach Bob Wilson told talent evaluator and scouting consultant Dave-Te' Thomas. "Deji is the most versatile back I've ever coached. He can do so many different things from different positions. He just had great skills, and he keeps getting better and better as he gets older."

> **C**oach (Jerry) Kill and his staff recruited me. He (Kill) said, 'We win championships here.' Then he showed me his ring.

Though he was on the radar of Division I-A schools like Iowa State, Kansas State and Texas A&M, academics were an issue when Karim came out of high school. Thus he signed with Northeastern Oklahoma A&M, the same junior college that Northern Illinois standout LeShon Johnson once attended.

After Karim starred for the Norsemen for two seasons, SIU landed him.

"Coach (Jerry) Kill and his staff recruited me," he said. "He (Kill) said, 'We win championships here.' Then he showed me his ring."

"He really got overlooked because of his past injuries," Kill said. "We were willing to take a chance."

However, Kill left Carbondale to take the head coaching job at Northern Illinois. The move didn't upset Karim.

"Coach Kill was a nice man, but I really didn't know him that well," he said.

Thus it was Lennon who benefited from Karim leading the SIU rushing attack.

"He has good strength where he can break tackles, (and) he also has the ability to stop and go," Lennon told Melinda Waldrop of the *Newport News (Va.) Daily Press.* "The thing there is, if he gets into the open, he can outrun everyone to the end zone. He has that breakaway speed."

So what memories will Karim take from his years as a Saluki?

"It's the relationships I've developed," he said. "It may be years down the road, but I'll never forget these people."

Karim also will remember SIU's 27-20 victory at Northern Iowa that snapped the Salukis' 11-game losing streak at the UNI-Dome. Northern Iowa came into the game ranked number two in the nation. Karim rushed for 125 yards and a touchdown. He also had a 48-yard reception.

"That (win) got the monkey off our backs," Karim said. "Before the win everybody asked when would we win at the UNI-Dome. After we won, everybody wanted to know what it was like to win in the UNI-Dome."

The conference title earned SIU an automatic berth in the Football Championship Subdivision playoffs. SIU entered the 16-team tournament as the number-three overall seed.

In the opening round, Karim went against an Eastern Illinois defense that hadn't allowed a 100-yard rusher all season. Karim changed that with a 155-yard, three-touchdown performance as the Salukis dominated 48-7.

However, a week later, SIU's national championship dreams ended in a 24-3 loss to William and Mary in the final game at McAndrew Stadium.

"Like I said in the postgame that day, they were tougher than us. They were more physical," said Karim, who was held to just 27 yards on 12 carries.

Despite the loss, Karim looked forward to giving pro football his best shot. Many experts compared Karim to NFL backs such as Brian Westbrook, Darren Sproles and Leon Washington.

"I'm just going to try my best and see where I can go," said Karim as he prepared for a pro career. "Whatever happens, it's this team that's helped me get there."

Like most NFL hopefuls, Karim's height and weight were altered by his college team. Listed by SIU as 5-foot-11, 205 pounds, Karim was measured at 5-foot-8½ and 209 pounds on his college pro day. However, Karim ran a 4.4 in his 40-yard timing.

The Jacksonville Jaguars selected Karim as the 180th overall pick in the 2010 NFL draft. Karim, a sixth-round draft choice, played in 11 games his rookie season. In July 2010 he signed a four-year, $1.9 million deal with Jacksonville.

Though sidelined by a thumb injury at the beginning of the season, Karim made an impact as a rookie. His main contributions came on special teams, where Karim averaged 25 yards per kickoff return. While he carried the ball only 35 times as a rusher, Karim averaged 4.6 yards per attempt.

Karim's NFL career lasted four years and was highlighted by a 101-yard kickoff return for a touchdown that sparked the Indianapolis Colts to a 2012 playoff victory over the Houston Texans. Karim's career ended with an injury the following season.

FOUR DOWN TERRITORY

Favorite Football Movies: *Any Given Sunday*, for the sheer look inside what football is like. *Friday Night Lights*, because my senior year in high school we started out the season 1-2 and the coaches took us to see it as a team. We didn't lose again until the state semifinals.

First Car—A 1995 Nissan Maxima. I loved that car.

Worst Summer Job—McDonald's. I worked there for two years in high school. I worked on the weekends and all summer.

Favorite Subjects in School—English and math.

BRANDIN JORDAN

Brandin Jordan came to Southern Illinois with a football pedigree.

His father Buford was a running back for the New Orleans Saints for seven years. His uncle Enis Hicks spent time with the Pittsburgh Steelers.

Yet Jordan didn't participate in tackle football until age 10.

"I played flag football," Jordan said from his parents' home in Louisiana. "My dad wouldn't let me play (tackle)."

Jordan's father wasn't worried about his son getting hurt.

"He figured that kids would get bored with it if they started too soon," he said.

Jordan didn't get bored with the game. Instead, he flourished in it.

Brandin Jordan became a star defensive player for the Salukis.

As a prep athlete, Jordan starred at John Curtis Christian High School in River Ridge, Louisiana. In fact, Jordan garnered Class 4A defensive and district Most Valuable Player honors his senior year as the Patriots rolled to a state championship and number-nine national ranking by *USA Today*.

"That taught me how to be a winner," Jordan said. "I hated to lose."

That happens when you taste defeat only four times in your prep career.

"I played in the state championship game every year," Jordan said. "We won it three times. The time we lost was my junior year. We lost by six points."

John Curtis is a well-known stop for college recruiters. In fact, Jordan played with Joe McKnight, one of the nation's top recruits in 2007. McKnight signed with the University of Southern California before leaving the program to turn pro following his junior year. McKnight was killed by gunshot in a road-rage incident in December 2016.

"I've known Joe since I was five," Jordan said. "My sister and I both knew him."

While the likes of USC chased McKnight, Jordan seemed a cinch to sign with the University of Arkansas.

"It was about 90 percent they were going to offer me," said Jordan.

However, following a bowl game blowout loss, Arkansas fired its defensive coordinator. Interest from the Razorbacks disappeared.

Other schools backed off because of Jordan's height.

"A lot of them said we don't even consider somebody (at linebacker) unless he's 6-(foot)-2 or taller," Jordan said.

"Brandin is a player who would have gotten a shot at a Division I-A school if he had just been a little taller," said former-SIU head coach Jerry Kill of the player listed on the Saluki website as 5-foot-11. "He's a kid who just loves playing football."

Five schools made Jordan offers: Louisiana Tech and Louisiana Monroe from Division I-A and McNeese State, Alcorn State and SIU from the I-AA ranks.

"Louisiana Tech pulled their offer," he said. "Most of my family went to McNeese State, but I didn't want that. I didn't want to be the next Jordan. I wanted to make a name for myself somewhere."

That somewhere ended up being SIU.

"I honestly had never really heard of them before they recruited me," Jordan said. "But my junior and senior years of high school, SIU was ranked number one. That caught my eye."

Jordan signed with the Salukis and was redshirted as a freshman.

"My goal was to start and get 100 or more tackles all four years," he said.

Following his redshirt year, Jordan got off to a roaring start. He was chosen as the Gateway Conference Freshman of the Year in 2006. In fact, the linebacker led the Salukis with 107 tackles, including a career-high 16 against Youngstown State.

Jordan's sophomore season brought second-team all-conference and honorable-mention all-American accolades. It also brought injury.

"I was on track (for 100 tackles)," he said. "I was averaging about 12 a game. Then one day in practice our deep snapper got bull-rushed and fell on my toe. I wound up getting turf toe."

That initial injury soon developed into other ailments.

"You start favoring one side, and it affects other parts of your body," Jordan explained.

His junior season brought a coaching change at SIU.

"Coach Kill was hard-nosed, similar to Coach JT, my high school coach," Jordan said. "Coach Kill would make you work hard and reach your potential."

Jordan, like many of his teammates, began to sense that Kill was about to leave.

"After our final game he was talking funny," Jordan said. "He had a nervous twitch in his voice. He kept talking to the seniors. He didn't say anything about next year. I knew something was up."

Kill left SIU to become the head coach at Northern Illinois University. Dale Lennon took over the Salukis.

But I have no doubts that I was one of the top linebackers in all of I-AA.

"There's a big difference between the two," Jordan said. "They both are good head coaches. Coach Lennon is more of a father-figure type of guy. He's cool and relaxed. He's not really going to yell at you so much as try to encourage you."

Regardless of the coaching change, Jordan's star continued to shine. The inside linebacker became the backbone of the Saluki defense. He earned first-team all-conference honors.

The best was yet to come. Jordan returned to SIU for his final and finest season. He not only led the team in tackles but also was named to the Walter Camp FCS All-America Team. Moreover, the two-time first-team all-conference performer was a finalist for the Buck Buchanan Award as the nation's top defensive player.

"I knew I wouldn't win the Buchanan, because other guys had bigger numbers," Jordan said. "Coach Lennon's staff plays a scheme that rotates people. But I have no doubts that I was one of the top linebackers in all of I-AA."

Lennon didn't have to be convinced.

"With Brandin Jordan, he's an instinctive player; that's what you want with your linebackers running a 3-4 scheme. They just go to the ball. He's a fun player to watch. When we bring him on the rush, he's difficult to block," the SIU head coach told Brian Nielsen of the *Mattoon Journal-Gazette/ Charleston Times-Courier.*

Eastern offensive coordinator Roy Wittke agreed.

"There's no question that the heart of their defense is the inside 'backer Brandin Jordan," said Wittke prior to playing SIU. "There's no question he's deserving of that (Buchanan nomination). He runs well. He really is a complete player and does a great job."

After losing its 2009 opener at Marshall, SIU won 10 straight regular-season games. The Salukis were unbeaten in Missouri Valley Conference play, earning their seventh straight playoff appearance.

SIU breezed past Eastern Illinois 48-7 in first-round playoff action. However, the Saluki season came to an abrupt end the next week as William and Mary defeated

SIU 24-3 in the final game at McAndrew Stadium.

"That was a disappointing end, but I'm proud of my career," Jordan said.

Having completed his degree in speech communication, Jordan prepared for his dream of following in his father's footsteps in professional football.

"I've just been working out, trying to catch someone's eye," he said following his final collegiate game. "I wasn't invited to any combines. I wasn't invited to play in any all-star games. It's just a matter of me doing whatever it takes to be ready."

Jordan spent weekends working at his father's speed camp. He also sought advice from former college players from his home state.

"Any little tip they can give me might make a difference," Jordan said. "It might seem like a little thing, but it just might be what puts me over the top."

Jordan's size, no doubt, worked against him.

"If he were 6-1 or 6-2, he would definitely play on Sundays," said Tom "Tuke" Matukewicz, who coached Jordan for two years at SIU.

His size didn't stop Jordan from finding a spot on the Jacksonville Jaguars roster for a brief time.

If playing football wasn't in his future, Jordan made plans to pursue a career in public relations.

"Maybe I'll work for the Saints," he said.

That seems fitting. After all, Brandin Jordan does have a football pedigree.

BRYAN BOEMER

Bryan Boemer had forgotten about the Rimington Award.

"Going into my senior year I was set on all-American goals," he said.

Boemer met those goals and more.

"I had gotten out of class and pulled into my driveway," he remembered. "I checked my phone and saw there was a voice mail from my offensive line coach."

The message, delivered by Phil Meyer, informed Boemer that he had won the Rimington, which is given annually to the top center in FCS football.

"I was shocked. I had completely forgotten about it," Boemer said. "I immediately looked on the SIU website, and they already had it posted. I texted my mom and called my coach back."

The award capped Boemer's remarkable Saluki career. The 6-foot-1, 315-pounder was a three-time all-American.

Bryan Boemer won the Rimington Award, annually given to the top center in FCS football.

Some may be surprised to learn that Boemer didn't start playing football until he arrived at St. John Vianney High School in Kirkwood, Missouri.

"It is a private all-boys school," he said. "It was a great experience. I wouldn't trade it for anything."

As a prep athlete, Boemer earned first-team all-conference honors at tackle. He also played lacrosse, basketball and golf.

"I wasn't one to sit around for six months waiting for football to roll around," he said. "I enjoyed those other sports too."

Yet it was football that captured his full enjoyment.

"We competed in Class 6A, which is the highest in Missouri," Boemer said. "We never made the playoffs. One year we were 9-1 and didn't make the playoffs. You had to win your district, and unfortunately, that one loss kept us out."

Playoffs or not, Boemer caught the eyes of numerous college recruiters. He had preferred walk-on offers from Missouri, Missouri State and Arizona State.

"(Missouri head coach) Gary Pinkel told me I was too short to play there. I talked to Arizona State, but then their coaching staff got fired and that pretty much ended things," he said.

Eastern Illinois did come through with a scholarship offer.

"I committed there on my visit," he said. "I had a full ride."

However, SIU invited him to visit Carbondale shortly afterward. Saluki assistant coach Pat Poore handled much of Boemer's recruitment.

"I came here (Carbondale) and really enjoyed myself," Boemer said. "The guys who hosted me were great. I liked the surroundings. I'm a guy who enjoys hunting and fishing. The weight room here was much better (than at Eastern). Coach (Jerry) Kill and his staff really had a reputation for success."

Thus Boemer informed both coaching staffs that he would pass on Eastern for a chance to play for SIU. There was one catch, however. Boemer had to walk on at Southern.

"I decided that I would pay for school for one year myself and earn my way into a scholarship," he said.

Consequently, after sitting out the 2007 season as a redshirt, Boemer worked his way into eight games the following year. The Saluki coaching staff moved him to center.

Boemer learned the position under former Saluki great and NFL center Carl Mauck.

"You had to be able to take criticism (from Mauck)," said Boemer. "I respected him. Look at his pro career; how could you not? He was tough and had his vulgar ways, but he was a boost to me too."

However, Kill left Carbondale following the 2007 season when he took over as head coach at Northern Illinois. His staff followed him.

"I saw it on the website that day," Boemer said. "I liked that staff, and it hurt when they left, but I also understood that it's a business. Those coaches had good reason to take the (NIU) job."

Meanwhile, in 2009, Boemer landed as a second-team All–Missouri Valley Football Conference selection. He also earned an MVFC Offensive Lineman of the Week award.

Boemer became a full-fledged star as a junior. He was honored as a First-Team All-MVFC performer, garnered another Offensive Lineman of the Week selection and was chosen as SIU's top offensive lineman seven times in 11 starts. Sportswriter Phil Steele recognized him as the sixth-best center in the FCS.

Such accolades made Boemer a player to watch entering his senior season. Named a team captain, Boemer played his way onto three different all-American teams. He anchored an offensive line that cleared the way for MVFC Newcomer honoree Jewel Hampton. The Salukis averaged 183.1 rushing yards per game.

"Nearly all of the offensive linemen came in together and left together. We didn't lose anyone along the way," Boemer said. "We were known for being the goofy bunch, but we took pride in doing our jobs. The quarterback and running back stats are our stats in a sense."

Though offensive line play often goes unnoticed by the average fan, Boemer and his line mates know all too well their value.

"(Most fans) don't understand the difference in pass blocking and run blocking," he said. "It's not one-on-one as many people think. We are working as a team. There are combination blocks. We have to be prepared for anything the defense throws our way. It all happens so fast that most people miss it."

Boemer also valued his friendship with quarterback Paul McIntosh.

"Maybe it's that center-quarterback relationship, but Paul and I really hit it off," Boemer said.

SIU lost McIntosh to injury midway through the 2011 season. Perhaps it's no coincidence that the Salukis stumbled to a 4-7 record.

Boemer listed beating conference rival Northern Iowa his sophomore season as one of the highlights of his career.

"We beat them up in the (UNI-)Dome, something that Southern hadn't done for 22 years," he said.

Shunned by Bowl Championship Series schools, Boemer also enjoyed playing against the University of Illinois and Ole Miss.

"We focused on those games," he said. "They really weren't that different from our other games, except that the attendance was much bigger. In retrospect, we performed pretty well in those games."

Saluki fans would readily say the same about Boemer's career. So would the folks who selected him as the Rimington Award winner.

"The Rimington was a symbol of everything in that final season," Boemer said. "It's something that means so much to me."

As with the Heisman Trophy, the Rimington included plaques for both Boemer and SIU.

"We have it on display," said Meyer. "It's something for our linemen to see."

Following his final autumn as a Saluki, Boemer remained in Carbondale to complete his marketing degree. In addition, he prepared for the NFL draft. Boemer attended Northwestern University's Pro Day, a showcase for all 32 NFL teams.

"Bryan won several awards at our year-end banquet," said Meyer. "He was picked as the 'Toughest Saluki.' That award seems to sum that kid up. I can't even remember a time he missed practice. He hardly ever missed any plays. He dished it out, but he also took a beating as a center. He didn't wear gloves, and he always had scraped knuckles."

"I would love to get a shot (at the NFL)," he said at the time. "Some projections have me as a late sixth- or seventh-round pick. I'm listed as undersized, but I'm used to that. I'm just preparing as best I can."

Meyer told scouts of Boemer's many strengths.

"He is smart, tough and quick," Meyer said. "If he were 6-2 or 6-3 he could have played for a lot of Big 10 teams."

Boemer later signed with the Iowa Barnstormers of the Arena Football League. He also had his eye on the future beyond his playing days, saying he would like to put his marketing degree to work with a pro sports franchise.

"I'd love to stay in sports," he said. "Maybe I can land an internship with the (St. Louis) Cardinals or Rams."

Whether it helps or not, having the Rimington Award on your résumé isn't something you see every day.

FOUR DOWN TERRITORY

Favorite Football Movie—I would have to say *Friday Night Lights.* It depicts the best of football.

First Car—A Chevy Silverado, a 1997. I put more dents in that thing.

Worst Summer Job—I worked for a landscaping company. We built retaining walls in all kinds of heat. If you didn't build them right, then you had to tear them apart and start all over again. You had to move around 80-pound stones.

Favorite Subject in School—I'd have to say science because of the way I learn. I like the hands-on learning of the experiments.

DALE LENNON

Following any highly successful person is never easy, whether that individual is a politician or a military leader or a businessman or a farmer. Or even a football coach.

Dale Lennon faced the difficult task of succeeding Jerry Kill, arguably the greatest coach in SIU history. Lennon was named the 20th head coach in Saluki football in December 2007.

There is an old saying in sports: "You don't want to be the coach who follows the legend;

you want to follow the coach who follows the legend." Lennon fell into the former rather than the latter.

Lennon grew up in Knox, North Dakota, near the U.S.-Canada border. There he worked at his father's grain elevator and starred at Rugby High School. After graduation, Lennon played fullback for the University of North Dakota from 1979 to 1983. He was a team captain for the Fighting Sioux.

Lennon began his head coaching career in 1997 at the University of Mary in Bismarck, North Dakota. In just one season he turned a losing program into an NAIA playoff qualifier.

That success landed Lennon back at North Dakota, where he became the winningest coach in school history. Lennon's UND team won the 2001 NCAA Division-II national championship. He also enjoyed seven playoff

Dale Lennon (shown with his team in 2015) ranks fourth among winning coaches in SIU history. His 2009 team became the first to go 8-0 in Missouri Valley Football Conference play.

appearances, a national runner-up finish and five conference titles.

All of that success led to SIU hiring Lennon as Kill's successor for the 2007 season. Lennon tasted success immediately, guiding the Salukis to consecutive Missouri Valley Football Conference titles and playoff berths. He won numerous coaching honors, and SIU set an MVFC record with 14 consecutive league victories.

Lennon ranks as the fourth-winningest coach in Saluki history. The SIU athletic website stated, "One of the most respected coaches in the country, Lennon was named to the American Football Coaches Association Board of Trustees in 2014."

Perhaps Lennon's biggest victories came in 2009 when SIU won 11 straight games and became the first team in MVFC history to go 8-0 in league play. Included in that collection of victories were convincing road wins at number-two-ranked Northern Iowa and at number-nine South Dakota State.

His players won awards for their accomplishments on and off the field. Pro contracts went to many of his players, including Ken Boatright, Korey Lindsey, Jayson DiManche and MyCole Pruitt. Lennon was also twice selected as MVFC Coach of the Year.

Yet his critics would argue that his success came on the heels of Kill's recruits and achievements. After posting a 20-5 record in his first two seasons at SIU, Lennon's teams were just 31-37 in the six seasons that followed. None of those teams made the FCS playoffs. His final six teams combined for a 21-27 conference record. His final team was 3-8 overall and 2-6 in the MVFC.

Team chaplain Roger Lipe said in an e-mail, "Coach Lennon and his staff arrived with a singular focus: to win a national championship. A few of his assistants had left head coaching roles to be a part of what they expected to be just such a run.

"In 2008 and 2009 we were very good and won conference championships. We also played well in the FCS playoffs. In 2010 we moved into the new Saluki Stadium but were significantly less talented than in the previous two years. We never did approach the level of success we enjoyed in '08 and '09."

Lipe further cited Lennon's changes as a coach upon his arrival in Carbondale.

"It was interesting to watch Coach Lennon adjust his coaching style to a totally different sort of player than what he had coached at the University of North Dakota. It was equally interesting to watch the players adjust to a coaching style radically different from that of Coach Kill. Both adjusted well, as affirmed by the two-year 15-1 MVFC record in those first two seasons."

Lipe also commented on Lennon's personality.

"Dale was a remarkably loyal person, both to staff and to players. He was very patient with people, allowing some second and third chances when most others were ready to quit on them. He was always very kind and accommodating to me. He bought in deeply to the team building I had begun with Coach Kill's teams and enabled me to do it throughout his tenure," Lipe said.

According to the official SIU release, Athletic Director Tommy Bell stated in November 2015, "On behalf of the University, I would like to thank Coach Lennon and his staff for their service to our institution. Dale and his staff directed the program with class and integrity. After a great deal of thought and consultation, I determined it was time for a change in the leadership of our football program."

Under the terms of Lennon's contract, which paid him an annual salary of $220,788, he received a $55,000 buyout.

Lennon also released a statement at the time. It read, "It is with deep disappointment and sadness that I leave Southern Illinois University. It has been a privilege to coach this team. I have greatly appreciated the support of so many members of the SIU administration, athletic department, faculty and staff, alumni and student body. Thank you all for your work with the football program through the years. Thank you to the citizens of Carbondale and the surrounding area for your support of Saluki Football as well.

"I have had the privilege of working with a number of great coaches during my time here, and I want to thank them sincerely for their efforts to coach and lead the young men on our football team. We have all tried to lead with honesty, integrity and hard work.

"To our Saluki football players I want to say that it has been an honor to be your coach. I have learned from you, as you have developed as athletes and future leaders. Thank you for doing your best, doing what is right, and giving your all. I have loved being your coach."

In a November 30, 2015 column, beat writer Todd Hefferman stated that Bell "was between a rock and (a) hard place." Hefferman pointed out that as a first-year athletic director, Bell had two options with Lennon—firing him or giving him one more try to "right the ship in the form of another extension."

Hefferman also noted that Lennon was "a very likeable guy who won two conference titles earlier in his tenure but had missed the playoffs the last six years." The *Southern Illinoisan* writer pointed out that Lennon "has won some games that he shouldn't have," citing a road win against Missouri State in which the Salukis were missing several starting players.

"The team's effort couldn't be challenged all year, even after several close losses that typically lead to a downhill spiral. The North Dakota native was one of the most approachable guy(s) you'd ever meet," wrote Hefferman.

Following his dismissal from SIU, Lennon returned to his roots, accepting a position as the director of public affairs at the University of Mary.

"My family and I have maintained close relationships with the school throughout the years," Lennon said in a statement released by the school in February 2016. "Returning to the university and the Bismarck community has been a scenario that we always hoped would become a reality."

Jayson DiManche (34) played with the Cincinnati Bengals after his standout SIU career.

2010s

JAYSON DIMANCHE

Jayson DiManche's Twitter handle is Di-MonsterXX. While that may fit his on-field play, it is the complete opposite of his demeanor off the field.

"Great guy. He actually worked in our office for a summer and was terrific," said SIU associate sports information director John Lock.

When asked what he wants to do after his NFL playing days are over, DiManche said, "I really just want to use my personality. I'm really outgoing. I'm not camera-shy; I'm not afraid to talk to people. I'm going to use my degree in communications and my minor in marketing at some point."

The former SIU linebacker seems like a natural. DiManche drew much attention for his part in the HBO reality series *Hard Knocks*, which featured the former Saluki star.

"Players were making so much fun of me, saying that the cameras were always on (me) more. There was a little bias because the creators of *Hard Knocks* are based in Jersey so they got me on there a little bit more than some others," he said.

While DiManche downplayed his scenes in *Hard Knocks*, the New Jersey native relished his screen time.

"It gave me a boost off the field, but you have to earn everything else on the field. My hometown loved it. SIU loved it. Everyone was really supportive. Those were some crazy days," he said. "It definitely helped my social media. I don't know how many followers I had before that, but I got thousands and thousands more followers after the show aired."

The show also allowed DiManche to work on his "personal bucket list" early in his life.

"I wanted to play in the NFL. I wanted to buy a new car, and I wanted to be on a TV show," he said. "I was able to cross three things off my list in about a year."

Growing up in Hamilton, New Jersey, as the son of Haitian immigrants, DiManche played virtually every sport available to him.

"I learned a little bit from every sport that I did, from the traditional sports to things like karate. Even what happens in gym classes in school," he said. "I didn't have any specific trainers or anything like that. I just had to take advantage of any opportunity I got. I would compete in any way that I could."

DiManche excelled at Hamilton West High School. His name appeared on a variety of all-county and all-area teams. He was named to the all-state team his senior year. DiManche racked up 253 tackles and 30 sacks in three prep seasons. Yet scholarship offers didn't pour in for DiManche.

"Southern was one of two full-scholarship offers that I had. Stony Brook was my other offer. I was not very highly recruited in terms of the national stage," he shared. "They (recruiters and coaches) always thought I was too small or too short, or they wanted me to play another position or my grades weren't quite good enough."

I *got more of a family feel at SIU, and that's why I ultimately decided to go there.*

When it came time to choose between Stony Brook and Southern Illinois, DiManche based his decision on what he thought was most important.

"I got more of a family feel at SIU, and that's why I ultimately decided to go there," he simply said.

After being named to the All–Missouri Valley Football Conference Academic Honor Roll his freshman year, DiManche came into his own as a player as a sophomore. He earned MVFC Defensive Player of the Week after recording three sacks in a win over 21st-ranked Western Illinois.

"That was my coming-out party," DiManche said. "I won the starting outside linebacker position in the 3-4 (defense). I beat out a guy that was older than me. It was

similar to what had happened back in high school. Once I got that first start I didn't look back. I was having a pretty average season until our game with Western Illinois. I had three sacks and two tackles for loss that game. I made some big plays. I'm pretty sure I had two sacks in a row that game. I realized that I could take over a game in college like I did in high school."

That game became a springboard to a stellar collegiate career. According to his NFL biography, DiManche "consistently wreaked havoc in offensive backfields in the FCS ranks, logging 38 tackles for loss and 16.5 sacks."

As a team captain his senior year, DiManche started all 11 games at linebacker and was named second team All-MVFC. He registered a tackle for loss in 10 different games and a sack in eight different games.

Despite all of his accolades, DiManche carries memories far beyond tackles and hard hits.

"It's really just about those moments, moments that you had with your teammates," he said. "College was so fun. It was the best time of my life. People are surprised when I say that because now I'm in the NFL. The relationships I made there were so special.

"I remember the big games that we had to pull out and the tough workouts that we had to push each other through. That's what I remember. You don't get that too much in the NFL."

The 6-foot-2, 229-pound DiManche said his thoughts turned to his NFL prospects following his junior year at SIU.

"I buckled down and chased it," he said. "There are so many players who helped me.

Kenny Boatright, who plays with the Dallas Cowboys. Eze Obiora, he's in Canada playing. Those guys stuck with me when others, whether they were coaches or even my former agent, doubted me. They kept me focused and gave me confidence throughout the workouts. I owe them a lot."

As the 2013 NFL draft approached, DiManche's agent, Joe Linta, told him he had "fourth- or fifth-round talent."

"Once he told me that, it really motivated (me) to be a highly rated player who could play in the NFL," DiManche said. "I knew that I was going to get an opportunity whether it was as a free agent or through a tryout or even if I was lucky enough to get drafted. I knew the opportunity would be there."

That opportunity came when DiManche signed with Cincinnati as a free agent in late April 2013. He played two seasons for the Bengals, including an appearance in a wildcard playoff game. After being released by Cincinnati following an injury, DiManche spent time with the Kansas City Chiefs and the Cleveland Browns.

"The fact he made the NFL is a testament to Jayson. There is no way anyone saw him as a pro when he came to Southern from New Jersey as a freshman," said SIU play-by-play broadcaster Mike Reis.

DiManche's biggest adjustment to the NFL centered on speed—both mentally and physically.

"The biggest adjustment is the learning curve. It's not so much that you have to learn a lot more, it's that you have to learn things a lot more quickly. Once something is installed you are expected to do it correctly

on the field right away," he said. "The speed to the game. Guys are just so fast. There are players that are just unbelievably fast. You have to learn quickly and learn to play quickly."

FOUR DOWN TERRITORY

Favorite Football Movie—*Remember the Titans*. Denzel Washington is one of the best actors ever. That movie was one of those that you can watch over and over, and I did as I was growing up as an athlete.

First Car—My first car was a 325 BMW. My dad gave it to me in high school. He had initially gotten it for my mom, but I needed a car so he gave it to me. I drive a Porsche Cayenne now. My dad's always been able to get his hands on a nice car for me.

Worst Summer Job—Working at Starbucks when I was in high school. That's when gas prices jumped up to something like $4 a gallon, and everybody needed a job to fill up the car. I did not like it at all. I will never work with food again.

Favorite Subject in School—Everybody always says you're a student-athlete, but I realized I'm probably an athlete-student. My favorite was always English. I like to read and I like do creative stuff.

THOMAS KINNEY

Though his name might suggest otherwise, when it comes to kicking, Thomas Kinney VI is his own man.

"It's a family tradition," Kinney explained. "My dad is Thomas John Kinney. My grandpa is Thomas Francis Kinney, and I'm Thomas Alan Kinney; I'm named after Thomas

Prior to his senior season Thomas Kinney was named a Preseason
First Team All-American by *Athlon's Football Magazine*.

Kinney III. It's a vague description, but he was a big part of establishing a union. He was a leader back then. He was offered a lot of bribes because people didn't want him to do it, but he instead chose to stand up for what he thought was right. He even got shot over it, but he kept his goals in mind."

Three generations later, Kinney feels the pride in his name. His goals, however, are measured as field goals. As a Saluki kicker, Kinney made 75 percent of his attempts in 2013. His 94 points were second-best in the Missouri Valley Football Conference that year.

Kinney developed his penchant for kicking at an early age.

"I was born in Flint, Michigan, and then we moved to Oklahoma and then to Maryland. When we moved to Illinois, we lived with my grandma. We lived on her farm for about a year before we found a place to settle," Kinney said.

It was on that farm that Kinney, then a third-grader, first kicked a ball on a regular basis.

"My uncle is a really good soccer player, and he used to make me play goalie when he practiced shooting. I didn't really enjoy it," he said. "My uncle is six years older than me. We would go outside and just kick balls against the broad side of the barn."

That activity paid dividends when Kinney played football a few years later.

"My coach, Coach Elliott, had the whole team line up to kick an extra point. I booted the first one. Ever since then he had me kick. He told me to try and make 10 extra points in a row before every practice," Kinney said.

By high school, Kinney had developed into a weapon for the Johnsburg Skyhawks.

He was a four-time special-teams player of the year. Kinney set an Illinois High School Association playoff record with a 52-yard field goal that beat rival Richmond-Burton.

Kinney's success didn't go unnoticed. He impressed Iowa and LSU coaches enough at their kicking camps that he was invited to be a preferred walk-on.

"I didn't think I could afford to pay my first full year, and didn't know if I would get a scholarship or not," he said.

Therefore, Kinney signed with Winona State, a Division-II school in Minnesota.

"They were the only ones to offer (a scholarship)," he said.

Winona State was coached by Bruce Carpenter, a Johnsburg native and former star Skyhawk quarterback.

Kinney hit 19 of 30 field goal attempts at Winona State, including a 45-yarder that fell just two yards short of the school record. As a sophomore, Kinney nailed 9 of 12 kicks.

With success, Kinney longed for what he termed "a bigger stage." Thus SIU became an option.

"Both my parents (Tom and Tracy) went to Southern, and so did my best friend. My parents always said good things about it," he noted.

"I went on a visit (to SIU) over the summer. Coach (Eric) Schmidt showed me around. I met a few of the players. They made it seem as though I would be challenged, which is what I wanted," he said.

"I took a chance because there were other (talented) kickers I had to compete against," he said. "It was a risk, but it was a risk I was willing to take."

Kinney sat out the 2012 season as a red-shirt due to the transfer.

"It was a good opportunity to get comfortable with the team and with school," he said.

Kinney responded by not only earning the starting kicking job for the Salukis but also excelling. He made 18 of 24 field goal attempts. He kicked a 52-yarder against Western Illinois, tying for the season's longest field goal at the FCS level. Kinney earned second-team All-MVFC honors and was named to the All-Newcomer team.

Kinney said he really felt he belonged at the FCS level following his performance against South Dakota State.

"We played the day after a high school game had torn the field up pretty good the night before," he said. "It had rained and was really muddy. The conditions were very difficult to play on. I went 2-for-2 that game. I had to change up my steps a lot and adjust to the mud, but I came through. Coach (Kyle) Sweigart came up to me after the game and said, 'Looks like we found our kicker.'"

Kinney was a key factor in the Salukis' victory over South Dakota State.

Prior to his senior season Kinney was named a Preseason First Team All-American by *Athlon's Football Magazine.*

"It makes me feel that I've been making progress and taking steps to become a better kicker, but other than that it doesn't really change my mentality or work ethic," Kinney said in the summer prior to his senior season.

Instead, Kinney spent the summer doing what he always did, trying to get better.

"Whenever I've worked with Philip Philipovich, my kicking coach, he's had me aim at a light post. I brought that with me to Southern," Kinney said. "He's taught me everything I know about kicking."

The 2014 season didn't play out as well as the previous one had for both Kinney and SIU. The Salukis missed the playoffs, and Kinney connected on just nine of 17 field goal attempts. In addition, his scoring fell from 94 to 71 points.

"I was more mentally prepared than I ever was before," Kinney told Barry Bottino of the *Northwest Herald.* "It's knowing how to handle successes and failures. I've been through a lot of both."

When asked his best attribute, Kinney named his leg strength. He compiled 42 touchbacks on kickoffs in his two SIU seasons. Kinney kicked in the inaugural FCS National Bowl in front of pro scouts at Florida International University.

FOUR DOWN TERRITORY

Favorite Football Movie—I'd have to say *Friday Night Lights* because even now just talking about it I'm getting shivers. It sums up the atmosphere of not only high school games but college too.

First Car—A '99 Grand Prix. I was 16 and my dad works for GM so he knows where to look for cars and how to get a good deal. I wanted a truck, but this is what he found. I wanted to wait for the truck, but I couldn't say no (to the car). My brother just got his license and his first vehicle was a truck, so I'm jealous.

Worst Summer Job—It was good experience but working for the township. I did landscaping. It was long days in the heat, pulling weeds and edging in hard dirt. Cutting grass, all that good stuff.

Favorite Subject in School—Motor behavior as a college course. I had a really good teacher. He worked with Carmelita Jeter and Olympic sprinters. He taught us a lot of fascinating stuff from his experiences.

MYCOLE PRUITT

MyCole Pruitt is one of those players you couldn't help but notice on a football field.

"No. 4 (Pruitt's uniform number) is difficult to defend out there. He's like a dominant rebounder in basketball with his ability to box out," said Illinois State head coach Brock Spack.

The Bleacher Report called Pruitt "the best 2015 tight end prospect you haven't heard of."

Pruitt, listed at 6-foot-2, 258 pounds by the NFL, caught the attention of pro scouts and general managers. He impressed at the NFL Combine when he ran the 40-yard dash in 4.58 seconds. In a 2015 *Chicago Tribune* postdraft story, NFL beat reporter Brad Biggs noted "he's got a thick lower half so he should prove effective as a blocker as he develops that skill, something he wasn't called on to do much of in school."

Biggs further noted that Pruitt "displayed good hands which was no surprise after he led all Division I tight ends in catches (81), yards (861) and touchdowns (13) last fall for the Salukis."

Ironically, Pruitt was selected in the fifth round of the 2015 NFL draft by Rick Spielman, a former Saluki-turned-NFL-general-manager. Spielman—once a Saluki linebacker and a member of the school's 1983 NCAA Division I-AA national championship team—has been the Minnesota Vikings' GM since 2012.

"Just because he was from Southern Illinois and I never drafted a Southern Illinois guy," Spielman said about the attraction to Pruitt. "There had to be one Saluki after all the UCLA and Notre Dame guys."

According to Biggs's *Tribune* story, "The Vikings have drafted four players from UCLA and Notre Dame since 2007 and they've also chosen four players from some other football factories like Florida State, Southern Cal and Oklahoma in that span."

Spielman was attracted to what draft experts the likes of Mel Kiper Jr. and Todd McShay saw on film.

"I think we have four really good tight ends, but bringing Pruitt into the mix to have that guy that can potentially be a mismatch," Spielman told Biggs. "Just some of the things he showed worked out really well at the combine and he caught the ball extremely well when you saw him on tape. And then (offensive coordinator) Norv (Turner) wanted to try to get another H-back type with some playmaking ability."

Former Saluki teammate and NFL player Jayson DiManche was thrilled for Pruitt.

"I stood up and clapped when he got drafted," DiManche said. "Going against him every day in practice, he's beating me up. I'm beating him up every day, just trying to make each other better. It was great to see him improve and become the player he has.

"I would go against (NFL) tight ends like Jermaine Gresham and Alex Smith every day in practice. I would tell MyCole that his talent was comparable to those guys. I told him many times 'you'll play in this league.'"

MyCole Pruitt (4) became the all-time leading receiver in SIU and MVFC history. Pruitt was drafted by the Minnesota Vikings.

Despite being one of the most decorated players in SIU history, Pruitt realized the NFL is on another level.

"As a rookie the number-one thing you have to do is stand out and make the coaches mention your name a few times and that is exactly what I have tried to do," Pruitt said.

Yet things weren't always so rosy for Pruitt and his NFL future when he arrived in Carbondale from Kirkwood High School in St. Louis.

"(Pruitt was) probably Coach Dale Lennon's best SIU recruit, (but he was) immature as a freshman," said Saluki play-by-play broadcaster Mike Reis. "Matured between his sophomore and junior season. Intelligent on and off the field."

Reis added that Pruitt appeared likely to leave SIU after his junior season for the NFL but decided to stay for his senior season in Carbondale.

"Quarterback Kory Faulkner's injury during the 2013 season impacted Pruitt's reception total," Reis noted.

Pruitt became SIU's all-time leading receiver during his senior season. He finished fourth in voting for Missouri Valley Football Conference Offensive Player of the Year after leading the league with an average 6.8 receptions per game.

Pruitt left Carbondale with a substantial list of accomplishments. The three-time All-American held the MVFC record for career receptions (211), receiving yards (2,601) and receiving touchdowns (25) among tight ends. Pruitt was named the top tight end on the MVFC's 30th Anniversary Team.

Saluki great and former Jacksonville Jaguar Damon Jones was impressed with Pruitt's skills and pro potential. The pair of Saluki stars met as Pruitt was closing in on Jones's school tight end receiving records.

"I wished him well and told him to set the bar high," said Jones. "I look forward to seeing him play on Sundays."

FOUR DOWN TERRITORY

Favorite Football Movie—*Remember the Titans*, because Denzel (Washington) is my favorite actor.
First Car—It was a Chevy Malibu. It was gold, classy.
Worst Summer Job—I've never had a bad summer job. My only real summer job was working with little kids at a basketball camp, teaching them how to play, and I loved it.
Favorite Subject in School—Lunch.

MARK IANNOTTI

Mark Iannotti put up huge statistical numbers as an SIU quarterback. Yet what comes to mind when he reflects on his storied football career is often a fallen friend.

Iannotti, a Schaumburg High School star, committed to Eastern Michigan, a Football Bowl Subdivision school that plays in the Mid-American Conference. Joining Iannotti were wide receiver Demarius Reed and cornerback Darius Scott of Chicago Simeon High School. The trio had become friends, even facing each other in the state playoffs.

Together they wanted to help restore glory to perennial MAC doormat Eastern Michigan.

"We wanted to be part of a big turnaround," Iannotti told Adam Jahns of the *Chicago Sun-Times.*

Their lives were forever changed when Reed was shot and killed during a robbery attempt at an apartment complex near the EMU campus.

"I was just in complete shock," Iannotti said. "I didn't quite know how to handle it."

As part of his grief, Iannotti used Reed as a motivator. Iannotti began to put extra time into workouts and film studies.

"He (Reed) was the guy calling me up to do those little things to separate (my)self from those competition battles," Iannotti said.

The winds of fortune again blew through Iannotti's life a few weeks after Reed's death. EMU head coach Ron English was fired. Iannotti made the decision to transfer to Southern Illinois.

The 6-foot-2, 218-pounder made the most of his fresh start. After a solid 2014 season,

Iannotti burst on the scene with a performance for the ages as SIU came within a point of upsetting Indiana University in the season opener.

Iannotti passed for 349 yards, rushed for 106 and accounted for five touchdowns in the 48-47 loss to the Hoosiers of the Big 10 Conference.

"That kind of put me on the radar and on the map, and I started having agents . . . contacting me," he told Jahns.

By season's end, Iannotti led all Football Championship Subdivision players in total offense per game. He passed for 5,436 yards and 46 touchdowns. Iannotti ran for 850 yards and 12 TDs. He landed on the All–Missouri Valley Football Conference team.

"He's the toughest football player I might've been around," coach Nick Hill told Thomas Donley of the *Daily Egyptian.* "In two years here, he never went into the training room. And if you watched us play, he took a lot of snaps and ran the ball a ton and he never slid."

Iannotti told Donley, "I've never been a big stat guy. After that game against Indiana, Coach Hill and I had a talk about how to handle all the accolades and the media that was going to happen. One of his points was, 'Don't think about it. In a few years, it'll be something you can look back on, but there's

Quarterback Mark Iannotti led a potent Saluki offense and drew the attention of NFL scouts during the 2015 season.

so much responsibility that the quarterback has, from preparation during the week and everything on game day.' So I never really thought about it until now."

Iannotti attended Northwestern's pro day and was invited to work out for the Chicago Bears. Though he most likely won't find himself in an NFL huddle, Iannotti's career path still is oriented to sports; he works as a promotions assistant for ESPN Radio in Chicago.

Through it all, his fallen friend and former teammate is still with him.

"Every time I'm thinking to myself that I don't want to do this extra workout or I don't want to go watch film, I think about him (Reed)," Iannotti told Jahns. "If he were here, he'd be dragging my butt to the film room or the field. I just always keep it in mind that he lost his opportunity and may he rest in peace. But he always has a special place in my heart. I'm always going out there, playing for him. I wish he could be out there with me."

CHASE ALLEN

It didn't take Chase Allen long to decide on Southern Illinois University.

"SIU was actually my second (recruiting) visit. I went to Tennessee-Martin for my first. I had others lined up: Illinois State, Southeast Missouri, and some other offers, but once I visited SIU, I felt like it was right. I felt like it was a family atmosphere here. The guys who hosted me showed me how the team was, how they interacted with each other and I felt like I could fit."

So why not take the other visits anyway?

"Once I committed, I was going to stick with (SIU)," Allen said before adding, "My dad went here. It was far away from home, but yet close enough if I needed to get home."

Allen grew up in Fairview Heights, Illinois, and attended Belleville East High School.

"I went to Grant Middle School in Fairview. Belleville is pretty far from Fairview; it's about a 20-minute drive. My sisters and I went to high school there."

Allen was an athlete from the time he could walk.

"I played baseball, basketball and when I was little, football, in my fourth- and fifth-grade year, but I didn't play again until high school."

As with most southern Illinois youths, Allen was an avid St. Louis Cardinals fan.

"My favorite sport growing up was baseball, for sure. I was always on a select team that traveled. By high school I started to get more serious about football and that became my favorite."

For many the middle school years are about finding yourself and figuring out who you are. For Allen, that factored into his decision not to play football during that period of his life.

"I was a bigger kid when I was younger and I didn't like playing offensive line," he explained. "(But), by high school I developed and started playing linebacker. I liked it a lot more."

St. Louis area fans also liked it. Allen developed into an all-state linebacker and was recognized as a *St. Louis Post-Dispatch* Super 30 recruit in 2012. He racked up 107 tackles and five interceptions on defense, while rushing for 700 yards on offense.

Those numbers and his game film brought recruiters to his door, including SIU assistant Eric Schmidt.

Chase Allen (5) emerged as one of the top linebackers in the Missouri Valley Football Conference. The Belleville East High School graduate also had a knack for blocking kicks.

"He wanted me to play defensive end, but he said I could come in and play outside linebacker (in SIU's 3-4 defense)," Allen said.

Allen wound up playing outside linebacker his first two years in Carbondale (including his redshirt year).

"We had some guys get in trouble at middle (linebacker) so we needed help there, so I moved inside. I had played middle linebacker in high school, so the transition was pretty easy."

Allen certainly made it look easy. By this junior year, Missouri Valley Football Conference opponents were scratching their heads trying to figure out ways to keep Allen away from their ball carriers and receivers.

The 6-foot-4, 241-pound Allen earned second-team All-MVFC honors in 2015. The management major also performed in the classroom, landing on the All-MVFC

academic list. Allen led the team with 120 tackles. He ranked third in the conference with 10.9 tackles per game. Statistically, his biggest game was a 19-tackle performance against Southeast Missouri, the most tackles for any SIU player since Bart Scott in 2002. Yet that game wasn't his favorite.

"It was tough because we kept getting up (on our opponent) and then turning the ball over. We had missed tackles and let them score. It was a pretty frustrating game," Allen said of the 27-24 loss. "I had a lot of tackles. I wasn't processing it at the moment, I was just concentrating on how we were going to win this game. And we ended up coming up short."

Instead, another game stands out far more in his memory. It was a 38-31 overtime victory against Youngstown State later that season.

"I got ejected from the Indiana State game for a late hit on the quarterback in the second half (the week before) so I had to sit out the first half of the Youngstown State game," Allen remembered. "I just remember sitting in the locker room because I wasn't allowed on the field (in the first half). It was killing me not to be on the field. I was watching the game on TV.

"The second half I was able to come back out, and I ended up having a pretty good game. I had two blocked kicks on special teams, and I had 10 tackles. We ended up winning with our defense making a stop."

Allen was named the MVFC Special Teams Player of the Week for his performance. It also showcased his knack for blocking kicks.

"Coach Schmidt did a great job coaching me when I was a freshman. He showed our get-offs and (stressed) no false steps. I really embraced that as a freshman. I feel like that's what helped me as a (kick) blocker," he said.

Former SIU quarterback Nick Hill took over as the Salukis' head coach for Allen's senior year when Dale Lennon was fired. Under Hill, SIU switched to a 4-3 defensive alignment. Allen was excited.

"I liked it a lot," he said. "It allows the linebackers to get those big guys (in the offensive line) off us so we can run around more. I feel like our system right now is a lot better than it has been in the past, depthwise. A lot of guys understand things a lot more."

Allen capped his career as one of the most decorated linebackers in SIU history. He was the team's leading tackler three straight seasons and was named All-MVFC honorable mention his senior year.

With an eye on a possible future playing in the NFL, Allen continued to work on improving his game in all phases.

"I think my understanding of the game and my maturity level have improved so much," Allen said of his time in Carbondale. "Becoming a man over the years at college, living on your own. It develops you on and off the field. My experience here has really developed and matured me both places."

Should pro football not pan out, Allen had a backup plan.

"I've always been into fitness. I want to open up a gym one day. I'd manage that and be a trainer," he said.

That's not surprising coming from a guy who makes his mind up pretty fast.

FOUR DOWN TERRITORY

Favorite Football Movie—*Friday Night Lights*, because high school football is the most fun. Once you get to college, it's more business. In high school, it's your friends and all that. I feel like that movie showed that. I could relate.

First Car—A 1996 Jeep Cherokee that my dad had and that he passed down to me.

Worst Summer Job—Pouring concrete with my uncle. He was a private contractor. He had me come and pour concrete. I was the guy with the wheelbarrow going up the hill, filling it up, and that was probably the toughest summer job.

Favorite Subject in School—I always enjoyed science. I like knowing how things work. I always paid a little more attention in science and math. I wanted to learn more (in those subjects).

NICK HILL, THE COACH

Upon the dismissal of Dale Lennon as SIU head coach at the end of the 2015 season, Nick Hill was hired as the 21st head coach of the Salukis. While many in the FCS world were surprised that a Missouri Valley Football Conference school would hire a 30-year-old with just three years of coaching experience, for Hill it was the dream job.

"If I thought 30 was a negative I wouldn't have applied for the job," Hill said. "When I stood there and interviewed for the job I had total confidence that I was the guy for this job.

"Am I standing here as an arrogant 30-year-old coach? No, I know I need to surround myself with a strong support staff."

Hill, the former Du Quoin standout and SIU star quarterback, views the SIU job as a regional position, not just one for the university and Carbondale communities.

"I want to get out and meet as many people as I can," Hill said. "This is their team too."

Hill further talked of changing the culture of Saluki football.

"I want my players to be part of the community, part of the region. There is more to being a football player than simply being on the field," he said.

Former SIU star quarterback Nick Hill, pictured here with athletic director Tommy Bell, was hired as the Salukis' head coach at age 30.

Hill, the former quarterback and offensive coordinator, talked of running an up-tempo offense.

"My philosophy (is) score points, play fast and have fun. I can promise you we will lead the country in attitude, effort and enthusiasm," Hill said.

Mike Reis has been around Saluki athletics since his days as a student in the 1970s.

"Hiring Nick Hill means SIU is betting on the come. His offensive intelligence, his way with players and his recruiting ability stand out immediately. His age isn't the issue. It's his lack of experience: just two years at college level and one at the high school level. The hire is a gamble. It is, however, a calculated gamble by athletic director Tommy Bell," Reis said.

All-conference linebacker Chase Allen described the coaching change from a player's perspective.

"It's two very different styles. Coach Lennon was more of an old-school type of guy," Allen said. "He's the guy who recruited me; he gave me a chance to play here, so I thank him for that. I loved him as a coach.

"Coach Hill is more emotional with us. He's more of our age. He was in the game not too long ago. He hired a young staff as well, so I feel like we can all relate to these guys."

Hill's inaugural season featured a high-energy approach with an exciting offense to watch. His passing offense averaged 332 yards per game. Mentors Jerry Kill and Carl Mauck were on hand for Hill's first coaching victory, a 30-22 win over rival Southeast Missouri State.

"I'll remember that for the rest of my life," Hill said afterward.

Illinois recruiting guru and SIU graduate Tim O'Halloran is high on Hill.

"Hill has a huge advantage because he's one of their own," O'Halloran said. "His age plays to his advantage. Kids tell you they really relate to him. He's young enough that he played the game not too long ago. It's a big advantage for him, and I also think he has some leeway because he's from down there. He's one of their guys. He's done well so far."

SIU fans show their support week after week each season.

EXTRA POINTS

MIKE REIS

From the mid-1970s to the opening of Saluki Stadium and beyond, SIU Salukis football has been a roller-coaster. And for much of that time, Mike Reis rode in the front car.

"I've see Southern experience the ultimate and the basement," said Reis, the radio voice of Saluki football since 1978. "I've seen the program on the ropes, on the verge of extinction at least once. I've seen the glory of the 1983 national championship season.

"Southern Illinois has been the ultimate roller coaster. Probably no other program has seen a more violent extreme than Southern."

Reis, a Cincinnati native, graduated from SIU's prestigious radio-TV department. He recalled his days as a student when "we laughed at SIU football."

Those were the days following the two-year, three-win coaching career of Doug Weaver. Rey Dempsey, the man who would eventually lead SIU to its national championship, took over in 1976.

"I cut my teeth when I covered him," Reis said. "I was a brash 23-year-old with a lot to learn. Rey Dempsey wasn't afraid to tell

Mike Reis (*left*) has experienced the highs and lows of SIU athletics firsthand for more than forty years.

me when I was wrong. He taught me many things about the game."

Whether as a student or as a professional, Reis has narrated some of the greatest moments in Saluki athletic history. He has called everything from the 1977 College World Series to the '83 championship to the basketball team's appearances in the NCAA Tournament.

Yet the memory of the near death of SIU football hasn't faded with time.

"McAndrew (Stadium seemed) beyond repair," Reis said. "The program was in real danger. In 1981 it was put to a student vote to increase fees (to raise funds for the athletic department). Had that vote been shot down, there was talk that the football program would have been eliminated. It's my opinion that football would have still existed, but most likely it would have continued as non-scholarship football. At that point in time, McAndrew was still salvageable."

The vote went through, breathing life into SIU football.

"The '81 team started the year 0-3 before winning seven out of the next eight," Reis recalled. "Dempsey felt that the September athletic fee vote was really a factor in the team's start."

Meanwhile, the Salukis had been competing at the Division-I level since 1972. SIU joined the Missouri Valley Conference in 1977. That experience paid dividends for Dempsey and the team when it joined the I-AA ranks in 1982.

A year later, SIU finished off a 13-1 season by routing Western Carolina 43-7 in the national championship game.

While the 1981 student fee increase vote and the '83 national crown marked the first rebirth of Saluki football, SIU head coach Jerry Kill resurrected the program two decades later.

"Rey Dempsey and Jerry Kill are very similar coaches, but some 25 years apart," said Reis. "In both cases, those coaches had administrative support. They had the support of the athletic director as well as other top campus officials. Not every Saluki coach had had that."

Reis also noted that Kill benefited from the program "being fully scholarshipped."

"Jerry mirrored the program of (Bill) Snyder at Kansas State," Reis said. "He got the administration to change the schedule. SIU played a softer schedule early and won games to build from there.

"Jerry Kill achieved what nobody thought he could for two reasons: one, no one knew him, and two, Southern hadn't won and no one expected it."

Following a 2002 season that ended with five straight losses, Kill's 2003 team won 10 games, a share of the Gateway Conference title and a playoff appearance.

"Two thousand three is the best story," said Reis, "to go from worst to first was remarkable."

During his time behind the microphone describing Saluki football, Reis said that he has "seen a lot of offense."

With 1983 firmly established as the greatest season in SIU football annals, Reis called the 2007 "the second best."

Asked to pick the best game, Reis gave two responses.

"For fans of Saluki football since 1970, it's the 2002 team versus Western Illinois," he said. "Southern had suffered 18 straight losses to Western. That game was back and forth the whole way. Southern won, 54-52. That game showed Southern could succeed under Jerry Kill.

"For Saluki fans before 1970, it's the 1967 game against nationally ranked Tulsa. It was Homecoming, and Southern pulled the (16-13) upset."

Reis also cited the 2007 national semifinal, played in Carbondale, against Delaware.

"It was Nick Hill versus Joe Flacco," he said.

Delaware prevailed 20-17 and advanced to the national championship game.

In 2008, SIU, coached by Dale Lennon, earned a share of the Missouri Valley Football Conference championship with a 17-10 overtime victory over Illinois State in Normal.

With the Redbirds driving for a potential game-tying score, a fourth-down play came down to a measurement. When the chains came out, ISU came up just short.

"That's the only game I've ever seen end on a measurement," Reis said.

The victory sent Southern into the playoffs.

Reis also recalled SIU's 35-28 win over Indiana University in 2006.

"It was the school's first win against a Big 10 school," he said.

Reis also mentioned a 1999 triumph over Murray State.

"The Salukis won 58-51 in a game that lit up the scoreboard like it had never been lit before," he said.

Reis has been inducted into the SIU Athletics Hall of Fame and the Illinois Basketball Coaches Association Hall of Fame. In 2011 Reis was named the Illinois Sportscaster of the Year.

No matter the score, Saluki fans have tuned into Mike Reis for more than three decades.

"If you can't be there, Mike is the next best thing," said former SIU star and athletic director Jim Hart from his Florida home.

FOUR DOWN TERRITORY

Favorite Football Movie—*The Replacements*. It wasn't as bad as other football movies I've seen.

First Car—1974 Ford Pinto. Interesting, and fortuitous, that I never got hit in the back end to see if the gas tank really would explode.

Worst Summer Job—Demolition for a construction company. 'Nuff said.

Favorite Subject in School—Radio performance classes in college. Geography in grade school.

ROGER AND SHARON LIPE

With all due respect to any SIU athletic department members, Roger and Sharon Lipe just might be the first family of Saluki football.

"Terrific people," said former SIU head coach Jerry Kill; "you'd be hard pressed to find a better pair than those two."

Saluki Hall of Fame receiver Cornell Craig played at Southern from 1996 to 1999 and returns to campus whenever he gets a chance.

Sharon and Roger Lipe head the "first family" of SIU football. *Photo courtesy of Roger Lipe.*

Craig said, "Anyone who has been a part of the SIU athletic family knows how vital Sharon is. She's a mainstay in the program no matter who the coach, winning seasons or losing seasons.

"Roger is definitely a benefit to the program as well. His work as team chaplain and with the Fellowship of Christian Athletes stands out. They are very important people to me, because they were always there for me and were definitely supportive."

While the Lipes have been associated with Saluki football since the mid-1990s, their personal relationship goes back even farther.

"She and I grew up next door to each other. She moved next to me when we were in third grade and it took me until our junior year in high school to get a date," Roger recalled in 2010. "But I finally got that date on April 19, 1973. Here were are, 37 years later with one son and a 14-month-old granddaughter."

Both are graduates of Carbondale High School. While Sharon took classes at SIU, Roger spent one year at a junior college.

"I got bored and went to work," he said.

That work turned out to be in the building industry for 15 years. He followed that by working for a short-term mission agency. The Fellowship of Christian Athletes came knocking on his door in the spring of 1994.

"It was a perfect fit for my love for sport, my love for God and the way they could be combined," Roger said.

Meanwhile, Sharon began working as the office manager for Saluki football under head coach Shawn Watson in 1995. She has worked hand in hand with SIU head coaches Jan Quarless, Jerry Kill and Dale Lennon.

Kill and Lennon rank highly on her list.

"Both men are very principled, caring men with great integrity who have a deep passion for the game and the athletes they coach," Sharon said. "Both men have made me feel like a valued member of the staff and have treated me with tremendous respect. I will always be indebted to Coach Watson for giving me the opportunity to transfer (jobs) to football. Unfortunately, I didn't get to work with him very long."

Watson and Lipe were together just one season because Quarless took over the SIU program in 1996.

"Shawn Watson, back in 1994, opened the door (for me to become team chaplain)," Roger said. "Shawn was in a tough spot. He was a 34-year-old head coach at a university with huge problems to solve and try to figure out how to win here."

Watson not only brought Roger Lipe in; he gave him freedom on the job.

"We kind of made it up as we went along," Roger said. "Shawn was kind and allowed me to experiment. We used trial and error, and I'm doing it all these years later."

The Lipes saw the hardships of Saluki football up close and personal in those early years.

"I came into the program at a time when there was discussion of discontinuing it," Sharon said. "It was woefully underfunded, and it was a major struggle for Coach Watson to try and build up. Coach Quarless faced the same issues Coach Watson did in the beginning. He was able to slowly get the program fully funded with scholarships but continued to have struggles gaining respect. He did not have a lot of support from the athletic administration, which put a lot of stress on the football staff."

Yet the Lipes also saw the Salukis return to glory when Kill rejuvenated the program.

"Coach Kill came in and was able to turn around the program in three years," Sharon said. "The first year we went to the playoffs (2003) was one of the high points. The first time SIU beat the University of Northern Iowa (2009) at the UNI-Dome was another high. Moving into the new football complex and watching the first game played at Saluki Stadium is definitely a high point (as well)."

Roger said, "One of the most exhilarating things was when we came into 2003. Jerry and I were sitting in his office in July talking about how to prepare for the season and he said, 'Rog, I think we're about a year away from being pretty good.' Turns out we won 10 in a row and didn't lose until we played at Northern Iowa in the last game of the season and then just got stomped by Delaware (48-7), which went on to win the national championship that year. The rapid acceleration to being good that year was something to see. That adrenaline rush every week was a pretty fun ride. Then we continued to be good for another seven years."

Roger, like his wife, developed a close relationship with Kill that remains in place today.

"I saw a depth of loyalty in Coach Kill that is really uncommon in college football. It's just the nature of the game, but with a lot of staffs it's just a turnstile of staffs, in and out, in and out," he said "I remember that we had a linebacker here play for five different linebacker coaches in four years. That's tough on a player because he never gets to play instinctively; he has to rethink everything because they change the name of what we're doing last week.

"Whereas with Coach Kill, he brought in the same bunch of guys from Emporia State, some of them were with him up at Saginaw. They were already together. There was a continuity and stability that immediately translated to better play, to better team building. Part of that is reflective of Coach Kill's nature just as a guy. He's deeply loyal but highly demanding at the same time. You can see it in his teams, in his family and in his personal friendships."

The Lipes were with Kill during the coach's diagnosis and fight against cancer.

"He just wouldn't quit when it might have been more expedient to change careers to some(thing) less stressful, because things like sleep deprivation, stress and dehydration tend to bring on the seizure disorder. All of those things come along with being a football coach. He's looked cancer right in the eye and dealt with it directly," Roger said.

While the general public may have seen Kill only on the Saluki sideline or at a public event, the Lipes have seen him wear many different hats.

"He and I are still close," Roger said. "There was a tragic situation with one of his players up at Minnesota. He and I talked into the night about how to handle that with his team and with the (player's) family.

"You see that side of him that is soft, but the other side of him is awfully intense, incredibly competitive and very demanding. Both of those things go together to make a unique package of a guy who knows exactly what he wants to get to and what he

is about. He has a dogged determination to see it completed."

With their lives revolving around SIU football, the Lipes see their jobs as more than simply a means to a paycheck.

"Working with the student-athletes and coaches (is the best part of my job)," Sharon said. "There have been very few coaches that I have not enjoyed working with. I have made some lifelong friends, and it is a joy to be around our players."

When Sharon says players, she notes that "it's very difficult to pick out specific players" that are her favorites because the list may be longer than Santa's list at Christmas. Still, Sharon managed to name former Salukis Kent Skornia, Walter Skeate, Sherard Poteete, Tom Koutsos, Bart Scott, Joel Sambursky, Brandon Jacobs, Deji Karim, Mike McElroy, Larry Warner, and Ryan and Andrew Kernes.

"I am still in contact with many of the players who have been here over the years," she noted.

Roger admires his wife and her dedication to the program.

"Sharon is unique, because in a place like a public university with civil service workers where the vast majority of them punch the clock and come 4:30 they're out the door, take off their work hat and disengage, she's not that way," he said. "She's as loyal and committed to that as any of the coaching staff. She goes way beyond the standard of what is expected of her. As coaches have come and gone, it's just like losing family to her."

Meanwhile, Roger lists the advantages to his job as getting to know the SIU players as young men and watching them grow into adults who do well in their careers and personal lives. Among those he has grown close to over the years are Ryan Hallahan and Mark Gagliano, as well as McElroy and Sambursky.

In fact, Roger officiated Sambursky's wedding.

Roger describes his job as one not only of ministry but also of motivation and team building.

"My job is mainly two things. First, I want to inspire. I want guys to love God," he said. "I am also trying to motivate. I want them to play well. My talks are going to be a blend of those two things. Scripture and I wind up being a problem solver."

Yet no job is without its challenges. For Sharon, coaching changes are never an easy transition.

"Since the secretary seems to be the one stable part of the program, a lot of responsibility falls on the position to assist the new staff in learning the ropes of the university," she said. "Earning their trust takes time. After working for the same person for several years, transition to a new staff is always stressful. The worst part of a coaching change is not knowing if the next person hired is going to be someone you will be comfortable working for."

For Roger, it is much the same.

"If they (coaching staff) trust me they bring me in to help with different situations. If they don't trust me, well then I have nothing to do," he said.

Roger's workload is often directly tied to how well or poorly a Saluki season is going.

"It's definitely different. When things are working and you're winning, there aren't usually a whole lot of things to be solved.

Then my role is one of dealing with more individual crises like an injury or illness to something going on in a family. When we're losing, everybody's needs go up significantly. Everybody's looking for answers, and sometimes they will look to me for answers when everything else has failed," he said.

If we were to play Alabama next week, I would be optimistic that we could play with them, and heck, might even win.

Moreover, not everyone sees faith the same way as Roger.

"Some men will treat matters of faith like a superstition," he said. "That's harder for me to talk with guys and not let them treat their faith like a rabbit's foot to be rubbed. Sometimes I have to challenge them by saying, 'Okay, are we going to pray as much when we're on a five-game winning streak as when we're on a five-game losing streak?'"

Yet, through good times and bad, the Lipes remain strong in their devotion to each other and Saluki football.

"With my personality, I'm incurably positive," Roger said. "If we were to play Alabama next week, I would be optimistic that we could play with them, and heck, might even win."

SHARON'S FOUR DOWN TERRITORY

Favorite Football Movie—I don't have a favorite football movie.

First Car—Plymouth Valiant.

Worst Summer Job—Sewing gloves in a glove factory. The factory wasn't air-conditioned, I was covered in lint from the gloves at the end of the day, and I had to be at work at 7 A.M.

FAVORITE SUBJECT IN SCHOOL—History. Love learning about what made our country.

ROGER'S FOUR DOWN TERRITORY

Favorite Football Movie—*Remember the Titans.* I have met a couple of those coaches, Boone and Yost, and some players on both sides of the ball. Knowing the significance of the issues that movie deals with adds another dimension. I have used clips from that movie when I do ministry talks with other chaplains. For instance, that scene when (Gerry) Bertier is lying in that hospital bed. What are you going to say to him? What are you going to say to his family, the coaches, his teammates? That movie is full of very real things.

First Car—A 1962 white Chevy Chevelle. I got it for $25 from my uncle. The first six months of insurance cost me $125, so it was five times more to insure the car than to buy it.

Worst Summer Job—Washing windows with a cleaning company. Man, I hated that. Baling hay was an infinitely better job than washing windows. Everybody complained about the streaks. As long as the hay got into the barn, nobody cared.

Favorite Subject in School—Math, in particular, algebra and geometry.

RECRUITING

Though recruiting is the lifeblood of any college football program, it has evolved just as much as any part of the game over the years.

"The biggest change (in recent years) is the pressure to commit before the senior year (of high school)," said Jerry Pettibone, who coached from 1966 to 1996 at six different universities, including Northern Illinois.

Today Pettibone maintains a personal evaluation service for high school and junior college athletes. The main focus of the service includes determining each athlete's level of playing ability and helping navigate him through the college recruiting process.

"The rules as far as contact are completely different today (than when I coached)," Pettibone said. "Now, coaches can only have contact once a week. They only get to see them play or practice a limited amount.

"There's not as much time in the player's living room. There's pressure to make an offer as soon as possible these days."

Much of that pressure comes from the growth of technology into the recruiting process.

"The Internet has changed it all," said Mike Sabock, who coached for 24 seasons at NIU and served as the Huskies' recruiting coordinator under head coach Joe Novak.

"There are no secrets out there," Sabock said. "Kids and parents now see who's getting offered scholarships. It's natural for them to say if so-and-so is getting an offer, what about me? I'm better than he is."

Prospective players are also now taking an active part in the process. Many of them make their own highlight DVDs or upload them onto YouTube or similar websites for college coaches and recruiters to see their skills.

"It's hard on coaches," Sabock said. "It takes time out of your day (to watch everything). But you've got to check them out, because you don't want to miss out on some-one. The kids now think it's easy to obtain scholarships."

Pettibone agrees.

"A lot (of recruiting) is done over the Internet and on websites," he said. "The official (campus) visit used to be the most import-ant part of the process. Now it's an after-thought."

Pettibone sees this as a huge negative.

"The personal side of it has been removed," he said.

As a result, the odds of coaches making mistakes in their offers have increased.

"The pressure to make those offers as soon as possible means the entire process is moved up," Pettibone said.

Thus coaching staffs around the nation are spending much of their time focusing on high school players that are not only up-perclassmen but also sophomores.

"That's just crazy to me," said Pettibone.

While coaches have always needed to es-tablish bonds with prospective players, that process has also changed in the fast-paced, touch-of-a-button society of today.

"You have to think like an 18-year-old kid," said PJ Fleck, who became the youngest head coach in FBS when Western Michigan hired him in 2013 at age 33.

"Texting, Facebook, Twitter, cell phones, that's how they communicate," said Fleck.

Thus coaches often use any and all of these tools in their attempts to sign the next re-cruiting class.

Yet coaches have to make sure their com-munication isn't too impersonal.

"You can't just mass-produce," Fleck said. "You have to be really careful."

SIU hired Nick Hill as its head coach when the former Saluki quarterback was just 30 years old.

"Recruiting is what I love," Hill said shortly after accepting the position. "There's not go-ing to be a head coach out there that recruits harder than me. I promise you that. If there's a day a head coach can be out on the road, I'm going to be on the road. I love kids. I love the relationships that you make with them. That's why I wanted to coach.

"When I'm sitting in those living rooms, it's coming from the heart."

In today's world, a big part of recruiting is impressing potential signees with updated facilities. In 2009, Eastern Illinois installed a $450,000 scoreboard complete with state-of-the-art audio and video capabilities. SIU opened the 2010 season in a brand-new sta-dium. Illinois State has renovated Hancock Stadium and is building an indoor practice facility.

"In today's economic climate it's a very tricky thing politically," ISU's Brock Spack said. "It's hard to me, even as the head football coach, to see a $40–$50 million investment when the library needs an up-grade or the chemistry building's roof is leaking. If you're going to do it, do it right. Make it a one-time thing, not an erec-tor set project that's going to need more later."

Yet not all see the modern recruiting game as being more difficult than those of yes-teryear.

Brodie Westen, who served as both an as-sistant and a head coach at Western Illinois in the 1970s, recalled the days of no limits on recruiting.

"It was worse back then because it was less restrictive," Westen said. "You had coaches who were practically living at high schools. There weren't any dead periods (for recruiting) like there are now. You could be on the road for 12 months. It got way out of hand. There was a lot of babysitting that went on."

According to Fred Huff's *Saluki Sports History: 100 Years of Facts and Highlights*, "recruiting was handled in somewhat of a unique fashion by some schools in the mid-1920s." To support his claim, Huff presented an illustration of a one-cent postcard used by Jackson University of Business located in Chillicothe, Missouri, in an effort to attract prospective players.

The postcard stated that the school "desires to get in touch with a few more football players. If you are interested in playing football or know of a good football player who is interested in playing, we would like to hear from you by return mail.

"When you answer, be sure to state the conditions under which you might join our football team immediately."

No matter the era, no matter the school, recruiting will always dominate a coaching staff's time and energy. It was true when players wore leather helmets; it remains true today.

FBS TRANSFERS

During the late 1980s, the NCAA changed its rules about transfers. Since that decision, the I-AA/FCS level hasn't been the same.

"(The rule) really changed the I-AA level dramatically," said former Northern Iowa head coach Darrell Mudra.

The change allowed players who met the requirements of a one-time transfer exception to go to I-AA/FCS schools and play right away regardless of how many years of eligibility they had remaining.

"As far as the impact of transfers, it's made FCS a lot better because there are some legitimate players that could play at FBS schools," said Kevin Capie of the *Peoria Journal-Star*, who has covered the Missouri Valley Football Conference since 1996. "The most common reason for transferring is that the player wanted to play."

One of the first high-profile players to take advantage of this rule was quarterback John Sacca who, having lost his starting job to Kerry Collins, left Penn State for Eastern Kentucky in 1994.

Opinions on the transfer rules vary as much as coaching philosophies.

"We didn't take a lot of them, maybe three or four," said Jerry Kill, who coached at SIU from 2001 to 2007. "You don't want to punish a kid, but then again, you don't want them to always have an easy way out. It's a fine line."

Brandon Jacobs is likely the most successful SIU transfer, despite playing just one season for the Salukis. With just one year of eligibility remaining, Jacobs was stuck behind future NFL first-round picks Carnell "Cadillac" Williams and Ronnie Brown at Auburn.

Thus Jacobs transferred to SIU for the 2004 season. He rushed for 922 yards and 16 touchdowns for the Salukis. He also attracted the attention of NFL scouts and was drafted by the New York Giants in the fourth round. Three years later, he was a Super Bowl champion.

Illinois native Mark Iannotti transferred to SIU from Eastern Michigan. The quarterback was both a passing and a running threat for Dale Lennon's Salukis.

Damon Jones transferred to SIU after first committing to the University of Michigan as one of the most heralded tight ends in the country in the 1990s.

"I had love for all the (SIU) coaches. Coach (Shawn) Watson and (assistant) Coach TJ Wrist were always special because they gave me a second chance," Jones said.

Over the years, SIU has landed its share of transfers, including Paul McIntosh (Army), De'Ron Flood (Purdue), AJ Hill (Northern Illinois), and Jewel Hampton and AJ Derby (Iowa).

However, the success of Jacobs and others like him led to the NCAA implementing a little-known rule in 2006. It prohibits seniors-to-be in Football Bowl Subdivision programs (formerly I-A) from transferring to FCS schools and being able to play immediately.

"A lot of these players at the I-A level would just be sitting on the bench for four years," said Mudra. "It's a nice opportunity for them to go and play right away without having to sit out. I'm all for giving kids a chance to play."

Former Illinois State head coach Todd Berry led the Redbirds to the 1999 national semifinals. His view of the transfer rules of his era contrast greatly with those of Mudra.

"I never liked it, because there are some I-AAs that are basically upper-level junior colleges," said Berry, the Redbird head coach from 1996 to 1999.

"Schools that consistently took transfers were certainly within the rules and had the right to do so," Berry continued. "One school in our conference in particular seemed like that's all they did. They'd lose players and

have a different team every year. It was easy to get rich every year."

The school Berry made reference to was Western Illinois, like SIU and ISU, a member of the Gateway/Missouri Valley Football Conference.

The rule first came into effect when the late Bruce Craddock coached the Leathernecks. It was most utilized, however, by Randy Ball, who took over the WIU program when Craddock died.

"We had our share (of transfers)," said John Smith, former WIU defensive coordinator under Ball.

One of the most successful Leathernecks transfers was running back Aaron Stecker from the University of Wisconsin. Stecker had seen his playing time diminish with the Badgers due to the emergence of future Heisman Trophy winner Ron Dayne.

Once Stecker became a WIU player, he enjoyed Dayne-like success. Stecker rushed for 2,293 yards en route to being named the Gateway Conference Player of the Year in 1997. Stecker, who later played more than a decade in the NFL, finished as WIU's career rushing leader with 3,799 yards in only two seasons in Macomb.

"Aaron Stecker proved to be a great recruiter for us," said Ball. "People knew of his reputation and what he had done in the Big 10. If he chose to come to Western, then it looked pretty good in their eyes."

Over the years, WIU accepted transfers from the likes of Carlos Daniels (Wisconsin), Sam Clemons (California), Jason McWilliams (Indiana), Mark Zanders (Wisconsin), David Bowens (Michigan), Frisman Jackson (Northern Illinois), Will Peterson

(Michigan), and RJ Luke and JR Zwierzynski (Penn State).

"Transfer U, that's what Western was labeled for a while," said former head coach Don Patterson, who took over the program in 1999. "It was hard to recruit guys to spend four or five years in Macomb. But a lot of them (transfers) you could get for a year or two. (WIU) got a lot of mileage out of those players, especially back in the '90s."

"Under Ball, there was no question that Western was 'Transfer U,'" said beat writer Kevin Capie of the *Peoria Journal-Star*. "The 1998 team had 42 transfers on the roster (21 from I-A and 21 from junior colleges). It took a few years, but Patterson eventually brought that number down and (Mark) Hendrickson has been that way. They'll still land a handful every year but not go overboard."

"I'm not going to deny the fact we didn't benefit from those transfers," said former WIU athletic director Dr. Tim Van Alstine.

However, Van Alstine is also well aware of the dangers of such transfers.

"From an academic standpoint, it hasn't always (worked out)," he said. "In those days (when players could transfer with one year of eligibility remaining), they came to play football. They didn't go to class. It was a hired-gun mentality."

It was that hired-gun mentality that spurred the NCAA to prohibit seniors-to-be in Football Bowl Subdivision programs from transferring to Football Championship Subdivision schools and being able to play immediately.

The rule change occurred because of concern that such players were transferring for purely athletic reasons and thus a market was being created for top-tier talent by FCS schools seeking one-year "hired guns."

As a result, transfers must now have at least two years of eligibility left to be allowed to play right away. Another option is that the player must already have a four-year degree and enroll as a graduate student in a program his current university does not offer.

"The way the rule stands now is probably the way it should be," Kill said.

Patterson agreed.

"I can understand why they changed that rule, because many of those guys had no motivation to take their academics seriously," he said.

Meanwhile, Berry has seen the rule from both levels. After his success at ISU, he fulfilled a lifelong dream as the head coach of Army, the Division I-A academy at West Point, New York. He also later coached at Louisiana-Monroe, another FBS school.

> **I** *always felt that you cheated players out of a bonding experience.*

"I always felt that you cheated players out of a bonding experience. I have nothing against giving kids a second chance. But too often, it's too easy (a) way out," Berry said. "It's easy for the I-AA schools, but it's also the Division I-A schools not taking responsibility for the guys they recruited."

Berry was especially bothered by the schools that didn't offer scholarships for football.

"I-AA is a great brand of football when it's played by the all-encompassing group that fully funded their programs," Berry said. "But there are schools that are only around because of Division I-A basketball and want to get into the (NCAA) tournament. They should be playing at the Division-III level (in football). They really dilute the (I-AA) level."

Despite the transfer rule, most coaches would still prefer to have players from the time they are freshmen.

"I'd like to be able to develop a kid from year one, but there are circumstances that don't always make that possible," said Bob Spoo, who coached Eastern Illinois for 25 years.

There are numerous cases where transfers have been more of a negative than a positive. The road is littered with players who have failed academically or been dismissed from schools for breaking team rules or being arrested for illegal activities.

"You've got to be careful who you bring in," said Illinois State head coach Brock Spack, the former Purdue defensive coordinator under Joe Tiller. "If you bring in the wrong guys you can rot your program from the inside out. You have to look at the motivation for the player who is leaving. Was he having off-the-field issues? Was he struggling academically? Was he stuck behind really talented players?"

Despite its risk, the transfer rule is not likely to disappear. Therefore, coaches must see its value.

"You've got to go after transfers these days (if you want to be successful)," said Smith, now an associate athletic director at Eastern.

Mudra agreed.

"That's true for all the top contending schools in I-AA," he said.

An example of the benefit of taking transfers is the FCS Championship game for the 2010–11 academic year. Eastern Washington and Delaware met for the title. Each team was quarterbacked by a Division I-A/FBS transfer: Bo Levi Mitchell from SMU and Pat Devlin from Penn State, respectively.

Ultimately, no matter one's view of the transfer rule, it has become part of today's college football world. If you're an FCS coach these days chasing a conference or national championship, or both, then transfers have become yet another aspect of the crazy world of recruiting.

SALUKI RIVALS

What constitutes a rivalry?

Randy Reinhardt of the *Pantagraph* has covered college football since his days as a student reporter at Illinois State University in the early 1980s. Moreover, he writes the annual Missouri Valley Football Conference preview for the *Sporting News.*

"Rivalry is difficult to define," Reinhardt said in an e-mail. "There's some sort of rivalry with every team in your conference, but I think having two teams close in proximity tends to make a good rivalry. If two teams have played several important games over a relatively short period of time, a rivalry usually develops."

Meanwhile, Kevin Capie has covered the MVFC for the *Peoria Journal-Star.*

"The first thing is a familiarity that breeds contempt," responded Capie in an e-mail. "But more than that, there has to be a competitiveness for the most part."

Rivalries have
changed over time
for SIU football.

Definitions aside, SIU rivalries have changed over the years, thanks to changing schedules and conference affiliations.

In the program's early days, Southern Illinois Normal University played a very modest schedule when compared with today's longer seasons. SINU essentially played other schools within a relatively close geographic proximity. Moreover, once SINU joined the Illinois Intercollegiate Athletic Conference in 1914, its opponents were the other state schools for the most part. The IIAC was at its peak in the late 1920s when 23 colleges were members, including a large number of smaller Illinois schools.

By the war years of the 1940s, only SINU, Eastern Illinois, Illinois State and Western Illinois remained. In 1950 the league became the Interstate Intercollegiate Athletic Conference when Central Michigan and Eastern

Michigan joined, upping membership to seven schools.

"We played some really tough games with Western Illinois," said Carver Shannon, the Salukis' do-everything back of the 1950s.

One of those games occurred on October 4, 1958, when Southern snapped a 10-game losing streak to Western with a thrilling 32-31 victory. The Salukis scored on the game's final play to move within a point of the Leathernecks. That final touchdown came on a 67-yard pass from Centralia native Bill Norwood to Lane "Night Train" Jenkins. Southern then won the game when Jenkins ran in the two-point conversion.

Mike Reis has been around SIU athletics since his time as an undergraduate in Carbondale during the mid-1970s.

"Saluki football is not fraught with long, intense rivalries," Reis said. "Illinois State is the biggest rival; the one that's lasted the longest. The rivalry withstands the teams' records. SIU's always viewed Northern Iowa as a rival, but UNI's only seen it as a rivalry when the two are competing for a conference title. That rivalry spiked from 2003 to '09. Missouri State sees SIU as a rival, but the Salukis do not view the Bears with the (same) disdain the Bears (have for) the Salukis.

"When Rey Dempsey was SIU's coach—and SIU was D-1—the rivalry with Northern Illinois was the strongest. When SIU won the 1983 national title, Indiana State was its biggest rival, as both were excellent programs. Eastern Illinois was probably the second-strongest then."

Back in the early 1960s, Sam Silas starred for the Salukis.

"In my time at Southern, Western Illinois was very tough," said Silas, who later played in the NFL. "Bowling Green was another. We never beat them. They were a step up for us, but still we didn't walk off of the field accepting second place."

Cornell Craig was a record-shattering Saluki wide receiver in the late 1990s. For Craig, one opponent stood out from the rest.

"Illinois State was always a big rival because of the proximity. There were a lot of students and players who knew people on the Illinois State team. That was definitely a big rival," Craig said. "Northern Iowa was just tough; I hesitate to call it a rivalry because when I was there we only beat them once."

Nick Hill became SIU's head coach at age 30. In his days as the Salukis' star quarterback, Hill and his teammates often went toe-to-toe with conference rival Northern Iowa.

"By far, it was Northern Iowa," Hill said. "We got into some real battles with them."

Bryan Boemer, the 2011 Remington Award–winning Saluki center, agrees completely.

"No doubt in my mind,' Boemer said. "Our two programs were neck and neck. Each time we played it was a close game. Sometimes it was the last second and the last play."

Thus rivalries will continue to evolve. For a variety of reasons, certain dates on the calendar will be circled and receive more emphasis.

"You can't beat a good rivalry game, that's for sure," said former SIU head coach Jerry Kill. "It's an intense week of preparation, and when the ball is teed up and the teams are ready to clash, you can't doubt something special is going on."

MONEY BALL

Scan your eyes down just about any SIU Salukis football schedule over the past three decades and you're likely to see it. There is nearly always an early season matchup with a Football Bowl Subdivision (FBS) opponent.

One year it might be Ole Miss. Another it might be Baylor. Perhaps it is Indiana or Northwestern or Illinois or Purdue.

"Why in the world are these games scheduled?" the average SIU fan might mutter.

The answer is mainly financial.

"Mostly for the paycheck," Stewart Mandel, formerly of *Sports Illustrated* and now with FoxSports.com, said in an e-mail. "These (FCS) schools are operating on a small budget to begin with, and the guarantees from those games ($300,000–$400,000) account

for a good chunk of it. It's also considered a big thrill for the players to be able to play a brand-name team in their stadium."

That's *their* stadium as in the big boys from the FBS stadium. You won't see any of these games taking place on the FCS fields.

So what's in it for the FBS schools? Why bring in a team like Southern Illinois?

"Mostly, because they are cheap," Mandel said. "A guarantee to get even a low-level FBS team is running around $800,000 these days, with some getting $1 million. Supply and demand. The FCS schools come cheap."

College football had been divided into Division I-A and I-AA in the late 1970s.

According to its media guide, SIU has played three ranked FBS opponents in its history: number 11 Oklahoma State in 1973, number 20 Florida State in 1982 and number 15 Illinois in 1990.

Again according to the media guide, SIU became an FCS member in 1982. The first official Saluki FCS versus FBS game was played on October 29, 1983, when SIU throttled New Mexico State 41-3.

The Salukis, however, lost their next 20 straight FCS-versus-FBS games. By the late 1980s, most of those defeats were by lopsided scores.

SIU, however, turned the tide with the hiring of head coach Jerry Kill. In 2002 Kill's

Over the years, SIU has played Football Bowl Subdivision (FBS) opponents for a shot at glory and a big payday. The Salukis recorded two victories over FBS schools, including one over Indiana in 2006.

Salukis narrowly lost 48-43 in overtime at Eastern Michigan. Two years later, a failed two-point conversion left the Salukis as one-point losers at Northern Illinois. Western Michigan defeated SIU by 34-28 in 2005.

Kill's Salukis broke through in 2006 with a 35-28 victory at Indiana. In 2007 SIU knocked off NIU 34-31. The rousing Saluki victory proved to be a factor in NIU's later hiring Kill. In 2009 Marshall struggled to hold off SIU 31-28 in Huntington, West Virginia. In 2015 Indiana narrowly slipped past the Salukis 48-47.

Thus such games have become a way of life for I-AA, or Football Championship Subdivision (FCS) programs, as they are now called.

Former SIU athletic director Mario Moccia is well aware that these games are a two-way street.

"I am all for playing one of these types of games each year for several reasons," Moccia said in a 2014 e-mail. "Our student-athletes look forward to the challenge, since many incorrectly perceive FCS as a much lower level of football. Our fan base loves the opportunity to see where we measure up with the teams they see on a regular basis on TV and have more traditionally established programs. Our philosophy has been to play schools with the best name possible that we have an opportunity to win while (being able to drive) to that location. As an example, it costs in the neighborhood of $100,000 to charter a plane, so a school offering $500,000 to Oregon versus $400,000 to Illinois is about the same deal (minus the opportunity to win and the travel distance with your alumni base).

"The negatives would be when you are playing a larger, heavier team with 22 more full scholarships; there is an increased possibility for injury from the standpoint of our starters being in the entire game versus the other team having the ability to bring in fresh players."

Most SIU players and coaches view these games as opportunities to prove themselves against the NCAA's top level.

"Certainly you point to those games on your schedule," said former SIU center Bryan Boemer, who played against Ole Miss and Illinois during his Saluki days.

Yet not all Salukis had the opportunities that Boemer and his teammates had.

"I would have liked to play a money game, because it would have been an opportunity to test my play against a Division I-A competition," said receiver Cornell Craig, who played at SIU from 1996 to 1999. "One thing we did have was the chance to play against schools in our conference that brought in transfers. Western Illinois was definitely one of those. They had some guys who had played in the Big 10, so in some ways I got to play against that talent."

In 2015 the Big 10 Conference announced it would no longer schedule FCS opponents because it hurt the league's strength of schedule in its bid to move up in the BCS standings and land a place at the playoff table.

SIU athletic director Tommy Bell said, "We've had a year to adjust to this new scheduling reality, and while it's disappointing that we'll be unable to continue to play in-state schools such as Illinois and Northwestern, the door is still open for us to play many other FBS opponents."

Bell, who previously worked in administrative positions at Northern Illinois and Western Illinois, added, "We've talked to teams in the MAC (Mid-American Conference), SEC (Southeastern Conference), AAC (American Athletic Conference), Conference USA, (and) Big 12, just to name a few. We'll keep an open mind when it comes to scheduling, although we'd ideally like to stay within driving distance of Carbondale in order to manage expenses and play opponents our fans can travel to see."

"The hope (of) many people is (that) Cinderella continues to get invitations to the FBS ball. But as the College Football Playoff grows in stature, if not teams, the FCS is at the mercy of the bigger conference decisions. The Pac-12, Big 12, SEC and ACC could come to agree with the Big Ten," wrote national FCS analyst Craig Haley.

THE NFL AND BEYOND: SALUKIS IN OTHER PRO LEAGUES

While most fans focus on SIU alumni who have played in the National or Canadian Football Leagues, plenty of former Salukis have seen action elsewhere.

According to football historian Bob Gill, 31 former Salukis played in the top minor leagues in the 1950s and 1960s.

Gill listed those players as Ike Brigham, Paul Brostrom, Ken Doyan, Jerry Frericks, Ralph Galloway, Bob Green, Dennis Harmon, Dave Harris, Sam Holden, Frank Imperiale, Al Jenkins, Mike Kaczmarek, Mitch Krawczyk, Tom Laputka, Bill Lepsi, John Longmeyer, Carl Mauck, Ken Moore, Mike Mosher, Dave Mullane, John Quillen, Ron Quillen, Sam Silas, Rich Slobodnick, Jim Thompson, Clarence Walker, Dave Wheeler, Gene Williams, Gene Wren and Ted Zahorberski.

"In the 1960s, the United Football League, the Pro Football League of America and the Continental Football League all had teams representing Chicago, and the PFLA also had other teams in the general vicinity," said Gill. "Dozens of players from Eastern, Western, Southern and Northern Illinois played for those teams."

Gill has written a series of books on minor league and independent football. In addition, he is a member of the Pro Football Researchers Association.

"I'm sure many more players from Illinois schools played in the Central States League (successor to the Tri-States League, which changed its name around 1962), since its teams were concentrated around the Great Lakes, but I don't have rosters for that league. It was a lower level, with teams in smaller towns and players making less money, but was still interesting—something like the Carolina League in baseball today. In that analogy, the Continental League or the Atlantic Coast League would be the equivalent of the International League or the PCL (Pacific Coast League)," said Gill.

Guard Russell Smith was the first former Southern Illinois player to see action in professional football. Smith, who played at Southern Illinois Normal University in 1914–15, began his pro career as a member of George Halas's Chicago Bears in 1922. Smith played the next two seasons with the Milwaukee Badgers, then a franchise in the

Running back Amos Bullocks earned First Team All–Interstate Intercollegiate Athletic Conference honors in 1960 and 1961. Bullocks, a member of the SIU All-Century Team, played three seasons with the Dallas Cowboys (1962–64) before joining the B.C. Lions of the Canadian Football League for the 1965 season. After spending 1966 with the CFL's Montreal Alouettes, Bullocks played two seasons with the Pittsburgh Steelers.

early days of the National Football League. Smith also played for Cleveland and Detroit before finishing his pro career by returning to the Bears for the 1925 season.

Running back Glenn "Abe" Martin was the next Southern player to appear in the NFL. Playing for the Chicago Cardinals in 1932, he rushed for 152 yards and one touchdown, and had 99 receiving yards and a touchdown.

Martin starred on Southern's only unbeaten team in 1930. Martin later coached SINU to the 1947 Illinois Intercollegiate Athletic Conference championship and a victory in the Corn Bowl. He also served as athletic director, coached basketball and revived the school's baseball program in 1947.

Running back Amos Bullocks earned First Team All Interstate Intercollegiate Athletic Conference honors in 1960 and 1961. Bullocks, a member of the SIU All-Century Team, played three seasons with the Dallas Cowboys (1962–64) before joining the British Columbia (B.C.) Lions of the Canadian Football League for the 1965 season. After spending 1966 with the CFL's Montreal Alouettes, Bullocks played two seasons with the Pittsburgh Steelers.

Saluki All-American defensive tackle Tom Laputka also played in the CFL, spending five seasons north of the border.

"Yes, the (adjustment) to three downs is tough," Laputka said. "You don't get much long offensive ball control, so possession changes hands a lot more. Players get much more playing time."

Laputka was one of three former Salukis who made their way into pro football by playing in the World Football League (WFL) in the 1970s. While Laputka played for the Philadelphia Bell, linebacker Mike Kaczmarek (Florida Blazers) and defensive tackle Sam Silas (Portland Storm) saw action in the 1974 WFL season. However, the league folded a year later.

In 1983 SIU won the I-AA national championship. Earlier that year, the United States Football League (USFL) played its inaugural season. Saluki linebacker John Harper was a third-round draft choice by the USFL's Denver Gold in 1983. Robert "Red" Miller, a Macomb native and former Western Illinois University player and coach, was the Gold head coach. Miller is most famous for coaching the 1977 "Orange Crush" Denver Broncos, a team that made it to the Super Bowl.

A year later, fresh off the '83 national championship, three former Salukis were USFL draft choices. Speaking to the strength of the '83 defense, all three players selected were defensive backs: Terry Taylor (Chicago Blitz, second round), Donnell Daniel (Chicago Blitz, eighth round) and Greg Shipp (Birmingham Stallions, sixteenth round).

Rick Johnson was the quarterback of the '83 team. Though undrafted by both the NFL and the USFL, Johnson earned a roster spot with the newly established Oklahoma Outlaws. Moreover, Johnson earned four starts over two USFL seasons with the Outlaws.

"(Broadcaster) Jim Lampley was interviewing me one time before a start against Steve Young," Johnson said. "He was really working the low-budget, free-agent quarterback versus the $40 million man angle.

He asked me if I felt any pressure. I told him no, that I didn't. He responded by saying. 'Really?' Sure, I said, because if I play half as well as Steve does, then I should get $20 million. He (Lampley) really liked that."

When the USFL closed its operations, its players were placed into a special dispersal draft for NFL teams. The Los Angeles Rams took Johnson in the second round. Despite that fact, Johnson instead signed with the Canadian Football League's Calgary franchise.

The move proved to be a wise choice. Johnson played five seasons in the CFL. In 1986 Johnson was the CFL's top passer and was named a league all-star.

Other ex-Salukis have also tasted success north of the border. Guard Jim Battle played for the 1965 Edmonton Eskimos after being a member of the NFL's Minnesota Vikings earlier in the decade. Again, according to Bob Gill, a football historian who has written books on both minor league football and the CFL, other Salukis played north of the border.

"Quite a few more," Gill wrote in an e-mail. "These are the Southern Illinois players I have in my Canadian Football League register, although it's not complete: Barclay Allen, Jim Battle, Amos Bullocks, Ralph Galloway, Bobby Hudspeth, Tom Laputka, Carver Shannon, Gene Wren."

Record-setting Saluki receiver Cornell Craig signed with the Montreal Alouettes of the CFL following his graduation from SIU.

"The (Canadian) game is a lot faster," Craig said. "There are only three downs, so it's often two downs and punt the ball and then the opposition has two downs and punts it back. With that huge field (wider and longer than the American football field), there is so much more running.

"There are times when you run 10, 15, 20 yards before the ball is snapped. There's a lot more running. Another thing that gets overlooked but is a major adjustment is that there are 12 men on the field. I had a mental picture of what the defense looks like from all my previous experience. So you'd beat the corner and think you were open, but in Canada there is another safety. You may think you're wide open, but there's another guy there in coverage."

Arkee Whitlock, a three-time all-conference player and Walter Payton Award finalist at SIU, played in three CFL seasons. Whitlock was the Edmonton Eskimos' Most Outstanding Rookie in 2009, when he rushed for 1,293 yards and 12 touchdowns. Whitlock also caught 44 passes out of the backfield that season.

Unfortunately, injuries took their toll on Whitlock. A foot injury limited his production in his second season. In 2011 a bad hamstring kept Whitlock off the field until the fourth week of the season. Once on the field Whitlock rushed for 92 yards on 17 carries, but he also dropped some passes and fumbled twice. Soon thereafter, Whitlock was released by Edmonton.

Defensive standout Eze Obiora also played in Canada. The 6-foot-3, 240-pound defensive lineman signed with the Hamilton Tiger-Cats in 2013.

Safety Anthony Thompson was drafted by the B.C. Lions in 2016. Thompson was the 12th overall pick in the CFL draft.

Arena football is yet another alternative. Former SIU standout quarterbacks Nick Hill and Chris Dieker played in the AFL—Hill for the Orlando Predators and Dieker for the Iowa Barnstormers and Cleveland Gladiators. Former Saluki wide receivers Alan Turner and Quorey Payne, along with linebacker Micha King, also played with AFL teams.

MCANDREW STADIUM

McAndrew Stadium served Southern Illinois University and its football program for 71 years. The official SIU athletics website states that McAndrew was "built by the Works Progress Administration during the Great Depression of the mid-1930s."

Costing $150,000, the new stadium seated 5,000 spectators. The first game played there was on October 1, 1938, against Southeast Missouri State. Two weeks later, Southern Illinois Normal University shut out Arkansas State 6-0 for the first win in stadium history.

When William McAndrew passed away in 1943, the university named the stadium in his honor. The most comprehensive renovation to the stadium took place following the 1973 season, when additional seating was erected on both sides.

"McAndrew was a very modest stadium," said Sam Silas, who played for the Salukis from 1960 to 1963. "It was a typical small high school stadium, not big-time at all. It was not much more than most of us had experienced playing high school ball."

Saluki fans were treated to many memorable games over the years, including an upset of nationally ranked Tulsa in 1967 and the I-AA national semifinal victory over Nevada-Reno that sent SIU to the national championship game.

SIU compiled this list of other memorable games:

McAndrew Milestones

Oct. 1, 1938
  SINU loses to SEMO, 27-0, in first game at stadium.

Oct. 15, 1938
  SINU beats Arkansas State, 6-0, for first win at stadium.

1943 Stadium is named for school's first coach, William McAndrew.

Nov. 10, 1950
  First night game is a 44-13 win over Eastern Michigan.

Oct. 20, 1973
  Last night game for nearly thirty years is a 25-23 loss to Tampa.

Sept. 13, 1980
  The biggest crowd in stadium history (17,150) watches SIU beat Eastern Illinois, 37-35. More than $30,000 is raised for former Saluki Mark Hemphill, who was paralyzed the previous year during a game with Illinois State.

2001 New AstroPlay turf is installed.

2002 Night football returns as Salukis trounce Kentucky Wesleyan, 78-0, on Aug. 29.

2004 Salukis beat Indiana State on Nov. 13, to set school record with 12th straight home victory.

2009 The stadium closes at the end of the 2009 football season.

2010 Demolition begins and is completed in February 2011.

Built as a WPA project during the Great Depression, McAndrew Stadium served Southern Illinois University and its football program for 71 years.

According to the SIU athletics website, the 2003 campaign saw SIU post a perfect 6-0 home record and record the highest average attendance (9,748) since the 1991 season, which drew 12,225.

In 2004 the Salukis ended the regular season with a 59-10 drubbing of Indiana State, stretching their home winning streak to a school-record 12 games.

After a 29-year absence, night football returned to McAndrew Stadium in 2002. The Salukis opened the season August 29 with a 78-0 win over Kentucky Wesleyan, followed by a fireworks show.

Local electrical union IBEW 702 installed the lights at no charge, saving the athletic department $100,000 in infrastructure improvements originally expected to cost $250,000.

Prior to 2002, the last night game at McAndrew was on October 20, 1973, when the Salukis hosted Tampa. The lighting system became inoperable the following year.

In 2003 the university's board of trustees approved a land-use plan for a new "gateway" to SIU, which would include a new football stadium. That study eventually led to the construction of Saluki Stadium, which opened in 2010.

Jim Hart not only quarterbacked the Salukis in the 1960s but also served as his alma mater's athletic director during the 1990s.

"The new stadium was such a long time in coming," Hart said in 2009. "We drew up plans in the mid-'90s. We didn't have the backing of the administration.

"Your stadium makes such a difference. You would look around the league and see places like Northern Iowa and Southwest Missouri State and envy the facilities they had."

Jerry Kill said, "McAndrew served Southern well for years, but the time had more than come."

SALUKI STADIUM

"I was at the opening game. It's an awesome facility," said former SIU quarterback Nick Hill, whose younger brother AJ also played for the Salukis.

"Coach Kill's name should be on there somewhere," Hill said of the stadium. "It's not just Southern or Carbondale; the whole region loves him."

Fellow SIU quarterback standout Joel Sambursky shares Hill's sentiments.

"When I look at the multi-, multimillion(-dollar) building on a college football Saturday, I know that if we had not been successful under Coach Kill and turned around the fortunes of Saluki football, then that stadium would not have been built," said Sambursky.

"There were discussions that we have a crumbling 70-year(-old) stadium and we can't win enough to get 5,000 people to a game. I can tell you there was not a lot of support saying, 'Let's invest more in this program,' and (there were) some who said, 'Let's drop it all together.' They had a Hail Mary attempt in hiring Jerry Kill, and within three years he turned it around, and not only did he turn it around from a losing program to a mediocre one but rather one of the best in the country. As a result of that, Saluki football became very popular. There was a ton of support in the community, and that directly tied into why you saw an upgrade in the facilities. And I don't know if many people would disagree with me on that."

Then–SIU athletic director Mario Moccia said the Saluki Way project—which encompasses Saluki Stadium—cost approximately $80 million. According to Moccia, the funds were raised by a student-fee increase, a general sales tax voted on by the city of Carbondale (valued at $20 million) and a capital campaign and private giving that raised around $12 million as of 2014.

"The linchpin came when the city of Carbondale voted to take a small portion of a penny of sales tax for revenue for the project," said team chaplain Roger Lipe, a lifelong Carbondale resident.

Further development continued in the years since the football stadium opened.

"Since the original Saluki Way plans (Saluki Stadium, the Boydston Center and the SIU Arena renovation), we have built a new track-and-field facility and throws area (named after Lew Hartzog and Connie Price-Smith, respectively) as well as the new baseball stadium (named after Richard "Itchy" Jones)," Moccia said.

"Moving forward we would like to build a facility over our six tennis courts at the law school to have our own indoor tennis facility and provide somewhere to go (during) inclement weather for baseball, softball and other sports when needed. Would like to build a locker room for both men's and women's swimming. Cover batting cages at baseball and softball. Create a men's golf locker room," Moccia added.

According to the official SIU website, at the time it was built, Saluki Stadium was the newest of 12 stadiums built by an FCS school since 2000. The horseshoe-shaped facility has a listed capacity of 15,000, including nearly 1,100 chair-back seats.

The two-story press box features 12 club suites, including a 2,500-square foot VIP

Southern Illinois University ushered in a new era when Saluki Stadium opened its doors for the 2010 season.

Club Room. A 20-by-40-foot scoreboard with video replay capabilities stands in the north end zone.

The Saluki players dress in a 5,000-square-foot locker room.

"It's a marvelous facility," said longtime Eastern Illinois head coach Bob Spoo, who was an assistant at Purdue prior to his days in Charleston.

Linebacker Jayson DiManche played at SIU from 2009 to 2012.

"It was really cool to be there for the transition (from McAndrew Stadium to Saluki Stadium). The new facilities were pretty amazing. It was like moving into a new home," he said.

For Sam Silas, a Saluki standout from the early 1960s, there is no comparison.

"(McAndrew) was not big-time by any stretch of the imagination," Silas said. "This new one is really something."

Homecoming has been an SIU tradition since 1922.

SALUKI TRADITIONS

HOMECOMING

Homecoming has been a part of Southern Illinois athletic tradition since 1922. In fact, according to Fred Huff's *Saluki Sports History: 100 Years of Facts and Highlights,* the inaugural Homecoming not only included an impressive victory for Southern Illinois Normal University but also marked the return of a favorite son.

"Another highlight was the Maroons' 12-7 homecoming win over Southeast Missouri State and the return that day of Russell Smith, 1915 team captain who went on to play for Navy and the University of Illinois before a professional career with Staley's, which by 1922 had become the Chicago Bears. Still playing with the Bears, Smith was SINU's first professional athlete. The previous spring he had returned to SINU and was in charge of practice with those athletes not participating in other sports," Huff's book states.

Homecoming means different things to different people. For players, it's a chance to shine in front of the season's largest crowd. For administrators, it's an opportunity to showcase the athletic department and bring in more revenue than a typical Saturday. For coaches, it's a week filled with heightened expectations and potential distractions. For alumni, it's a chance to reconnect with old friends and acquaintances.

Sam Silas starred at SIU in the early 1960s. He later played in the NFL and was named to the SIU Football All-Century Team.

"Everybody tried to make Homecoming special," Silas said. "There were more people at the game. There was more excitement, more fanfare."

Nearly a half century later, Bryan Boemer excelled in the Saluki offensive line as a Rimington Award–winning center. He echoed Silas's thoughts.

"(Homecoming is) more dramatic," Boemer said. "It projects an image of your team. It's more intense. It seemed like the game came down to the end about every year I played."

Former Saluki defensive star Jayson DiManche said, "Homecoming is awesome because all of the old players come back. They're egging you on and cheering you on; they expect so much. Some of my biggest disappointments came on Homecomings because we didn't always win. You want to win your Homecoming game. Those are big-time games."

Du Quoin native Nick Hill has seen Homecoming from both a playing and a coaching perspective.

"For me, every game was Homecoming, since I grew up 20 minutes down the road," Hill said. "You're representing your school and your alumni."

Cornell Craig, a member of the Saluki All-Century Team as a receiver, also welcomed the return of Homecoming each fall.

"Homecoming was always special," Craig said. "It was a bigger crowd, a lot more energy. There were all the festivities and the homecoming court attached to it.

"During my time we never played the traditional homecoming team (where you got an easy win). We played Northern Iowa or Illinois State, a rival team, so it was always a good game."

While Southern Illinois first celebrated Homecoming in 1922, other state schools had enacted the tradition in prior years. Yet the origins of the first Homecoming are shrouded in mystery. In fact, like many modern traditions, there are as many stories and claims as there are floats in the annual parade.

For years the University of Illinois has either claimed or been given credit for establishing the Homecoming tradition. For example, the *ESPN College Football Encyclopedia* states, "Homecoming weekend originated at Illinois in 1910, created by undergraduates W. Elmer Ekblaw and C. F. "Dab" Williams. The first celebration was held Oct. 14–16, and the Fighting Illini beat Chicago 3-0 in a game that served as the weekend's

main event. Other schools adopted homecoming . . ."

Furthermore, the University of Illinois website stated that homecoming at the school "is the longest continuously running such collegiate event, beginning in 1910 and marking its 100th anniversary in 2010. The occasion has taken place in each of those 100 years, with the exception of 1918, when the event was canceled because of the exigencies of World War I."

Documented research by former Northern Illinois University sports information director Mike Korcek, however, showed that NIU played its first Homecoming game in 1903.

"What is a quick definition of the word 'homecoming'?" Korcek said in an interview.

According to *Merriam-Webster's Collegiate Dictionary*, "homecoming" is defined as "a return home" and "the return of a group of people usually on a special occasion to a place formerly frequented or regarded as home; *especially*: an annual celebration for alumni at a college or university."

Thus, through documented university archive records, Korcek dated the origins of the Huskie Homecoming celebration to an alumni football game played on October 10, 1903. Called "the Eventful Game" by the student newspaper, the Northern Illinois State Normal School varsity shut out the Alumni 6-0.

Further research set the beginning of the University of Michigan's homecoming in 1897. In addition, Marshall University (1906), the University of Wisconsin (1908), Indiana University (1909) and Baylor University (1909) also were ahead of the U of I's "first" Homecoming.

"Let me make this also perfectly clear: Northern Illinois did not invent or create the first Homecoming," stated Korcek in an e-mail, "but ours (or our form) was prior to Illinois. My goal was to diplomatically discredit the U of I on their Homecoming claim. Upon calling the other Midwest schools (some Big Ten and some MAC), it was also obvious that Michigan with an 1897 date also beat the vaunted U of I."

Meanwhile, the University of Illinois website also stated that "Homecoming's original concept—designed by two University of Illinois students, Clarence Foss Williams, Class of 1910, and W. Elmer Ekblaw, Classes of 1910 and 1912—was to offer an annual event geared specifically to alumni and centered around a football game. Its inaugural launch was an unqualified success, drawing more than 10,000 participants."

When asked to comment on Korcek's research, Robin Kaler, the associate chancellor and director of public affairs at the University of Illinois, sent an e-mail response.

Kaler wrote, "In 1910, the students who organized the first such celebration on our campus claimed 'Illinois may well pride itself on being the originator of the plan for drawing home the alumni.' Over the years, we have learned of similar and earlier efforts at other institutions, but the University of Illinois certainly has one of the longest college traditions called 'Homecoming.'"

Further complicating matters was an exhibit featured at the NCAA Hall of Champions in Indianapolis in the early 2000s. The exhibit claimed that Indiana University had invented the Homecoming concept.

In an e-mail response, Hall of Champions associate director of public and media relations Gail Dent stated, "Unfortunately, none of the staff who worked on that project are with the NCAA today and the Hall of Champions was completely renovated following a fire a couple of years ago so the information is no longer in house. Generally, we reach out to schools for their information, which they provide for various exhibits, but we rely on their facts and figures and give them credit.

"I don't believe there was extensive research done on this subject, at least that I've been able to find, so we couldn't officially confirm that one school versus others was the first to host a Homecoming."

Dent also brought up schools at levels below Division I.

Dent wrote, "Since those schools don't get as much coverage as D-I schools, it is possible they were also hosting 'official or unofficial' homecomings in years past. It is also possible that some schools held 'homecomings' for basketball too.

"That said, I'd suggest getting the comments for your project from our member schools directly, as opposed to the Hall of Champions. I'd also look at what was done over the years in Division II, which includes HBCUs (historically black colleges and universities), and in Division III. I hope that helps to some degree."

According to the 2004 NIU football media guide, university historian Glen Glidemeister put NIU's first formal Homecoming on the weekend of October 12–13, 1906. The term "Homecoming" first appeared in the October 1906 issue of the newspaper *Northern Illinois.* In 1907 the NIU Alumni

Association's constitution stated "there shall be a social meeting of the alumni and guests, following the annual football game, on the evening of the second Saturday in October."

Again, according to the 2004 football media guide, the first 11 NIU Homecoming football games were against the alums.

"That continued until 1913 when the series was curtailed by the alumni team because 'few of the members (were) in condition,'" stated the media guide's article written by Korcek.

The following year, 1914, the first Northern Illinois game against an intercollegiate football opponent at Homecoming took place on October 24, when the hosts defeated Wheaton College 29-3.

Meanwhile, Eastern Illinois played its first Homecoming game in 1915. Illinois State Normal School began its tradition in 1921 and Western Illinois in 1923.

Ironically, Princeton and Rutgers, the first two combatants in what has been recognized as college football's first game back in 1869, did not celebrate Homecoming for many years.

Princeton first had a Homecoming in 1918, 50 years after that inaugural game, to celebrate the landmark contest's anniversary.

Harvard, the nation's oldest university, held its first Homecoming in 2009. The Crimson began playing football in 1874.

MARCHING SALUKIS

No college football experience would be complete without the pulsating sounds of a marching band.

"It's one of those sounds that stays with you," said former Saluki head coach Jerry Kill. "It's part of the crisp fall game day experience that makes college football the spectacle it is."

Former SIU defensive back Terry Taylor said, "You know it's fall and school is back in session. It's game day when you hear the band strike it up."

According to the band's official website, "The Marching Salukis provide entertainment and school spirit at countless SIU athletic events. Over 150 strong, the members of the band represent every college and major in the University. They take part and are leaders in an incredible variety of academic and extracurricular pursuits. Discipline, teamwork, dedication—all are lessons learned on the marching band field."

The marching band performs at all home Saluki games, and occasionally travels to an away game each year. The Marching Salukis have also performed at professional football games, generally those of the St. Louis Rams.

Michael Hanes began his work with the SIU marching band during the 1964–65 academic year. Just a year later, he was promoted when his predecessor moved on to a new position.

"I was able to take over as assistant director of bands, director of the Marching Salukis and percussion teacher in 1965," Hanes said in an e-mail.

His timing was fortunate.

"At the time I took over the band, they were one of the most unique marching bands in the country," Hanes said. "They played mostly jazz and contemporary pop music

using, largely, custom arrangements. The band dressed in tuxedos—half the winds in red dinner jackets, and half in black, and the percussion was in plaid."

Hanes noted that the idea of wearing tuxedos developed out of 1950s and '60s professional jazz musicians.

"In 1965, the Marching Salukis were all male, with the only women being a twirling corps," Hanes added.

The SIU percussion section was unique, as its drums and other pieces were on carts that had bicycle wheels.

"The carts allowed us to have various-sized snare drums and tom-toms, as well as suspended cymbal, high-hat cymbals, timbales, bongos, a conga drum, xylophone," Hanes said. "Rather than sounding like a military marching band, the carts allowed the section to sound like a giant drum set, or a

For many years, the Marching Salukis played mostly jazz and contemporary pop.

concert percussion section. This was 15 or more years before drum corps and marching bands started expanding from the standard percussion instrumentation.

"The band maintained this style and instrumentation into the mid-1990s."

Hanes knows firsthand the importance of a top-notch marching band and its impact on a university as "an excellent public relations entity providing public exposure of the school throughout the region with performances off campus, at professional sporting events, (in) parades (and at other gatherings)."

Just like a university's athletic teams, the marching band does numerous hours of preparation for Saturday's game.

"The average fan has no idea (of) the amount of planning, organization and rehearsal that is involved in the operation of an effective university/college marching band," Hanes noted. "They assume that college marching bands are mostly music students. This is not the case—most college marching bands have many more players who are not majoring in music, but rather use the marching band as a social and creative outlet."

As someone involved professionally in music for over three decades, Hanes found many aspects of marching band that were gratifying.

"For me, it was developing a close relationship with the students as they are members of the group, and watching them grow throughout their memberships. We have an active Alumni Marching Saluki Group, with members from as far back as the early 1960s, that still stay in contact and return to campus every Homecoming to perform with the current band," Hanes said.

Being a member of the Salukis marching band has always been a unique experience.

"The Marching Salukis have always been considered a group that will 'try anything once,' as long as it is fun, entertaining and unique," Hanes said. "They had the first-ever 'Marching Baby Grand Piano,' a marching violin player and other similar gimmicks that the public enjoyed. At a time that all marching bands were military style, they put on tuxedos and performed jazz and contemporary popular music. When you see the band in action, you can see the players are totally involved in what they are doing and are having fun doing it."

SIU CHEERLEADING

Another key component of SIU game day is the cheerleading squad.

According to their official website, SIU cheerleaders view themselves as ideals of what a strong university should be.

"We are a program that is in the rebuilding process at SIU, and we're not running a 'cheer factory,'" states the group's website. "We care about your education and your personal development because those are the main factors in how enjoyable and successful your life will be."

The cheer squad's vision "is that we work together, have fun together, and encourage and support one another like family. We treat people how they want to be treated, and when conflicts arise we handle them with open honest communication. Preparing our team for competition we steadily

progress our skills and fitness level by working hard at practice and outside practice, and we go out of our way to help our teammate's progress. At games, we believe we can help the team win by leading the crowd, and we will do it better than anyone in the country."

Cheerleaders usually practice two or three times per week, with each practice lasting two hours. In addition, the cheer squad has two one-hour strength and conditioning workouts.

"SIU cheerleaders are front-line representatives of the university, so they are expected to be in excellent physical shape," further states the website.

KING TUT'S TOMB

King Tut became the first official SIU mascot during the 1953–54 academic year. The original King Tut was the first live Saluki dog to represent the team from the region

SIU cheerleading has long been a part of Saluki tradition. Here the Saluki Shakers perform at halftime.

Above: Before each home game the players pat Tut's Tomb for good luck as part of the Saluki Walk to the stadium. *Right*: According to the SIU media guide, 22 Saluki dogs served as mascot from 1953 to 2005. Multiple dogs have served since then.

Grey Dawg, one of two human versions of the Saluki mascot—the other is Brown Dawg—is a fan favorite around campus and at athletic events.

known as Little Egypt. On his death, the dog's remains were buried in the northeast corner of McAndrew Stadium.

When Saluki Stadium was built, King Tut's tomb was moved to its present spot between the stadium and the team's locker room in the Donald Boydston Center.

SALUKI DID YOU KNOW?

- **William McAndrew** was appointed as the first director of athletics at SINU on July 15, 1913, by President Shryock. He has been called "the father of intercollegiate athletics" at Southern Illinois. McAndrew's 1913 football team posted a 4-2-1 record despite having only 14 players when it opened the season. His 1930 Maroons remain the only untied, undefeated team in the school's history.
- **Harry Warner** of Vincennes, Indiana, became the first out-of-state player to letter in SINU football.
- **Ed Parker** played every minute of every game for three seasons (1913–15). **Glenn Fishel** later duplicated the feat (1921–23).
- In 1916 SINU printed its first football schedule card, which featured a full-length picture of captain **Arlie Boswell**.
- October 5, 1916, ushered in **Bayliss Field** as the new SINU football facility. It was "east of what later became known as Lincoln School, just east of the railroad tracks and northeast of campus," according to Fred Huff's *Saluki Sports History: 100 Years of Facts and Highlights.* SINU

defeated Cape Normal (Southeast Missouri State) 34-0 in the inaugural opener.

- SINU's defeat of Southeast Missouri State in 1919 proved to be an odd rarity. The Maroons won 4-0, the only time in SINU history and possibly the only time in college football history that the losing side gave up two safeties while being shut out.

- The **1927 SINU** 50-man roster featured 48 players from within a 50-mile radius of Carbondale. Twenty-three of the players hailed from Carbondale itself. The team featured **Raymond "Cabbage" Floyd,** long recognized as the finest drop kicker in school history.

- **McAndrew Stadium** was completed in 1937 and served the football program through 2009.

- When World War II shut down the SINU football program in 1943, **Carbondale High School** and **Pinckneyville High School** played in McAndrew Stadium for SINU's "Homecoming."

- The **Henry Hinkley Award** was established during the 1945–46 school year. Annually given to the top athlete at SINU/SIU, the accolade was announced at the banquet for "I" club members and was given by the Carbondale Businessmen's Association. Hinkley, an honor student, a sophomore representative to the student council and a letterman in football, basketball and track, was killed in the Pacific theater of operations during World War II. **Sam Milosevich** was the first Hinkley Award recipient.

- **Willie Brown** was a four-time lettermen for the Salukis. The 1959 team MVP was named to the All-Conference First Team *on both offense and defense.* In addition, Brown made the dean's list every term for four years at SIU.

- When SIU left the Interstate Intercollegiate Conference after the 1961–62 school year, the Salukis held three team, single-game conference records: most rushing attempts (66), net rushing yards (550) and total offense (594 yards). All of these records occurred in a 1960 game against Eastern Illinois. **Amos Bullocks** held the record for most rushing attempts in a single season (122 in 1960).

- Former Saluki running back **Ernie Wheelwright** played seven years in the National Football League after leaving Carbondale. In addition, Wheelwright served as a member of the 101st Airborne Division, also known as "the Screamin' Eagles." Wheelwright later appeared in films such as *The Longest Yard* and *The Greatest*. Perhaps most interesting, Wheelwright was also the owner of one of Atlanta's premier nightclubs in the 1960s, the Pink Pussycat Club. Wheelwright died of cancer in 2001 at age 61.

- SIU's 1963 game versus Fort Campbell pitted 19-year-old **Jim Hart** against ex-Army star **Tom Blanda**. Fort Campbell won 14-13.

- SIU's final game of the 1963 season, scheduled to be played at North Texas State, was canceled due to the assassination of **President John F. Kennedy**.

- SIU All-American defensive tackle **Tom Laputka** flew planes in Alaska for two years following his days in professional football.

- Safety **Adrian White** played one season at SIU (1983). After transferring to the University of Florida, White became a three-year starter for the Gators. He also anchored Florida's 400-meter relay team that included Olympian Dennis Mitchell. White later played seven seasons in the NFL before returning to Carbondale to start his coaching career as an SIU assistant in 1999.
- Record-setting receiver **Cornell Craig** is a graduate of the same Louisville high school as sports icon **Muhammad Ali**.
- All-time leading SIU scorer and record-setting kicker **Craig Coffin** nailed three field goals, including a game-winning 23-yarder in overtime as the United States defeated Japan 23-20 in the title game of the 2007 World Championship of American Football at Todoroki Stadium.
- SIU and Southeast Missouri State squared off in the first college football game ever played at **Busch Stadium**, home of the St. Louis Cardinals. The Salukis scored 17 unanswered points and cruised to a 39-16 victory on September 21, 2013. The announced attendance was 14,618.
- All-time leading SIU receiver **MyCole Pruitt** caught at least one pass in 43 of his 44 career collegiate games.
- Females must run an eight-minute mile to be considered for the Saluki cheerleading squad. Males need to run a mile at a rate dependent on their size.

WHAT IF?

Most likely the subject has come up at various tailgates around Saluki Stadium or in the restaurants or watering holes around Carbondale. Some pause over the next bite of a bratwurst and sip of a drink to ponder the question.

"Which Salukis team was the best in school history?" one maroon-clad fan asks another.

Mike Reis has broadcast SIU football since 1978. Before that, the Cincinnati native was a student in Carbondale.

"The 1983 team was the best," he said. "That team had pros on it. Terry Taylor was a first-round NFL pick. Donnell Daniel and Rick Johnson played pro football. That secondary all got shots in either the NFL or the USFL, the two pro leagues at the time."

Reis cited the '83 team's stout defense as its strength.

"Opponents just could not score on that team," he said. "The playoffs proved that. Look at the championship game. They had seven interceptions and only gave up seven points (in a 43-7 victory over Western Carolina)."

Les Winkeler, sports editor of the *Southern Illinoisan*, agrees with Reis.

"The Salukis had a tremendous defense led by cornerback Terry Taylor, who played about a dozen years in the NFL. Donnell Daniel, the other corner, also played professionally. SIU had a great quarterback in Rick Johnson, big play receivers and a bruising running back in Corky Field," Winkeler said in an e-mail.

Southern Illinoisan beat writer Todd Hefferman considers the 1983 and 2004 Salukis as the best in SIU history. He also gives a nod to the 2007 national semifinalists.

"The 1983 squad had what we now call a Football Bowl Subdivision–caliber roster

The 2004
SIU Salukis

and played in Division I-AA," said Heffer-man in an e-mail.

While noting the offensive contributions of Johnson, Hefferman highlighted the '83 Saluki defense.

"SIU's defense intercepted 41 passes that season and allowed less than 226 yards of total offense per game," Hefferman said. "Taylor, center Tom Baugh and linebacker Fabray Collins all made it to the NFL."

Meanwhile, Reis chose the 2007 Salukis as his second-best team. SIU, under head coach Jerry Kill, posted a 12-2 record and won two playoff games before falling to Delaware 20-17 in the national semifinals.

"The 2007 team also deserves mention," said Winkeler. "Led by quarterback Nick Hill, the Salukis' only loss was 30-24 at num-ber-two Northern Iowa. Many Saluki fans believe a bad call cost SIU the game on a last-minute drive."

Kill's 2003 and 2004 Salukis each won 10 games and lost in the first round of the playoffs.

"Two thousand three provided a great moment when Southern won the confer-ence championship," Reis said. "It came out of nowhere and was a truly special moment."

The 2004 team repeated as conference champions and had won nine consecutive games entering the playoffs.

"Southern was the number-one seed and got bounced in the first round by Eastern Washington (35-31) at home," Reis said.

Hefferman noted the 2004 Salukis "beat people with balance."

"For the first time in seven years, the Sa-lukis didn't have a 1,000-yard rusher that season, because they had two with more than 950, two-time Super Bowl champion Brandon Jacobs (992 yards on 150 carries) and SIU Hall of Famer Arkee Whitlock (959 yards on 151 carries)," Hefferman said.

Jacobs averaged a school-record 6.6 yards per carry, while Whitlock averaged 6.4 yards per rush. Quarterback Joel Sambursky, another SIU Hall of Famer, threw for 2,224 yards and 19 touchdowns while being intercepted only five times.

The '04 Salukis lost by one point at Northern Illinois in a September 11 game.

"They went for a play-action pass instead of a Jacobs handoff with the game on the line on a two-point conversion attempt," Hefferman noted.

SIU won nine straight games to end the regular season before falling to Eastern Washington at McAndrew Stadium in the playoffs. Jacobs rushed for 166 yards and four touchdowns in the loss.

"It was one of the most bitter pills SIU ever swallowed in the postseason," Hefferman added.

The 1999 SIU team, coached by Jan Quarless, was just 5-6.

"You might not have seen a better offense," said Reis. "They could not be stopped, but also they could not stop anybody."

The '99 team scored 424 points but yielded 342. SIU scored more than 50 points three times. However, the Salukis gave up more than 50 points four times, including 68 to Western Illinois and 66 to Indiana State.

Conversely, Winkeler added, "Old-timers will tell you the 1947 7-2-1 was one of the best in SIU history."

That '47 team capped its season by shutting out North Central College of Naperville 20-0 in the Corn Bowl, held in Bloomington.

There you have it; the experts have weighed in with their assessments of Salukis football. Fans and former players have no doubt done the same. Yet is there a way to determine the greatest Southern Illinois Salukis football team ever?

While none of these debates will ever be completely resolved, technology does provide some interesting possibilities.

Game designer Dr. Wayne Poniewaz and programmer Richard Hanna are the creators of Second and Ten (SAT) Football, a highly acclaimed computer simulation lauded for its statistical accuracy. The game contains a ratings adjustment to allow for teams from different eras to compete against one another on an even footing.

"It adjusts each team's defensive ratings based on the average of the season averages of the two teams playing," explained Poniewaz, who has a PhD in experimental psychology.

Thus SAT is the means by which the All-Time SIU Salukis will be crowned as the greatest team in school history.

SIU has enjoyed storied success throughout its history. Though the Salukis won Interstate Intercollegiate Athletic Conference (IIAC) championships in 1960 and 1961, the game played in those days was a far cry from the so-called modern era. The same goes for the '47 team that Winkeler referenced.

Thus our field begins with Rey Dempsey's 1979 Salukis, which posted an 8-3 mark and finished second in the Missouri Valley Conference. After losing three of its first five games, Dempsey's team ran off six straight victories.

The 1983 national championship Salukis and their impressive 13-1 record come next. Only a late-season loss at Wichita State kept SIU from a perfect season. The Salukis overwhelmed Western Carolina 43-7 in the national championship game.

Jerry Kill revitalized the program and re-kindled the Salukis as a national power. His 2003, 2004, 2005, 2006 and 2007 teams all make the cut.

"I think every team was important and each was different. From the 1-10 team (in 2001) to the five straight years of 10-win seasons, they all had to sacrifice to get us better and take us to national prominence," said Kill in 2014.

When Kill left Carbondale to succeed Joe Novak at Northern Illinois, Dale Lennon arrived from North Dakota to keep the SIU winning ways aflame. Lennon's 2008 and 2009 teams round out the field.

So, it's time to tee up the ball with the click of a mouse and the stroke of a keyboard . . .

The All-Time SIU Salukis Tournament was played out in a round-robin format, with each team playing the other on a neutral field in ideal weather conditions. For the sake of statistical reliability, each "game" was simulated 1,000 times. The results are an average of those results and are presented as one game that represents the entire simulation.

As you can see, the 2004 SIU Salukis ran the table. Coach Jerry Kill's team won in dominating fashion. In fact, the '04 Salukis won four of their "games" in 90 percent or more of the simulations. The closest game came against the 1979 Salukis, with the '04 team winning 54 percent of the matchups by an average score of 25-21. The '04 team

All-Time SIU Salukis Tournament Final Standings

2004	8-0
2009	6-2
2003	5-3
1979	4-4*
2007	4-4
1983	3-5*
2005	3-5
2006	2-6
2008	1-7

denotes head-to-head tie-breaker

showed balance with the rushing of Arkee Whitlock and Brandon Jacobs setting up the passing of Joel Sambursky. The '04 Salukis averaged 31.3 points per game while yielding 17.7 points per matchup.

The 2009 Salukis stumbled only twice, falling to the '04 team (79 percent, 29-19 average score) and to the 2007 team (55 percent, 25-23). Deji Karim averaged 116 rushing yards per game.

Kill's teams claimed two of the top three spots, while Dempsey's 1983 national champions finished a disappointing sixth in the tournament field. The '83 team gave up just 18.1 points per game but scored at just a 16.8-points-per-game clip.

The 2008 team scored its lone victory in an "upset" of the 2005 squad (57 percent, 25-23).

Thus, by virtue of the computer world, the 2004 team wears the crown as the All-Time Greatest in Saluki history.

Let the debates begin (or continue) . . .

APPENDIX

BIBLIOGRAPHY AND RESOURCES

Muhammad Abdulqaadir

APPENDIX

SIU ALL-CENTURY TEAM (1913–2013)

(Selected by an online fan vote)

QUARTERBACKS

Jim Hart (1963–65)

Nick Hill (2005–7)

Rick Johnson (1980–83)

Joel Sambursky (2002–5)

RUNNING BACKS

Muhammad Abdulqaadir (2002–3)

Amos Bullocks (1958–61)

Andre Herrera (1974–76)

Brandon Jacobs (2004)

Deji Karim (2007, 2009)

Tom Koutsos (1999–2003)

Burnell Quinn (1976–79)

Arkee Whitlock (2004–6)

WIDE RECEIVERS/TIGHT ENDS

Lionel Antoine (1969–1971)

Cornell Craig (1996–99)

Kevin House (1976–79)

Damon Jones (1994–96)

OFFENSIVE LINEMAN

Tom Baugh (1982–85)

Bryan Boemer (2008–11)

Will Justice (2003–6)

Aaron Lockwood (2005–8)

Jim Lovin (1946–49)

Elmer McDaniel (2003–4)

David Pickard (2008–11)

UTILITY

Jim Battle (1959–62)

Glenn "Abe" Martin (1929–31)

Carl Mauck (1966–68)

Marion Rushing (1954–57)

Carver Shannon (1955–58)

Jim Battle

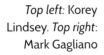
Top left: Korey Lindsey. *Top right*: Mark Gagliano

DEFENSIVE LINEMEN

Houston Antwine (1957–60)
Bryan Archibald (1998–2001)
Andre Bailey (1997–99)
James Cloud (2006–8)
John Harper (1979–82)
Sterling Haywood (1982–85)
Sam Silas (1959–62)

LINEBACKERS

Fabray Collins (1981–83)
Brandin Jordan (2006–9)
Carl Mauck (1966–68)
Marion Rushing (1954–57)
Bart Scott (1998–2001)

DEFENSIVE BACKS

Oyd Craddock (1976–79)
Donnell Daniel (1982–83)
Korey Lindsey (2007–10)
Alexis Moreland (2001–4)
Greg Shipp (1980–83)
Terry Taylor (1980–83)

PUNTERS

Mark Gagliano (1993–96)
Scott Ravanesi (2006–9)

KICKERS

Craig Coffin (2002–6)
Kyle Dougherty (2007–10)

RETURN SPECIALISTS

Craig Turner (2004–7)
Larry Warner (2007–8)

HEAD COACHES

Rey Dempsey (1976–83)
Jerry Kill (2001–7)

SALUKI HALL OF FAME

(in alphabetical order)

Muhammad Abdulqaadir
Lionel Antoine
Houston Antwine
Cecil Bass
Jim Battle
Tom Baugh
Gene Bricker
Frank Bridges
Bill Brown
Willie Brown
Amos Bullocks
Harry Canada
Bob Colburn
Verdie Cox
Oyd Craddock
Cornell Craig
Donnell Daniel
Ralph Davison
Rey Dempsey
Russell Emery
J. T. English
Frank Eovaldi
Raymond Floyd
William Freeberg
Scott Gabbert
Mark Gagliano
James Gray
Jim Hart
John Harper
Andre Herrera
Lynn Holder
Kevin House
Rick Johnson
Jerry Kill
Tom Koutsos
Jim Lovin

William McAndrew

Glenn "Abe" Martin
Carl Mauck
William McAndrew
Tom North
Bill Norwood
Bill O'Brien
Burnell Quinn
Bob Reeves
Marion Rushing
Joel Sambursky
Bart Scott
Carver Shannon
Sam Silas
Clint Smothers
Clarence Stephens
Quentin Stinson
Charles Strusz
Terry Taylor
Bill Townes
Charles Warren
Arkee Whitlock
Wayne Williams

RETIRED SIU JERSEY NUMBERS

23	Harry Bobbitt (1961–63)
30	Mark Hemphill (1979)
78	Jim Lovin (1946–49)

SIU HEAD FOOTBALL COACHES

Coach	Years	Record
William McAndrew	1913–16, 1921–38	83-79-20
Sam Patterson	1917	2-2
No teams in 1918 and 1920		
William Lodge	1919	2-2
Glenn "Abe" Martin	1939–49	31-42-5
Bill Waller	1950–51	3-14-1
William O'Brien	1952–54	6-20
Al Kawal	1955–58	20-15-2
Carmen Piccone	1959–63	28-20
Don Shroyer	1964–65	4-16
Ellis Rainsberger	1966	4-5-1
Dick Towers	1967–73	30-37-2
Doug Weaver	1974–75	3-18-1
Rey Dempsey	1976–83	54-37
Ray Dorr	1984–87	17-27
Rick Rhodes	1988	4-7
Bob Smith	1989–93	17–38
Shawn Watson	1994–96	11-22
Jan Quarless	1997–2000	14-30
Jerry Kill	2001–7	55-32
Dale Lennon	2008–15	51-42
Nick Hill	2016–present	

SIU FOOTBALL CLASSIFICATIONS

1937–72	NCAA College Division
1973–77	NCAA Division I
1978–81	NCAA Division I-A
1982–present	NCAA Division I-AA/FCS

SIU FOOTBALL CONFERENCE MEMBERSHIPS

1913–24	Independent
1925–49	Illinois Intercollegiate Athletic Conference
1950–61	Interstate Intercollegiate Athletic Conference
1962–72	Independent
1973–76	Division I Independent
1977–84	Missouri Valley Conference
1985–2007	Gateway Football Conference
2008–present	Missouri Valley Football Conference

SIU FOOTBALL CONFERENCE CHAMPIONSHIPS

1947	Illinois Intercollegiate Athletic Conference
1960	Interstate Intercollegiate Athletic Conference
1961	Interstate Intercollegiate Athletic Conference
2003	Gateway Conference
2004	Gateway Conference
2005	Gateway Conference
2008	Missouri Valley Football Conference
2009	Missouri Valley Football Conference

SALUKIS SELECTED IN THE NFL DRAFT

Player, Position	Team	Round	Year
Bob Ems, RB	Chicago Cardinals	28	1955
Wayne Williams, WR	New York Giants	30	1956
Carver Shannon, RB	Los Angeles Rams	19	1959
Houston Antwine, DT	Detroit Lions	3	1961
Amos Bullocks, RB	Dallas Cowboys	20	1962
Dennis Harmon, DB	Chicago Bears	8	1963
Jim Battle, OT	Cleveland Browns	6	1966
Al Jenkins, OT	Cleveland Browns	3	1969
Bob Hudspeth, OT	New Orleans Saints	4	1969
Carl Mauck, C	Baltimore Colts	13	1969
Lionel Antoine, OT	Chicago Bears	1	1972
Tom Laputka, DT	San Francisco 49ers	11	1972
Bill Story, OT	Kansas City Chiefs	9	1973
Andre Herrera, RB	Kansas City Chiefs	6	1977
Kevin House, WR	Tampa Bay Buccaneers	2	1980
John Harper, LB	Atlanta Falcons	4	1983
Terry Taylor, DB	Seattle Seahawks	1	1984
Rick Johnson, QB	Los Angeles Rams	2	1984
Tom Baugh, C	Kansas City Chiefs	4	1986
Ralph Van Dyke, OT	Atlanta Falcons	4	1987
Tom Roth, G	Los Angeles Raiders	12	1992
Damon Jones, TE	Jacksonville Jaguars	5	1997
Brandon Jacobs, RB	New York Giants	4	2004
Deji Karim, RB	Jacksonville Jaguars	6	2010
Korey Lindsey, CB	Cincinnati Bengals	7	2011
MyCole Pruitt, TE	Minnesota Vikings	5	2015

SALUKIS SELECTED IN THE AFL DRAFT

Player, Position	Team	Round	Year
Houston Antwine, DT	Houston Oilers	8	1962
Sam Silas, DT	Boston Patriots	6	1963

SALUKIS SELECTED IN THE CFL DRAFT

Player, Position	Team	Round	Year
Anthony Thompson, S	B.C. Lions	12	2016

SALUKIS SIGNED AS NFL/AFL FREE AGENTS

Player, Position	Team	Year
Russ Smith, G	Chicago Bears	1922
Abe Martin, RB	Chicago Cardinals	1930
Marion Rushing, LB	Chicago Bears	1959
Sam Silas, DT	St. Louis Cardinals	1963
Clarence Walker, RB	Denver Broncos	1963
Ernie Wheelwright, RB	New York Giants	1964
Jim Thompson, DT	Denver Broncos	1965
Jim Hart, QB	St. Louis Cardinals	1966
Mike Kaczmarek, LB	Baltimore Colts	1973
Tommy Thompson, RB	San Diego Chargers	1974
Fabray Collins, LB	Minnesota Vikings	1987
Sebron Spivey, WR	Dallas Cowboys	1987
Adrian White, DB	New York Giants	1987
Dave Smith, OT	Cincinnati Bengals	1988
Yonel Jourdain, RB	Buffalo Bills	1994
Bart Scott, LB	Baltimore Ravens	2002
Jayson DiManche, LB	Cincinnati Bengals	2009
Nick Hill, QB	Chicago Bears	2010
Chris Dieker, QB	Pittsburgh Steelers	2011
Jewel Hampton, RB	San Francisco 49ers	2012
Ken Boatright, DE	Seattle Seahawks	2013
Adam Fuehne, TE	Detroit Lions	2016
Brandon Williams, LB	Atlanta Falcons	2016
Chase Allen, LB	Miami Dolphins	2017
Deondre Barnett, DE	Tampa Bay Buccaneers	2017

Note.—Lists first team and year the player signed as a free agent

SALUKIS SIGNED AS CANADIAN FOOTBALL LEAGUE FREE AGENTS

Player, Position	Team	Year
Rick Johnson, QB	Calgary Stampeders	1987
Alan Turner, WR	Edmonton Eskimos	2009
Arkee Whitlock, RB	Edmonton Eskimos	2010
Eze Obiora, DE	Hamilton Tiger-Cats	2013

Note.—Lists first team and year the player signed as a free agent

SALUKIS IN THE WORLD FOOTBALL LEAGUE (WFL)

Player, Position	Team	Year
Mike Kaczmarek, LB	Florida Blazers	1974
Tom Laputka, DT	Philadelphia Bell	1974
Sam Silas, DT	Portland Storm	1974

Note.—Lists first team and year the player signed as a free agent.

SALUKIS SELECTED IN THE USFL DRAFT

Player, Position	Team	Round	Year
John Harper, LB	Denver Gold	3	1983
Terry Taylor, DB	Chicago Blitz	2	1984
Donnell Daniel, DB	Chicago Blitz	8	1984
Greg Shipp, DB	Birmingham Stallions	16	1984

Note.—Lists first team and year the player signed as a free agent.

SALUKIS IN ARENA FOOTBALL

Player, Position	Team	Year
Nick Hill, QB	Orlando Predators	2010
Micah King, LB	Iowa Barnstormers	2010
Quorey Payne, WR	Spokane Shock	2010
Alan Turner, WR	Chicago Rush	2010
Bryan Boemer, C	Iowa Barnstormers	2012
Chris Dieker, QB	Iowa Barnstormers	2012

Note.—Lists first team and year the player signed as a free agent.

BIBLIOGRAPHY AND RESOURCES

BOOKS

Bell, Taylor H. A. *Dusty, Deek, and Mr. Do-Right: High School Football in Illinois.* Urbana: University of Illinois Press, 2010.

ESPN College Football Encyclopedia. Michael MacCambridge (ed.). New York: Hyperion, 2005.

Huff, Fred. *Saluki Sports History: 100 Years of Facts and Highlights.* Peoria: MultiAd Sports, 2005.

Lahman, Sean. *The Pro Football Historical Abstract: A Hardcore Fan's Guide to All-Time Player Rankings.* Lyons Press, 2008.

Maxymuk, John. *The Quarterback Abstract: The Complete Guide to NFL Quarterbacks.* Chicago: Triumph Books, 2009.

Miller, Jeff. *Going Long: The Wild 10-Year Saga of the Renegade American Football League in the Words of Those Who Lived It.* New York: McGraw-Hill, 2004.

ONLINE SOURCES

Associated Press. "Herrera Revives Memories for Sayers." October 28, 1976. Google News website. https://news.google.com/newspapers (accessed May 27, 2016).

Bennett, Dean. "Eskimos RB Arkee Whitlock Finds His Stride Heading to CFL Playoff Game vs Stamps." November 11, 2009. MSN Sports website. http://sports.ca.msn.com (accessed July 7, 2014).

Biggs, Brad. "SIU Connection on Vikings with Addition of MyCole Pruitt." *Chicago Tribune,* August 17, 2015. http://www.chicagotribune.com/sports/football/ct-mycole-pruitt-vikings-20150817-story.html (accessed December 9, 2015).

Bishop, Greg. "The Last Word in Trash Talking." *New York Times,* December 19, 2009. http://www.nytimes.com/2009/12/20/sports/football/20jets.html (accessed August 4, 2015).

Bode, Gus. "Mike Dunbar Woke Up Monday Morning Thinking the Worst of His Worries Was Facing Youngstown State University." November 3, 1998. http://www.daily egyptian.com (accessed June 3, 2016).

———. "Football Team Awaits Carpenter's Comeback." *Daily Egyptian*, August 22, 1999. http://www.dailyegyptian.com (accessed June 1, 2016).

Bottino, Barry. "On Campus: Johnsburg Grad Kinney Keeps on Kicking." *Northwest Herald*. January 25, 2015. http://www.nwherald.com/2015/01/23/on-campus-johnsburg -grad-kinney-keeps-on-kicking/akgeeph/ (accessed July 14, 2015).

Byers, Barry. "Good News, Bad News for Former 'Cats." *Herald*, September 8, 2010. http:// www.heraldonline.com/sports/high-school/prep-football/article12259289.html (accessed July 5, 2013).

Cunningham, Steve. "Former Saluki Cornell Craig Signs with CFL." *Southern Illinoisan*, April 18, 2001. http://thesouthern.com (accessed December 22, 2015).

———. "Remember Me? With Coach Quarless Gone, SIUC Defensive Star Bart Scott Is Back on the Field." *Southern Illinoisan*, April 19, 2001. http://thesouthern.com (accessed July 14, 2015).

Donley, Thomas. "Tragedy, Transfer, Touchdowns: The Mark Iannotti Story." *Daily Egyptian*, May 10, 2016. http://www.dailyegyptian.com (accessed June 29, 2016).

Dreilinger, Danielle. "St. Aug Seeks New President, as Oyd Craddock Plans to Retire." *New Orleans Times-Picayune*, February 18, 2016. http://www.nola.com/education/index .ssf/2016/02/st_aug_new_president.html (accessed May 27, 2016).

Engster, Jim. "LSU Has History of Puglistic Running Backs." *Tiger Rag Magazine*, August 12, 2013. http://www.tigerrag.com/engster-lsu-has-history-of-pugilistic-running-backs / (accessed May 25, 2016).

Greenstein, Teddy. "Tight End Prospect Aware of His Precarious Position." *Chicago Tribune*, April 18, 1997. http://articles.chicagotribune.com/1997-04-18/sports/9704180053_1 _jones-attitude-farrell-jones-damon-jones (accessed July 15, 2015).

Haley, Craig. "Reality Still Hovers over FCS-FBS Dreamin'." *Yahoo! Sports*, September 6, 2015. http://sports.yahoo.com/news/reality-still-hovers-over-fcs-fbs-dreamin -160746895—ncaaf.html (accessed January 21, 2016).

Hefferman, Todd. "Mac Moment No. 4: Emotional Hemphill Day Moved Salukis." *Southern Illinoisan*, July 26, 2009. http://thesouthern.com (accessed January 27, 2017).

———. "SIU Hall of Famer Rushing Dies." *Southern Illinoisan*, April 27, 2013. http://the southern.com (accessed July 14, 2015).

———. "Bell Makes Bold Statement with Lennon's Dismissal." *Southern Illinoisan*, November 30, 2015. http://thesouthern.com (accessed June 14, 2016).

Jahns, Adam L. "SIU QB Mark Iannotti Won't Take Bears' Pro Day for Granted." *Chicago Sun-Times*, April 13, 2016. http://chicago.suntimes.com/sports/siu-qb-mark-iannotti -driven-to-impress-bears-at-local-pro-day/ (accessed June 29, 2016).

Merkin, Scott. "Tight End's Tight Squeezes Over." *Chicago Tribune*, January 24, 1997. http://
articles.chicagotribune.com/1997-01-24/sports/9701240057_1_jones-performance
-tight-damon-jones (accessed December 12, 2015).

Mishow, Marty. "Salukis Put 34-7 Thumping on SE in Season Finale." November 15, 1998.
Google News website. https://news.google.com (accessed June 3, 2016).

New York Giants website. http://www.giants.com.

Oberhelman, Dave. "Marmion Grad Koutsos Joins SIU Hall of Fame." *Daily Herald*, January
14, 2010. http://www.dailyherald.com/article/20100114/sports/301149855/ (accessed
December 22, 2015).

Southern Illinois University Salukis website. http://www.siusalukis.com.

Williams, Jonathan. "Arkee Whitlock: A Diamond in the Rough." April 19, 2010. http://www
.examiner.com/article/arkee-whitlock-a-diamond-the-rough (accessed July 5, 2013).

Dan Verdun grew up in Odell, Illinois, and holds degrees from Eastern Illinois University and Northern Illinois University. He is the author of books about football at Northern Illinois, Eastern Illinois, Southern Illinois, and Illinois State Universities. He is a coauthor of the *Prairie State Pigskin* blog for *Chicago Now*. Currently he teaches in public school district 204 in Naperville, Illinois, where he lives with his wife, Nancy; son, Tommy; and daughter, Lauren.